Crab Decks & Tiki Bars
of the Chesapeake Bay

By Susan Elnicki Wade and Bill Wade

This book is dedicated to Max and Nicholas,

who tolerated their parents
during the making of this book

ISBN: 978-1-4635-5201-5

Authors: Susan Elnicki Wade and Bill Wade
Photographs by Susan Elnicki Wade
Maps by Bill Wade
Illustrations by Samantha Simon

Printed in the United States of America

For additional copies of this book visit www.crabdecksandtikibars.com

Or contact us at
2916 Northampton Street, NW
Washington, DC 20015
(202) 531-7136
susan@crabdecksandtikibars.com
bill@crabdecksandtikibars.com

Table of Contents

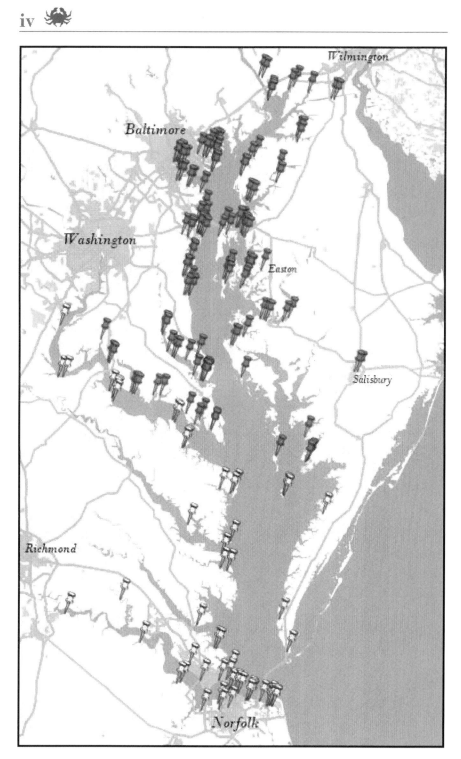

Crab Decks & Tiki Bars of the Chesapeake Bay

Introduction

We're not kidding when we say we consumed at least 11 gallons of crab soup, 300 oysters, 85 crab cakes, 40 pounds of mussels, 25 rockfish, 200 steamed shrimp, and an undisclosed amount of beer and rum in 7 months.

But that's what it took to make this book. Even though we'd been regulars around the Bay for quite a while, we needed to resample the wares, rub shoulders with the locals, and get a clearer picture of what's the buzz around the Bay today.

It all started in August of 2010 on our back porch while celebrating our friend Rich's new iPhone app on Rehoboth Beach. He asked why we hadn't considered writing something about our favorite Chesapeake crab decks and tiki bars.

Rich pointed out that we had unique perspectives. Bill is a true son of Maryland, who knows the Bay intimately and has fond childhood memories of boating around with his family. That speaks to credibility.

I was one of those people who sped across the Bay Bridge, growling at traffic and hoping to reach Rich's beach house in time for happy hour. I'd blow past the Bay without stopping to enjoy its treasures.

But thanks to Bill, Route 50 became more than an expressway from DC to the Atlantic shore. He opened my eyes to the wonders of the Bay by taking me to romantic B&Bs in Kent County, camping on St. George Island and fishing off

Kent Narrows. Now I've grown fond of those murky Chesapeake waters and the blue-collar folks of the Bay who remind me of the blue-collar workers back home in Pennsylvania.

I was a transplant like the palm trees that have been popping up around the Bay for the past decade or so — not an indigenous species, but now blended into the scenery amidst the rusty crab pots and rickety oyster-shucking houses. That speaks to conversion.

Most important for writing a book was how much we enjoy being at the Bay. For years we've taken friends and family to our favorite spots, so how hard could it be to share our knowledge with strangers?

Bill and I looked at each other and thought ... well, maybe he's on to something. We have tons of publishing experience, so we know how to throw a book together. Plus all those years of Bay visits and restaurant work give us a leg to stand on while talking about eateries.

But could we find time to write a book while raising two boys? And how would we pay for it? Ah what the hell, we'll figure that out later. Let's do it! With a burst of naive gusto, we charged full-steam ahead into our great Bay adventure.

Ok now, game on. We made a list of our favorite crab decks and tiki bars. How many more could there be? Maybe 30 or 40? After using maps and online resources, we uncovered more than 150 in Maryland and 60+ in Virginia. How could we possibly hit them all before the 2011 summer season?

We fine-tuned our criteria and only included waterfront restaurants that served crabs in some form or another. We also decided that just covering Maryland crab decks would be a major undertaking, so full details on Virginia would have to wait until the next edition.

We hit the road to visit every crab deck and tiki bar on our list. Sometimes we'd plan a family trip around our Bay research. All too often we'd tell the kids that we were just going to a county fair; no crab decks this time. They quit believing us. So we'd kiss our boys good-bye at friends' houses and jump in the car with destinations charted and goals to reach.

Things didn't always go as planned: "I thought you brought the map! ... Dang, my phone just died along with our only GPS system. ... I'm positive I put extra batteries for the camera somewhere in my purse. ... It's raining again?"

Hectic as it was, this project took us from the graceful farmlands of St. Mary's County, to Baltimore's busy port, up to the pristine Susquehanna headwaters, and down to Crisfield's the austere marshlands – and we cherished each place for its unique beauty. Even better than the places we saw were the people we met. Watermen, waitresses, restaurant owners and boaters welcomed us with open arms and shared their stories.

So as we prepare our book to send to the printer, we breathe a sigh of relief for a mission accomplished yet harbor a touch of sadness that it's over.

And now we challenge you to get off the couch and start your own adventures on the Chesapeake waters. Pick a region, a town, a creek you've never seen before. Revisit authentic gems you already know and look for new places along the way.

Use this book to explore one of the most magnificent, quirky, and fun-loving places in the country. Most of all, we hope you learn to love the Bay as much as we do. Be sure to check out our website www.crabdecksandtikibars.com!

— Susan Elnicki Wade

Bay Travel Tips

At times during our trips around the Bay, we felt like seasoned explorers, successfully navigating the back roads and hidden creeks without a hitch. Other times, well, let's just say we made some mistakes that took a little wind out of our sails. To make your trips run smoothly, consider a few Bay travel tips:

- **Call first.** Most destinations are family-run businesses that can have irregular hours, especially in the off-season. Give them a ring to see if they're open when you plan to arrive. And ask if they take reservations so you can avoid long waiting lines.

- **Use every navigation tool.** Grab a detailed map, your GPS, nautical charts, and charge up your smart phone. Many crab decks are located off the beaten path where roads are poorly marked and locals give directions by telling you to turn right where the fire station burned down 10 years ago. Charting a course in advance can reduce frustration.

- **Plan ahead but be flexible.** It's a safe bet that the Bay Bridge will back up on Friday afternoon in peak season. Avoiding predictable traffic gridlock will put you in a better state of mind for when the unexpected happens – like waiting for a parade of boats to pass under an old drawbridge or getting stuck on a two-land road behind a dilapidated chicken truck. But those are part of the Bay's charm and add color to your travel tales.

- **Eat food that's in season.** Chesapeake aficionados say you should only eat oysters in months with an "r," and crabs bought off-season are rarely local. So look at the chalkboard or ask your server about what's fresh, even if you had your heart set on something else. Every season along the Bay offers delicacies that are unique and delicious – and worth waiting for.

About the Authors

Bill Wade was born in Bethesda, raised in Montgomery County, MD, and attended University of Maryland. His blood runs red, black, yellow, and white, just like the state flag. His father, a former D.C. fire fighter, hadn't intended to become a waterman — until Bill's mom entered a jingle-writing contest for a Wheaton car dealership and won a boat. The family started with a 16-foot fiberglass run-about, upgraded every time a child was born, and ended up with a more spacious 34-foot wooden cabin cruiser. Their boat, "Limey," was built on the Chesapeake Bay, and they docked at Kent Narrows. Summers were spent cruising around the remote necks of the Bay and catching crabs with chicken necks tied to the end of strings. Bill can still pick a crab faster than most workers at a Phillips processing plant.

Susan Elnicki Wade grew up in Oil City, a small blue-collar town in western Pennsylvania, eating native brook trout that she and her brothers caught from Allegheny mountain streams. The closest she'd come in her youth to a blue crab were the crawfish they used as bait. She worked in restaurants in Pittsburgh and later in New York while getting her Masters at NYU. She first experienced the Bay during her courtship with Bill when he whisked her off on weekend adventures to such far-flung places as Chestertown, Cambridge, and Ridge, MD. Picking crabs still doesn't come easy to her, even after visiting every Maryland county along the Bay over the past two decades. But she can whip up a mean batch of fried oysters and recently baked her first Smith Island Cake.

Bill and Susan live in Washington, D.C., with their two sons. For years, they've brought their boys to the Bay, revisiting the same necks on the Eastern and Western shores where their father used to play and teaching them to appreciate the charms of the Chesapeake. Bill and Susan each have 20+ years experience in the publishing industry and hope to make enough money on this book to buy a boat.

About the Book

Crab Decks & Tiki Bars of the Chesapeake Bay is a comprehensive destination guide to authentic seafood restaurants, crab shacks, and tiki bars on the Bay. The eateries chosen for this book are located near the water's edge, have outdoor seating, and serve Maryland blue crabs.

Crab Decks & Tiki Bars of the Chesapeake Bay is divided into nine geographic regions of the Bay. Each entry starts with general contact info (address, phone, web site), followed by:
- County in Maryland where it's located,
- Latitude and Longitude,
- When It's Open (year-round or seasonal),
- Body of Water, and Dockage.

Every crab deck and tiki bar profile includes a map that was painstakingly created by co-author and wannabe cartographer, Bill Wade. Photos were taken on site by co-author, Susan Elnicki Wade, who braved driving rain and 35 m.p.h. winds in her role as designated photographer. A unique Atmosphere Meter assesses the ambience, ranging from casual to formal on a scale of one to 10 (frosty beer mugs to crisp martinis).

Crab Decks & Tiki Bars of the Chesapeake Bay provides in-depth descriptions that paint a vivid image of each restaurant's décor, atmosphere, cuisine, surroundings, and specialties to help you know what to expect when you arrive. Many profiles include colorful bonus data on the history, folklore, culture, and traditions unique to each neck of the Bay.

Additional features include an appendix listing 63 Virginia locations and 3 indexes: Alphabetical by Restaurant, City, and Body of Water.

Crab Decks & Tiki Bars
of the Chesapeake Bay

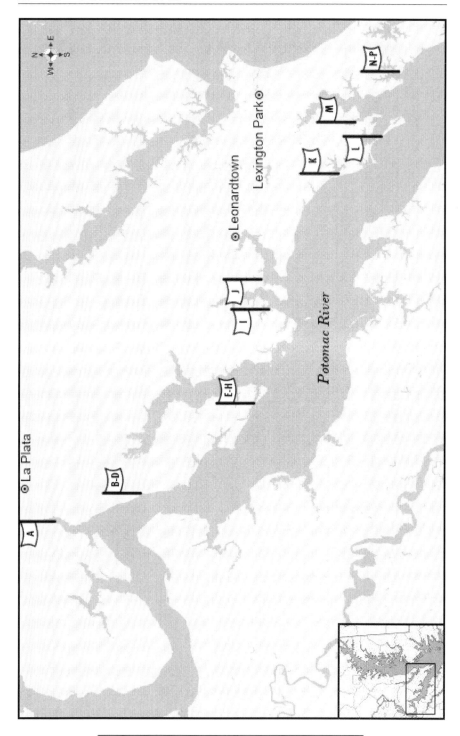

Potomac River

Crabby Dick's
at Port Tobacco Marina

7610 Shirley Boulevard
Port Tobacco, MD 20677
301-870-3133
www.crabby-dicks.com

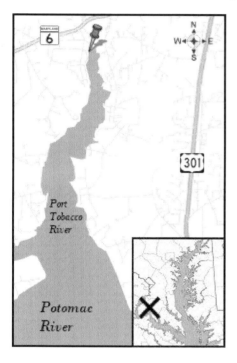

County: Charles County

Open: Year Round

Latitude: N 38° 29' 52"

Longitude: W 77° 1' 36"

Body of Water: Port Tobacco
River off the Potomac River

Dockage: Yes

Picture Code: CD at
www.crabdecksandtikibars.com/
pix

Atmosphere Meter

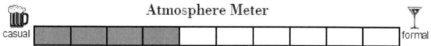

casual ◻◻◻◻◻◻◻◻◻◻ formal

Grab a map and keep your eyes on the GPS when you drive to Crabby Dick's. It's easy to get lost and you don't want to miss this tucked-away treasure. Your reward for successfully navigating through scenic southern Maryland and the tiny town of Port Tobacco (population 13) is the spectacular view at Crabby Dick's. Chesapeake grassy marshlands create a serene backdrop as boats chug along the river. It won't take long for you to spot a blue heron plucking a dinner of minnows or baby crabs from the water's edge.

Two-tiered decks that wrap around the restaurant give everyone a perfect view. But don't worry if an unexpected rainstorm sends you inside. The atmosphere is fun, cozy, and friendly. Knotty pine walls are decorated with a menagerie of nautical items: crabs, fish, waterfowl, mermaids, pirates, and more. And big-screen TVs help you catch the score of a Nationals or Redskins game.

The menu plays with local fare, teasing you with specialties such as Crabby's Famous Balls, Topless Oysters, Harry Dick's Steamed Clams, and Anita's Breasts of Chicken. The Cream of Crab soup is so amazing, that it should be used as a benchmark for all others — velvety smooth with big chunks of crab meat.

The restaurant's name might sound familiar, because it's owned by the same folks as Crabby Dick's in Delaware City and Rehoboth.

History buffs might want to check out nearby Port Tobacco. It was the original county seat of Charles County (moved to La Plata in 1895), and until the end of the Revolutionary War, it was the second largest river port in Maryland (first was St. Mary's City). The harbor gradually silted up due to excessive tree cutting and crop planting, particularly tobacco, so river trade became restricted to small boats.

To learn more, visit the Port Tobacco Historical Society and an archaeological dig that's currently underway to unearth nuggets of early American history.

Pope's Creek Waterfront Rawbar & Restaurant

11455 Popes Creek Road
Newburg, MD 20664
301-259-2710

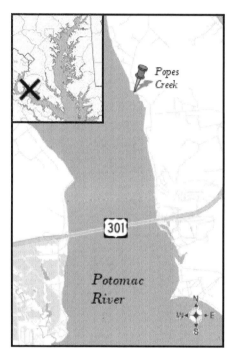

County: Charles County

Open: Year round

Latitude: N 38° 23' 55"

Longitude: W 76° 59' 29"

Body of Water: Popes Creek off the Potomac River

Dockage: Yes

Picture Code: PCWRR at www.crabdecksandtikibars.com/pix

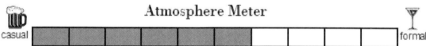

Atmosphere Meter

casual   formal

The new kid on the block in Newburg, MD's waterfront dining row is Pope's Creek Rawbar & Restaurant. It opened in spring 2010 at the former site of Robertson's Crab House and offers a fresh, new approach to Chesapeake cooking.

The dining room wood is stained in rich, warm colors and accented nicely with deep blue tiles. Exposed wooden ceiling rafters supported by a massive I-beam and the clean, simple decor give the restaurant a relaxed contemporary feel.

On the outside deck, placed inches above the water, patrons lean back on tall-backed wooden benches to soak in a gorgeous view of the Potomac River. Shade is provided by big black umbrellas.

The menu features fresh seafood with an innovative twist. Appetizers take things up a notch: fried oysters are coated with panko bread crumbs, crispy wonton shrimp comes with adobe aioli, and mussels lounge in a bowl with basil, garlic, and tomato broth.

Sandwiches include tuna burger with soy and shallots, chicken breast topped with crab imperial, and Angus beef burgers with aged cheddar. Entree standards like crab cakes and filet mignon lay a solid foundation for newcomers like spicy shrimp and grits or sun-dried tomato and lobster pasta.

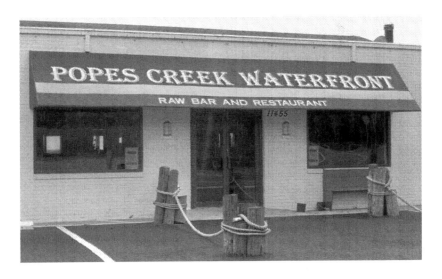

Captain Billy's Crabhouse

11495 Popes Creek Road
Newburg, MD 20664
301-932-4323
www.captbillys.com

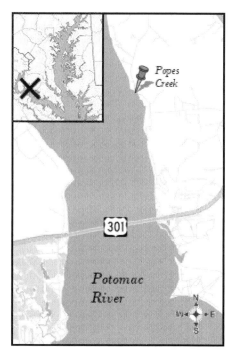

County: Charles County

Open: Seasonal

Latitude: N 38° 23' 53"

Longitude: W 76° 59' 27"

Body of Water: Popes Creek off
the Potomac River

Dockage: Yes

Picture Code: CBC at
www.crabdecksandtikibars.com/
pix

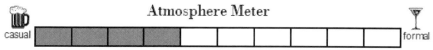

Atmosphere Meter

casual | | | | | | | | | | formal

As you stand on the shore at Captain Billy's Crab House,
imagine a pair of unrelated historical events taking place
near this spot.

To escape capture after shooting President Lincoln, John
Wilkes Boothe looked at those same waters hoping to cross
the river into Virginia, where he thought he'd be heralded as a

hero of the Confederacy. Fast-forward about a century, to a time when electricity had just arrived in Popes Creek and construction had just started on the Potomac River Bridge.

A boy named Billy Robertson caught his first crab and soon started selling them around town. When Billy grew up, he became a waterman and eventually opened this restaurant, considered by locals to be among the best crab houses in the area.

For 60 years, a giant neon crab sign out front has pointed the way for diners who come to enjoy fabulous waterfront views from the outdoor deck or the cool air-conditioned comfort of the spacious indoor dining area.

Chesapeake seafood dominates the menu with oyster stew, fried shrimp baskets, hardshell crabs, and steamed clams — all accompanied by homey touches such as hush puppies or corn fritters with honey.

Landlubbers can opt for BBQ ribs, steak, or chicken if they want, but when the place mats give instructions for picking crabs, you might want to stick to what Captain Billy's does best — fresh seafood feasts served with warm Southern Maryland hospitality.

Gilligan's Pier

11535 Popes Creek Road
Newburg, MD 20664
301-259-4514
www.gilliganspier.com

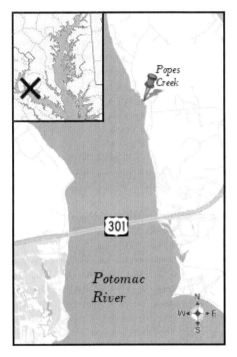

County: Charles County

Open: Year Round

Latitude: N 38° 23' 47"

Longitude: W 76° 59' 17"

Body of Water: Popes Creek off the Potomac River

Dockage: Yes

Picture Code: GP at www.crabdecksandtikibars.com/pix

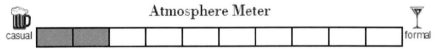

Atmosphere Meter

When you pull into Gilligan's, you might be tempted to blink your eyes to make sure it's real, not a mirage. Tucked in amid Southern Maryland's rural landscape of farms, corn fields, and old tobacco barns is an oasis of tiki island fun.

The building, painted neon pinkish-purple, is flanked by tall palm trees and plush tropical plants. A band plays rock-and-roll or reggae, while cold specialty drinks are poured at the tiki bar, and volleyball players rub on sunscreen before slamming a ball over the net.

Children build sand castles and dabble in the water along the 1.5 acre beach (a rare find along the Potomac), and boaters tie up at the pier. The Route 301 bridge in the distance adds a special Bay charm to breath-taking sunsets.

Inside, the ceilings are draped with fish nets, crab bushels serve as lamp shades, and brown paper on the tables catches shell carnage from hot steamed crabs.

The food is good — nothing fancy but always fresh and plentiful, with local seafood, salads, sandwiches, steaks, and steamers.

And if you want to share this tiki experience with a group of friends, Gilligan's rents out its island — palm trees and sandy beach included — for weddings, receptions, family reunions, or corporate retreats.

Captain John's Crab House

16215 Cobb Island Road
Cobb Island, MD 20625
301-259-2315
www.cjcrab.com

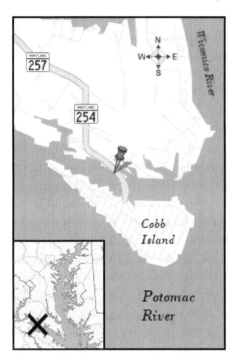

County: Charles County

Open: Year Round

Latitude: N 38° 16' 4"

Longitude: W 76° 51' 5"

Body of Water: Neale Sound between the Wicomico River and the Potomac River

Dockage: Yes

Picture Code: CJCH at www.crabdecksandtikibars.com/ pix

Atmosphere Meter

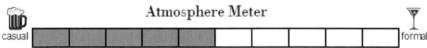

casual / formal

Deep in Charles County on the last stretch of mainland before the bridge to Cobb Island are a pair of family-owned restaurants that represent the best of Chesapeake seafood tradition: Captain John's and Shymansky's.

Captain John's is located on the right side of the road overlooking Neale Sound. Built in 1963 by John Shymansky and currently run by his grandson, Skip Yates, this place continues an almost 50-year legacy of excellent home-style cooking.

Heartwarming old family pictures — including a robust portrait of the captain himself — hang on the walls. A string of lights made of red and white fishing bobbins brightens the outside waterfront deck.

During a recent visit, a 30-year veteran waitress pulled down a collage of before-and-after Hurricane Isabel photos that showed extensive flood damage and how hard the family and community worked to keep the business going.

A market in the back sells fresh seafood brought in daily by local watermen. The famous seafood buffet offers a cornucopia of Bay specialties: steamed or fried shrimp, crabs, clams, oysters, rockfish, mussels, hush puppies, and corn fritters.

The crispy fried chicken gets high approval ratings from any Southern Maryland native who takes a bite. No matter what you order, you won't leave hungry or unhappy.

Shymansky's Restaurant

16320 Cobb Island Road
Cobb Island, MD 20644
301-259-0300

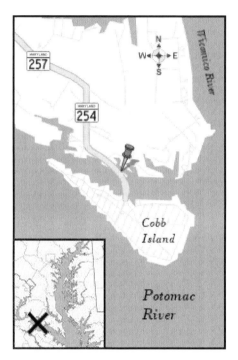

County: Charles County

Open: Year Round

Latitude: N 38° 16' 2"

Longitude: W 76° 51' 0"

Body of Water: Neale Sound
off the Potomac River

Dockage: Yes

Picture Code: SR1 at
www.crabdecksandtikibars.com/
pix

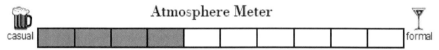

Atmosphere Meter

casual   formal

At the tip of Charles County where the Potomac and Wicomico Rivers meet, a southern Maryland family is working hard to keep Bay traditions alive. On the left side of the road just before you reach Cobb Island is Shymansky's Restaurant and Marina (Captain John's across the street is owned by other family members).

The long one-story white building was bought by Bruce Shymansky in the 1950s, and his clan has been making Chesapeake water lovers happy ever since. The restaurant's dining room and bar have a homey casual feel that make you want to linger a while at your table and gaze out at the expansive waterfront view.

Plump steamed crabs are delivered daily and couldn't get much fresher. The menu also features other local seafood selections of shrimp, oysters, rockfish, mussels, and clams. Hearty sandwiches and juicy burgers come with crispy fries.

If you're willing to leave terra firma and experience some of the best fishing in the region, walk over to Shymansky's Marina. They'll set you up with boat rentals, bait and tackle, slips, or gas — everything you need for a perfect day on the Bay.

The Scuttlebutt Restaurant

12320 Neale Sound Drive
Cobb Island, MD 20644
240-233-3133

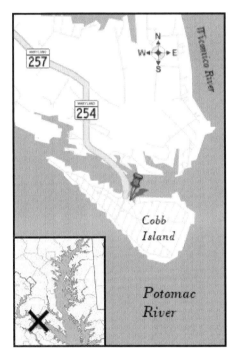

County: Charles County

Open: Year Round

Latitude: N 38° 15' 49"

Longitude: W 76° 50' 57"

Body of Water: Neale Sound
between the Wicomico River
and the Potomac River

Dockage: Yes

Picture Code: TSR at
www.crabdecksandtikibars.com/
pix

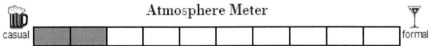

Atmosphere Meter

casual ▮▮▮ formal

The word "scuttlebutt" originally referred to a drinking fountain or cask on a ship that held the day's supply of drinking water. It's kind of like the office water cooler or village well, where people gather to gossip about the latest buzz around town.

It's the perfect name for Scuttlebutt Restaurant on Cobb Island. This cozy little restaurant has a special charm that makes you want to stay for a while and hear local residents and watermen tell tales about life in their island community.

Bright yellow walls are decorated with palm trees on a sandy beach with red crabs and a blue heron. Rosy pink impatiens overflow the edges of stone planters near the front door.

On a warm summer evening, the outdoor deck at the water's edge gives you a front-row seat to crimson sunsets. Good food at affordable prices features delicious soups of the day and fresh seafood caught nearby.

When you leave Scuttlebutt, be sure to take a spin around Cobb Island. Don't worry; it won't take long. This tiny piece of land (only 290 acres) offers big natural beauty and a lovely community where the Potomac and Wicomico Rivers meet.

You won't see a sprawling shopping mall or high-rise buildings. Instead, you'll pass a post office, market, and vintage cottages interspersed with newer homes among tall oak trees.

The 825 residents own more boats than cars, and they gather for bingo night, oyster and ham dinners, or the Friday fish fry at the fire hall. It's a slice of pleasant Bay living that you won't want to miss.

Drift Away Bar & Grill at Pirates Den Marina

12364 Neale Sound Drive
Cobb Island, MD 20644
301-259-0333

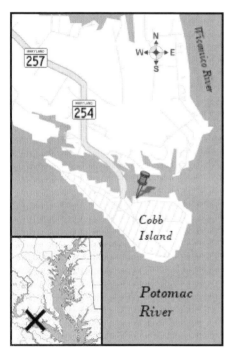

County: Charles County

Open: Year Round

Latitude: N 38° 15' 49"

Longitude: W 76° 50' 50"

Body of Water: Neale Sound between the Wicomico River and the Potomac River

Dockage: Yes

Picture Code: DABG at www.crabdecksandtikibars.com/pix

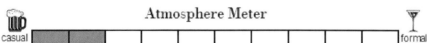

Remember the '70s song by Dobie Gray that went "Give me the beat boys and free my soul, I want to get lost in your rock-and-roll and drift away...?"

Well, the Drift Away Bar & Grill on Cobb Island is named after that tune, and it's certainly living up to the lyrics. It's the kind of place where music, the water, and a bit of Bay history merge into one upbeat get-away experience. Run by the bass player and manager of Southern Maryland's Sam Grow Band, this place features live local bands on weekends.

Bright orange walls with a tropical theme, a pool table, and a good jukebox set the stage for a lively rock-and-roll night on the Bay.

The atmosphere is laid-back casual, and the crabs are plump and fresh. The outdoor deck overlooks Pirate's Den Marina, which bustles with fishermen and pleasure boaters cruising through Neale Sound.

So, are you wondering where that body of water got its name? How about Cobb Island? In 1642, the island was owned by James Neale, a ship captain who was notorious for capturing Spanish treasure ships in the West Indies and returning home with his stolen bounty.

The large Spanish coins that Neale confiscated were cut into pieces called "cobbs" and used as coins by the early colonists.

Thanks to the exploits of James Neale, we're forever graced with Neale Sound flowing between the mainland and Cobb Island.

Frank Morris Point Restaurant

38869 Morris Point Road
Abell, MD 20606
301-769-2500
www.morris-point.com

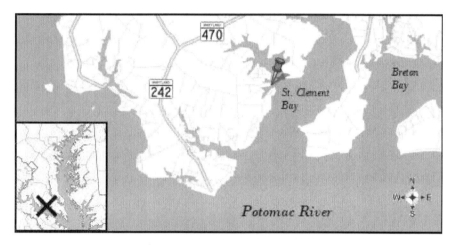

County: St. Mary's County
Open: Year Round
Latitude: N 38° 15' 7" Longitude: W 76° 43' 57"
Body of Water: Canoe Neck Creek off St. Clements Bay
off the Potomac River
Dockage: Yes
Picture Code: FMPR at www.crabdecksandtikibars.com/pix

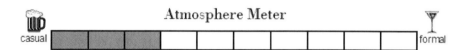

Frank Morris Point is an ideal destination for adventurers seeking the authentic Bay experience. It's a tiny wisp of a place, probably more deck than building.

The restaurant is nestled in a remote part of St. Mary's County, not far from Leonardtown, and is surrounded by working boats, modest houses, and mobile homes. It rests on pylons above Canoe Neck Creek, and offers a dazzling duck's eye view of the water. On this spot in 1885, Stewart Morris ran a general store and oyster packing house. Years later, it was converted into a restaurant called the Ebb Tide (which burned down), and eventually retired waterman Frank Morris built his own eatery.

Everything about it says "Classic Chesapeake," but they toss in a few surprises that make this place special. The yard in front of the restaurant is landscaped with the standard oyster shells, pea gravel, and local foliage, but someone placed a few unexpected abstract stone statues of human figures around the lawn. The decor inside is casual and comfortable, with enough space for about eight oilcloth-covered tables neatly arranged in the dining room. Homey blue curtains with a sailboat pattern line the top of the windows, and colorful nautical flags add a dash of cheer.

The menu is anchored in family tradition, proudly serving Grandma's chili, made-to-order oyster stew in a quaint iron pot, and shrimp stuffed with lump crabmeat and broiled in a homemade butter sauce. Seafood feasts featuring fresh catch from the Patuxent or Potomac Rivers are unforgettable, and the "Fatty Crab" entree packs a plump crab cake into a soft shell body. Pleasant surprises include the smoked trout platter, homemade lasagna, and blackened ahi tuna in a teriyaki reduction.

To create a perfect Southern Maryland day, include a visit to St. Clement's Island Museum or visit one of the four state parks nearby after indulging in Morris Point's wonderful family-style cooking.

Fitzie's Restaurant

21540 Joe Hazel Road
Leonardtown, MD 20650
301-475-1913

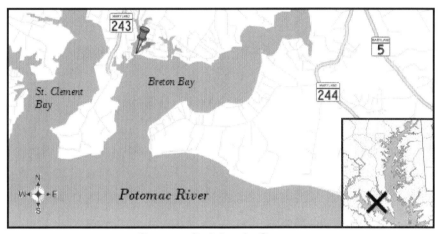

County: St. Mary's County
Open: Year Round
Latitude: N 38° 15' 33"　Longitude: W 76° 41' 42"
Body of Water: Breton Bay off the Potomac River
Dockage: Yes
Picture Code: FR at www.crabdecksandtikibars.com/pix

Atmosphere Meter

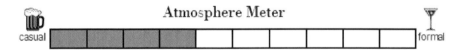

casual　　　　　　　　　　　　　　　　formal

Is it kosher to mix tiki and crabs with shamrocks? In that "anything goes" Chesapeake spirit, the odd combo works well at Fitzie's.

It's a large building, newly renovated and expanded after Hurricane Isabel damaged the former structure in 2003. Its cream-colored siding with kelly green accents provides a contrasting backdrop for three tiki huts stationed in the sand near the water. The view of Breton Bay is expansive and spectacular, and there's plenty of space for parking or docking.

Inside, an Irish theme plays throughout. The lounge, equipped with a pool table, a few pinball machines, and a long wooden bar, is decorated with flags from the Emerald Isle, hand-stitched shamrock craft art, and a lighted palm tree.

Above the red brick fireplace, green needlepoint testifies that Fitzie's was established in 1993. Two floors accommodate dining needs: the top floor is reserved for special events and the lower level provides regular service. Walls of windows let in ample light to brighten the main dining area where tables are covered with pale green oilcloths.

The menu takes traditional Bay dishes and dresses them up with a little Gaelic flare. Entrees include Leprechaun's Dream (char-broiled New York strip with steamed shrimp), and the Erin Go Braugh (Cajun-seasoned shrimp, scallops, and crab over pasta).

The Killarney fries a half chicken Southern Maryland style. Jumbo lump crab cakes are legendary, and sandwiches are robust and filling.

So go figure ... at the Bay, it's perfectly fine to enjoy red crabs with green beer.

Reluctant Navigator

18521 Herring Creek Road
Tall Timbers, MD 20690
301-994-1508
www.talltimbersmarinasomd.com/index_files/
ReluctantNavigator.htm

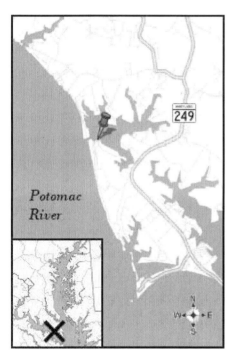

County: St. Mary's County

Open: Seasonal

Latitude: N 38° 10' 37"

Longitude: W 76° 32' 38"

Body of Water: Herring Creek off the Potomac River

Dockage: Yes

Picture Code: RN at www.crabdecksandtikibars.com/pix

Atmosphere Meter

casual ▭▭▭▭▭▭▭▭▭▭ formal

If Reluctant Navigator claims to be the best kept secret on the Potomac, then why is it packed with scores of fishermen, boaters, and locals having a good time on the water?

Some early bird patrons like to jump-start their morning with what the bar proudly calls, "The Best Damn Bloody

Mary" at the Sunday breakfast buffet. The cook lays out a mighty spread of biscuits with creamed chipped beef, bread pudding, spiced apples, pancakes, cheesy eggs, grits, corn beef hash, and breakfast burritos.

Other guests hold out until later in the day for a frosty beer with their favorite dish on the regular menu. Steamed shrimp, crab cakes, and the catch of the day are fresh local treasures. Juicy burgers, grilled chicken, thick steaks, home made meatloaf, and pasta are a landlubber's delight.

Some folks have so much fun at Reluctant Navigator that they forget to take their personal stuff. The owners hold what's left behind in safe keeping at "The Museum."

From floor to ceiling this room overflows with an astonishing collection of oddities such as wooden oars, boat motors, duck decoys, old signs, fishing poles, rusty tools, knotted ropes, oyster tongs, beaded necklaces, and banged-up kids' toys. It's a hoarder's heaven that boggles the imagination.

When you're done surveying the long-forgotten artifacts, head out to the deck to watch the boats cruise by and raise a glass to the wonderfully quirky ways of the Chesapeake Bay.

The Island Inn Bar & Grill

16810 Piney Point Road
Piney Point, MD 20674
301-994-9944
www.stgeorgeislandinnandsuites.com

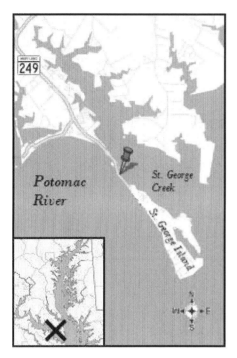

County: St. Mary's County

Open: Year Round

Latitude: N 38° 7' 48"

Longitude: W 76° 29' 39"

Body of Water: between St. George Creek and the Potomac River

Dockage: Yes

Picture Code: TIIBG at www.crabdecksandtikibars.com/pix

 Atmosphere Meter

casual | | | | | | | | | | formal

You can come for a meal, spend the day, or enjoy an entire weekend at Island Inn Bar & Grill. It's nestled on a thin strip of land leading to St. George Island, with St. George Creek on one side presenting spectacular sunrises and the Potomac River on the other side dishing up gorgeous sunsets. The lovely decor is understated, soothing, and casual. The menu features fresh local seafood. You can start with mussels, smoked bluefish dip, or shrimp. Fried oyster fans should place an order right away. They're lightly dredged in flour and fried to a golden brown, crispy on the outside and juicy on the inside. If sandwiches float your boat, you can go with crab cakes, po boys, or burgers. Entree choices include shrimp linguini, sizzling rib eyes, and Chesapeake steamer platters. At Sunday brunch, you get to build your own omelet.

If you don't want to head home after a meal, the inn has 28 rooms with balconies overlooking the water. Folks looking for more adventurous accommodations can drive down the road and pitch a tent at Camp Merryelande on St. George Island. It offers sites in the forest or on the beach and concierge camping where they do all the work for you.

While you roast hotdogs over the campfire, you can tell tales of St. George's history. This tiny island was host to the first battle on Maryland soil during the Revolutionary War. During the War of 1812, the British claimed the island as their home base for raiding local shipyards and plantations.

If you really get hit with island fever, there's another one nearby that delights nature lovers and history buffs alike — St. Clements Island. In 1634, a pair of ships called the *Ark* and *Dove* brought the first English-speaking settlers to Maryland's shores and celebrated the first Catholic Mass in the colonies.

At Coltons Point you can visit a museum that chronicles the region's history and then ride on a water taxi out to the island. It's fun to bring a picnic lunch, then hike the trails that lead to the recently restored Blackistone Lighthouse and a 40-foot cross erected in memory of those early Catholic settlers. Or you can bring your own boat on the first weekend of October for the annual Blessing of the Fleet.

Torpedo Bar & Grill

46555 Dennis Point Way
Drayden, MD 20630
301-994-2404
www.torpedobarandgrill.com

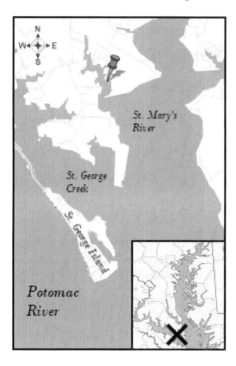

County: St. Mary's County

Open: Year Round

Latitude: N 38° 9' 25"

Longitude: W 76° 28' 8"

Body of Water: Carthagena Creek off the St. Mary's River off the Potomac River

Dockage: Yes

Picture Code: TBG1 at www.crabdecksandtikibars.com/pix

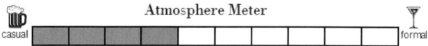

Atmosphere Meter

casual ———————————————— formal

The sight of kids crawling all over a 20-foot metal torpedo tipped on its side near the parking lot speaks volumes about the atmosphere at Torpedo Grill.

It's all about summer fun in Southern Maryland. Located at St. Mary's Yachting Center, the restaurant's cozy indoor dining room, wooden deck, and thatched roof tiki bar offer good food and a great view of the water.

The menu is laced with local seafood options such as steamed crabs or shrimp, oyster po boys, clams with garlic butter, and fish tacos. Hell Bound Wings are so hot that "you'll have to stick your head in the Bay."

Meat lovers can opt for 12-ounce New York strip steaks, chicken caesar wraps, BBQ pulled pork, or juicy burger bomb sliders.

French fries covered with cheese and crab meat, crispy hush puppies, jalapeno poppers, and chips with homemade salsa are available for folks who want a snack.

And that's not all. Torpedo Grill picks up the pace at this bustling marina with events like Hooters & Scooters (bikini contest and motorcycle show), pizza chow down, live bands on weekends, and power boat races. Next to the deck, there's a swimming pool for dipping, a pier for crabbing, and rental canoes for spying osprey nests.

Charter boats take you to deeper waters for a chance at catching your limit of rockfish. And if you want to stay for more than a day, reserve a spot at one of the campground's 75 sites surrounded by tall shade trees.

Spinnakers Waterfront Restaurant

16244 Millers Wharf Road
Ridge, MD 20680
301-872-5020
www.pointlookoutmarina.com/spinnakers

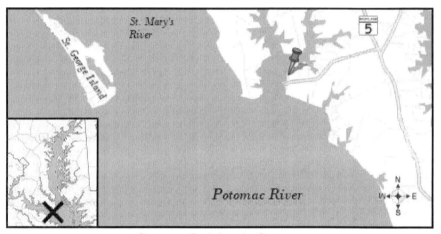

County: St. Mary's County
Open: Year Round
Latitude: N 38° 6' 54"   Longitude: W 76° 24' 4"
Body of Water: Smith Creek off the Potomac River
Dockage: Yes
Picture Code: SWR at www.crabdecksandtikibars.com/pix

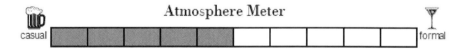

Every small town or marina should have a place like Spinnakers — a local gathering spot where people can grab a bite to eat, share a laugh, and catch up with their neighbors.

To create that community feel, Spinnaker's has Thursday pizza night with discounted pitchers of Bud, hosts a pig roast on July 4th, and whips up stuffed ham and oysters for the holiday season. Everyone's invited.

It's located at Point Lookout Marina and recent renovations have spruced up the restaurant and grounds. A wooden cabana bar now stands outside with a string of green and purple lights hung overhead.

On the deck, patio furniture with round glass-top tables offer front-row seats for a gorgeous view of Smith Creek. The decor inside is comfortable, homey, and sports a traditional maritime theme.

When you step into the Mermaid Bar, a stained-glass screen shows a pair of mermaids frolicking in the water among the coral, sunfish, and conch shells. On the bar's sign, a blond lady of the waves with a curled pink fin lounges in a martini glass.

A mural near the ceiling paints palm trees and hibiscus flowers in dreamy tropical pastels. Framed pictures of Chesapeake sailboats and working vessels hang on the white walls.

The menu presents classic regional fare pulled fresh from the local waters. Crab cakes have only a dusting of filler, rockfish is grilled to perfection, and shrimp are steamed with a generous dose of Old Bay. And you'll have a tough time choosing between a crispy fried oyster sandwich or a juicy cheeseburger.

When you're done, take a stroll around the charming marina and enjoy a lovely sunset over the water.

Scheible's Crab Pot
Seafood Restaurant & Lounge

48342 Wynne Road
Ridge, MD 20680
301-872-0025
scheibles.homestead.com

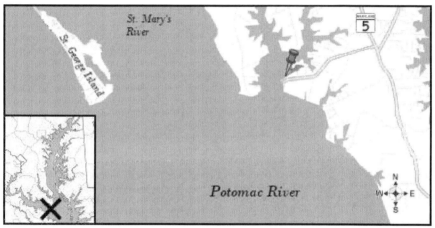

County: St. Mary's County
Open: Seasonal
Latitude: N 38° 6' 36"   Longitude: W 76° 24' 17"
Body of Water: Smith Creek off the Potomac River
Dockage: Yes
Picture Code: SCPSRL at www.crabdecksandtikibars.com/pix

Atmosphere Meter

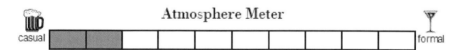

casual | | | | | | | | | | formal

   Scheible's is the one-stop shop for people who are crazy
about Chesapeake seafood. Since 1946, this family-owned
fisherman's paradise has been the epitome of life in Southern
Maryland – laid-back, hard-working, and always connected
to the water.

It's located on Smith Creek where the Potomac meets the Bay. From April to November, charter boats at Scheible's Fishing Center go chumming, trolling, or jigging in some of the region's best saltwater fishing spots to reel in trophy-worthy rockfish, blues, flounder, and whatever else takes your bait.

If you want to be on site to head out before sunrise, you can book a room in the hotel and enjoy a country-style breakfast in the morning.

The restaurant is in a simple, blue, one-story building that can't possibly prepare you for what's inside. Upon entering, you meet two monster-sized taxidermied fish mounted on a wood-paneled wall. Seriously, they are longer than a table and look fierce enough to send a chill down Captain Ahab's spine. The menagerie of crabs and other fish used for decoration pale in comparison. Blue-and-white plaid curtains hang above the windows, matching the nautical-print oilcloths on the tables.

The Fishtale Bar is decorated with fish nets, lighthouses, sea captains, crabs, and photos of fishermen proudly holding up their prized catch.

The food evolves around what's in season and is cooked Southern Maryland style. Rockfish and flounder are regulars on the menu, crabs and shrimp are steamed just right, and fried oysters couldn't get much crispier or fresher. Pizza and wings get washed down with a cold pitcher of beer, and steaks and chicken are on hand for meat lovers.

Homemade desserts, like apple dumplings, bread pudding, and chocolate lava cake, are a heavenly, calorie-rich treat. In a nutshell, at Scheible's you're in for a genuine Bay experience, and it's all about the fishermen.

Courtney's Restaurant & Seafood

48290 Wynne Road
Ridge, MD 20680
301-872-4403

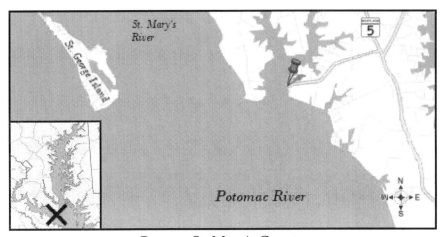

County: St. Mary's County
Open: Year Round
Latitude: N 38° 6' 34"   Longitude: W 76° 24' 21"
Body of Water: Smith Creek off the Potomac River
Dockage: Yes
Picture Code: CRS at www.crabdecksandtikibars.com/pix

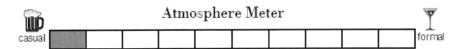

Atmosphere Meter
casual — formal

If you want to get away from the city noise and traffic, Courtney's might be the answer. And when you see the restaurant's red stenciled sign planted next to a rusty propane tank and a six-pack of mobile homes, you'll know you're as far from urban life as you can get.

Courtney's is all about simple country living — no fuss and very rustic. The white cinder block building's low drop ceiling looms over wood-paneled walls that are decorated with a hodge-podge of old photos, nautical artifacts, and beer signs. A radio, almost tuned in to the local country station, plays staticky tunes by Elvis, Hank, and Patsy. Shelves are stacked with dusty vintage knickknacks.

Tables lined up on a time-worn wooden floor are covered with red cloths and paper place mats that disclose fun facts about the Bay.

You'll likely be seated and served by the owner or his wife, who also do the cooking. When a patron asks for ketchup or another condiment, they grab one from an old refrigerator in the back of the dining room, next to the salad bar and a pair of black fat-belly pots that keep the soup-of-the-day warm. Likely candidates inside the cauldrons would be Boston clam chowder, vegetable crab soup, or creamy oyster stew.

What Courtney's lacks in fancy decor, it makes up in home-style food at very reasonable prices. Crab cakes are just-caught fresh, huge, and a third the price of their urban counterparts.

Lightly breaded fried oysters, rockfish, shrimp, and other local seafood taste like they've just been pulled from the Bay. Land lovers can choose fried honey-dipped chicken, T-bone steaks, or cheeseburgers.

If you venture out early, Courtney's serves up a hearty country breakfast with eggs, pancakes, chipped beef, scrapple, grits, corned beef hash, or creamed sausage and biscuits.

Now, that's down-home cooking worth traveling for.

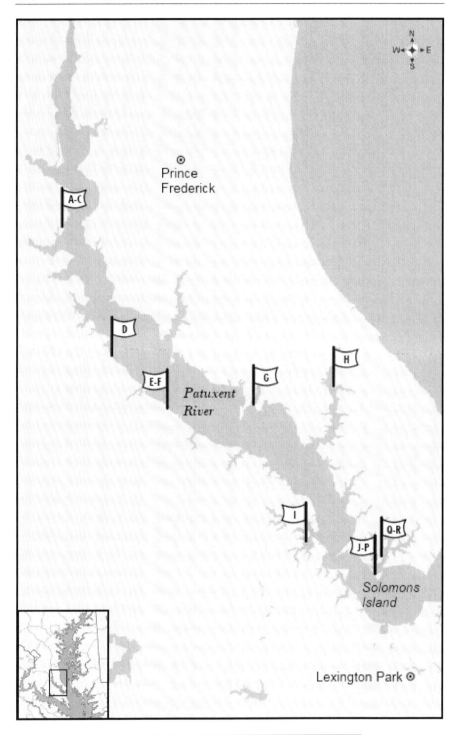

Patuxent River

Ray's Pier Restaurant

18170 Desoto Place
Benedict, MD 20612
301-274-3733

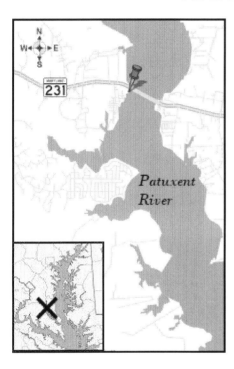

County: Charles County

Open: Year Round

Latitude: N 38° 30' 46"

Longitude: W 76° 40' 34"

Body of Water: Patuxent River

Dockage: Yes

Picture Code: RPR at
www.crabdecksandtikibars.com/
pix

Atmosphere Meter

casual | | | | | | | | | | formal

There's a timeless feel to Ray's Pier, where old and new seem to blend together in a seamless continuum of life directly connected to the water. Maybe it's the hard work behind a family-owned business that give Ray's such a warm, comfortable atmosphere.

You almost feel like you're in your grandmother's house when you walk inside the one-story white building. Lobsters,

crabs, geese, fishnets, and pictures of boats garnish the walls.
A giant blue and silver marlin with slightly chipped paint
hangs from a string above the doorway.

Table-to-ceiling windows open up to a grassy lawn with
old trees and picnic tables near the water's edge. The smell of
fresh steamed crabs and shrimp gets your taste buds excited
about an authentic Chesapeake feast.

Crab cakes and rockfish are fried to perfection — crispy
on the outside yet still moist and tender inside. Country-fried
steak is blanketed in a velvety smooth gravy. Homemade
coleslaw and potato salad are sprinkled with just a dash
of Old Bay.

And the waitress — who often juggles the tasks of serving
patrons and helping steam crabs in the kitchen — makes
everyone feel right at home.

Maybe Ray's gets its special charm from the location. The
tiny town of Benedict was established in 1683 and originally
named Benedict-Leonardtown after the 4th Lord Baltimore,
Benedict Leonard Calvert.

It was a fishing village in the late 17th Century and grew
into a ship-building port that constructed a vessel for George
Washington in 1760.

Steamboats, tomato-processing plants, and
seafood-packing houses once stood on its shores, but today
Benedict is home to watermen, farmers, sports fishermen,
and duck hunters.

River's Edge

7320 Benedict Avenue
Benedict, MD 20612
301-274-2828

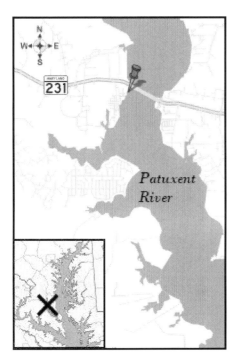

County: Charles County

Open: Seasonal

Latitude: N 38° 30' 36"

Longitude: W 76° 40' 41"

Body of Water: Patuxent River

Dockage: Yes

Picture Code: RE at
www.crabdecksandtikibars.com/
pix

Atmosphere Meter

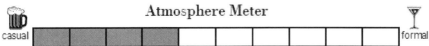

casual — formal

At Rivers Edge, the present and past converge to create a memorable experience in the quiet town of Benedict, MD.

You can enjoy what's right before your eyes — a cozy restaurant with a wooden deck and spectacular waterfront views – or you can recall important events that happened here long ago.

Good food at reasonable prices appeals to local seafood lovers and landlubbers alike. Mouthwatering shrimp, fresh oysters, crab soups, creamy oyster stew, and golden-brown crab cakes the size of baseballs are served with homemade hush puppies. Also from the kitchen come steaks, chicken, ribs, and sandwiches. Ladies who order an entree get a free dessert.

All of that would make your trip worthwhile, but there's more to this spot than meets the eye. Right where you're sitting, events occurred that changed the course of American history.

In August 1814, after fierce battles with U.S. naval forces, British ships sailed up the Patuxent River and unloaded scores of soldiers, right near the spot where River's Edge stands today. Those British troops marched from this point north to Washington where they burned and looted the White House, Capitol, Treasury, War Department, and Naval Yard.

But wait, there's more. This place also played a role in the Civil War. In 1863, Camp Stanton was built on this site to train Maryland's 7th Regiment and help squelch Southern aggression.

The 19th Regiment of Colored Troops also trained here. It was comprised of slaves whose freedom was purchased by the U.S. government, enabling them to join the Union cause.

A school was later created by Samuel Armstrong, war hero and abolitionist, to educate freed slaves and help them become teachers.

Just some food for thought while you're picking crabs in Benedict.

Goose Landing
Restaurant & Bar

19311 Wilmott Drive
Benedict, MD 20612
240-254-2006
www.gooselandingbar.com

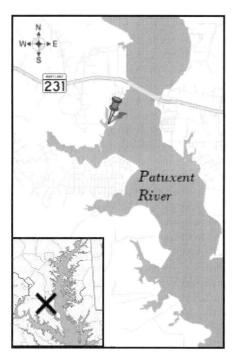

County: Charles County

Open: Year Round

Latitude: N 38° 30' 16"

Longitude: W 76° 40' 52"

Body of Water: Patuxent River

Dockage: Yes

Picture Code: GLRB at
www.crabdecksandtikibars.com/
pix

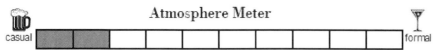

Atmosphere Meter

casual | | | | | | | | | | | formal

If you want to let loose and experience a little Southern Maryland night life, stop by Goose Landing. In this trinity of restaurant, bar, and nightclub, you can work up a sweat dancing to a band and then let the Bay breezes cool you down.

The walls and ceiling are painted jet black, with deep red accents on the rafters, door frames, windows, and carpet.

Locals gather for pool leagues on Thursday night and Texas Hold 'em tournaments on Sunday after church. You might even rake in some easy money playing Keno, the lottery, or betting on the ponies.

It's got a come-as-you-are feeling and a good view of the water. The menu features classic American pub fare with fresh treats from the Bay, such as steamed crabs, shrimp and oysters in season.

Other tasty munchies include wings, nachos, pizza, and chili. Burgers, sandwiches, and spaghetti and meatballs are a carnivore's delight. A kids' menu with hotdogs, fish fingers, Mac and cheese, and chicken tenders keeps the little ones busy while adults let off some steam and have fun.

Drift Inn

6240 Delabrooke Road
Mechanicsville, MD 20659
301-884-3470

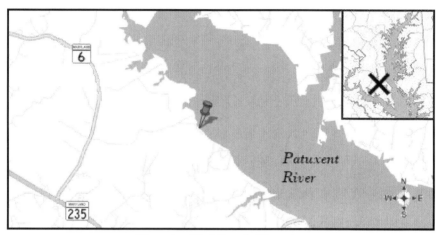

County: St. Mary's County
Open: Seasonal
Latitude: N 38° 26' 20"   Longitude: W 76° 38' 43"
Body of Water: Patuxent River
Dockage: Yes
Picture Code: DI at www.crabdecksandtikibars.com/pix

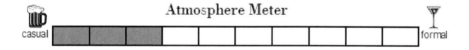

Finding Drift Inn by boat is no big deal, but arriving by car presents some interesting challenges. Even if you lock in your GPS and bring along a map, the roads aren't particularly well marked, so it's easy to lose your way.

But it's well worth the adventure. Winding through these scenic rural back roads is like an appetizer to an authentic Bay experience. Some say Drift Inn is the oldest crab house in operation in Southern Maryland.

For about 50 years, it has been run by generations of the Copsey family, who have deep roots in the community and longstanding traditions with Chesapeake seafood.

You'll know you've successfully reached your destination when you see the big hand-painted sign with bright red letters and plastic seagulls perched on top.

A red tin roof sits on top of the one-story white cinder block building. Red and blue crabs point the way to the entrance.

Because it's only open Friday, Saturday, and Sunday from May to October, you might run into a crowd during peak dining hours. But that's okay. The wait gives you a chance to let your eyes gaze down the long wooden pier that stretches out into the Patuxent River or witness the kaleidoscope of colors from a summer sunset reflected on the water.

And when the waitress finally places a tray of hot steamed crabs and delicious homemade sides on your table, you'll remember that good things in life don't come easy. And you'll be glad you took the time to experience this treasure on the Bay.

Sandgates Inn

27525 North Sandgates Road
Mechanicsville, MD 20659
301-373-5100

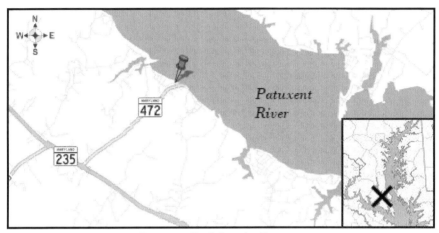

County: St. Mary's County
Open: Year Round
Latitude: N 38° 24' 47" Longitude: W 76° 36' 32"
Body of Water: Patuxent River
Dockage: Yes
Picture Code: SI1 at www.crabdecksandtikibars.com/pix

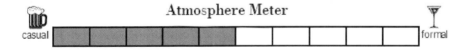

At Sandgates Inn, pictures of crabs seem to be everywhere
— on the doors, the walls, the front sign, the windows, and
the menu. Even a red crab made of lights shines bright
outside near the roof.

The charming crab infestation underscores the top priority
for this traditional Maryland seafood house. But the crabs

that merit your full attention are the hot steamy ones piled high on the table in front of you.

They're cooked to order with a house-specialty seasoning mix that enhances their delicate flavor and makes them a favorite dish for locals. Also worth a try are the jumbo lump crab cakes, creamy seafood chowder, steamed shrimp, fried oysters, and tender clams. Hearty sandwiches and exceptional fried chicken are big crowd pleasers.

You can eat inside this family-friendly restaurant or venture out to its waterfront deck that reveals a spectacular view of the Patuxent River and the rolling grassy lawns of its quaint neighborhood.

After dining, you might want to take a stroll on the wooden pier that stretches out on the water, sit back to catch a summer sunset, or play a game or two of horseshoes at Seabreeze next door.

Seabreeze Restaurant & Crab House

1505 North Sandgates Road
Mechanicsville, MD 20659
301-373-5217

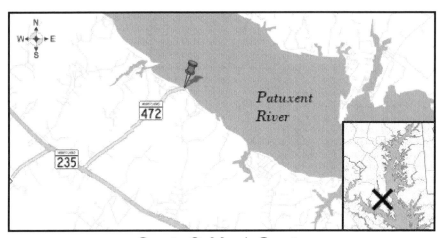

County: St. Mary's County
Open: Year Round
Latitude: N 38° 24' 47"   Longitude: W 76° 36' 26"
Body of Water: Patuxent River
Dockage: Yes
Picture Code: SRCH at www.crabdecksandtikibars.com/pix

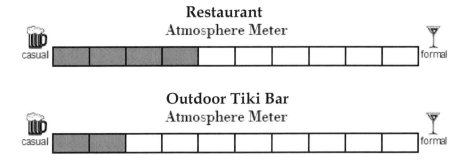

Restaurant
Atmosphere Meter
casual   formal

Outdoor Tiki Bar
Atmosphere Meter
casual   formal

Don't eat and run when you visit Seabreeze. Stay awhile and enjoy everything this crab house has to offer. There's easy docking for boaters and ample parking for cars and motorcycles.

Located next door to Sandgates Restaurant, the one-story blond-brick building houses bar and dining areas with table-to-ceiling windows that open up to a gorgeous view of the Patuxent River.

Seabreeze specializes in hot crabs and cold beer — good, no-frills Maryland cooking at reasonable prices. Local seafood, steaks, prime rib, and steamers of shrimp and crab legs arrive with mounds of corn fritters and coleslaw.

After you've picked your fill, head over to the tiki bar. It's a simple wooden structure with beer posters plastered all over its walls and Harleys lined up in front.

Bar tenders hand out cool cocktails and frosty beers to a mixed crowd of friendly bikers, thirsty boaters, and suntanned fishermen who meander out to the deck or pick up a game of darts inside.

The fishing piers and horseshoe pits keep folks busy for hours. When the bands start to play on Friday and Saturday nights, you'll be tempted to dance on the sandy beach under the moonlight. Go ahead. At Seabreeze, it's all about enjoying life at the water's edge.

Stoney's Broomes Island Seafood House

3939 Oyster House Road
Broomes Island, MD 20615
410-586-1888
www.stoneysseafoodhouse.com/broomes_island.php

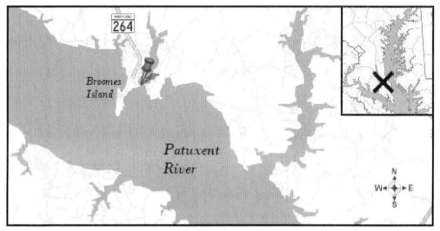

County: Calvert County
Open: Seasonal
Latitude: N 38° 24' 46"   Longitude: W 76° 32' 42"
Body of Water: Island Creek off the Patuxent River
Dockage: Yes
Picture Code: SBISH at www.crabdecksandtikibars.com/pix

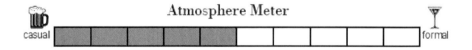

Whether you arrive by boat, jet ski, or car, it's hard to imagine a more pleasant place to spend a warm summer day than at Stoney's Broomes Island.

Tucked away in a lovely residential neighborhood on a narrow street appropriately named Oyster House Road, this charming place has been serving up good Maryland seafood for almost 20 years.

As a sister restaurant of Stoney's Kingfishers and Solomons Pier in nearby Solomons, jumbo lump crab cakes with only a dash of filler and served on a soft roll are the house specialty.

Clams, steamed shrimp, and oysters are local and fresh, and the rockfish basket has the right mix of crunch and flavor. Steaks, sandwiches, salads, and crab soups expand your dining options.

The newly renovated indoor dining rooms offer a visual display of waterfowl replicas and other aquatic wildlife dangling from the rafters. Floor-to-ceiling windows open up to a fantastic view of Island Creek and Solomons Bridge.

But if you're seeking the outdoor Bay experience, give in to the temptation to walk through the back doors. Along the water's edge, decks with wooden picnic tables are lined up like an archipelago of crab-covered islands. Boaters and landlubbers alike belly up to the tiki bar for icy rum cocktails or beer.

Keep strolling the grounds and you'll discover a waterfall surrounded by lush green landscaping and a white-sand beach that creates a picturesque setting to watch the tide come in or the sun set in the West.

The quaint inn is available to rent by the night or longer if you want to extend your time on the Bay.

Vera's White Sands Beach Club Restaurant

1200 White Sands Drive
Lusby, MD 20657
410-586-1182
www.verasbeachclub.com

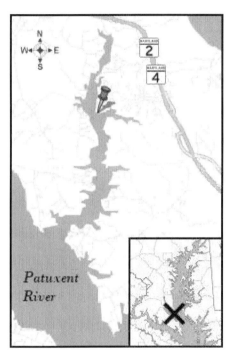

County: Calvert County

Open: Year Round

Latitude: N 38° 25' 16"

Longitude: W 76° 29' 11"

Body of Water: St. Leonard Creek off the Patuxent River

Dockage: Yes

Picture Code: VWSBCR at www.crabdecksandtikibars.com/pix

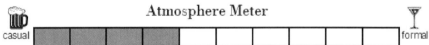

Atmosphere Meter

casual ▢▢▢▢▢▢▢▢▢▢ formal

It all started over a half-century ago when an adventurous young woman named Vera left her small town in Montana for the bright lights of Hollywood. While Vera never found fame as a movie star, she did marry optometrist Effrus "Doc"

Freeman. The couple explored the world aboard his yacht, visiting exotic ports-of-call from India to Indonesia.

Crates filled with mementos from their journeys came to rest at their home in Southern Maryland among the farmers and watermen. After WWII when Tiki became the rage, Vera and Doc opened a restaurant showcasing their Polynesian art and collectables.

In its heyday, celebrities from Baltimore, Washington, and Annapolis came by yacht or limo to this tropical paradise where Vera held court. In 2006, when Vera reached her nineties and the upkeep became too challenging, she relinquished her tiki throne and sold the place.

After extensive renovations, White Sands reopened with a casual, beach party style but still adheres to tiki tradition. Upon arrival, you're welcomed by a massive granite statue of Poseidon. Behind the god of the seas, a huge stone Easter Island head stands guard over the boats in the marina below.

Inside, dark wooden tiki masks stare out from bamboo walls, faux leopard-skin stools encircle the bar, and palm branches and sea shells add a splash of color to the dining rooms. Water trickles down a mermaid fountain on the patio. On the menu, casual pub fare is mixed with more ambitious dinner entrees. Mountains of steamed shrimp, sandwiches, chicken tenders, and fried seafood in cheery baskets rests on tabletops next to steaks, crab cakes, and sautéed rockfish.

In tribute to the former owner, a glamorous portrait of Vera hangs on the wall. Perched on top of her golden blond hair is a tall seashell headpiece, while she wears a dress made of peacock feathers and jewelry laden with oyster shells and emeralds. That alone is worth the trip.

Clarke's Landing Restaurant

24580 Clark's Landing Lane
Hollywood, MD 20636
301-373-8468
www.clrestaurant.com

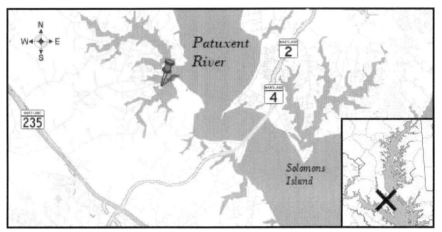

County: St. Mary's County
Open: Year Round
Latitude: N 38° 20' 33"   Longitude: W 76° 30' 13"
Body of Water: Mill Creek off the Patuxent River
Dockage: Yes
Picture Code: CLR at www.crabdecksandtikibars.com/pix

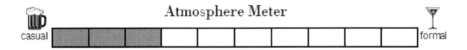

Atmosphere Meter

casual | formal

On one side of the Gov. Thomas Johnson Bridge is busy bustling Solomons; on the other side, life is a bit more laid-back. The epitome of this easy Southern Maryland living is Clark's Landing.

Whether you arrive by boat or car, you'll have no problem finding this quaint waterfront restaurant. The one-story building is painted a calming sky blue, with bright blue and white awnings and umbrellas protecting diners from the scorching August sun on the deck.

A crab holding a wooden spoon and wearing a chef's hat gives a splash of red to the restaurant's sign. A rickety wooden duck blind rests at the end of a nearby pier.

Inside, a nautical theme plays out with giant marlins, crabs, and ships mounted on the wood-paneled walls. Cement planters shaped like rowboats hold clusters of pink impatiens by the door.

Country music plays softly in the background while locals belly up to the bar by noon. The atmosphere is friendly and casual.

The menu offers classic Chesapeake seafood. Steamed crabs, crab cakes shrimp, pan-seared mussels, and fried oysters are accompanied by hush puppies, fries, crisp salads, or creamy crab soup. Steaks, chicken, sandwiches, and pasta round out your dining options.

Stoney's Kingfishers Seafood House

14442 Solomons Island Road South
Solomons, MD 20688
410-394-0236
www.stoneysseafoodhouse.com/kingfishers.php

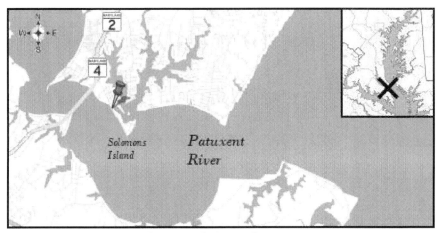

County: Calvert County
Open: Year Round
Latitude: N 38° 19' 26"   Longitude: W 76° 27' 37"
Body of Water: between The Narrows and the Patuxent River
Dockage: No
Picture Code: SKSH at www.crabdecksandtikibars.com/pix

Atmosphere Meter

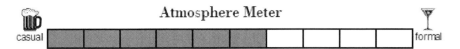

When you see a bait and tackle shop next door, signs for charter fishing boats inside, and six types of oysters on the menu (steamed, raw, or fried), you know you're in the right place for Chesapeake seafood.

Sandwiched between the Patuxent River and the Narrows, Stoney's Kingfishers has Bay tradition written all over it.

On the walls are murals accented with hand-crafted wood carvings of Maryland estuary life, including geese, eagles, ducks, herons, and osprey.

The atmosphere is casual-nice: the kind of place where you'd feel comfortable meeting colleagues after work, rather than the gritty crab shacks where you worry about feisty seagulls swooping down to steal a French fry.

The food is fresh, well-prepared, and seafood-centric. A steaming bowl of crab soup (your choice of tomato-based or creamy) with a salad is enough to fill you up. Sandwiches give a token nod to chicken and beef, but focus more on crab, tuna, and rockfish. Burgers are made with a whopping half-pound of cow.

But the seafood entrees are where Stoney's Kingfishers really shines: crab in cakes or creamy imperial, soft shells lightly sautéed, Neptune platters with mixed delicacies from the Bay, and fried oysters and shrimp with a crispy outside coating.

In case the name sounds familiar, this is a sister restaurant of Stoney's Broomes Island and Solomons Pier.

Catamarans Restaurant

14470 Solomons Island Road South
Solomons, MD 20688
410-326-8399
www.catamaransrestaurant.com

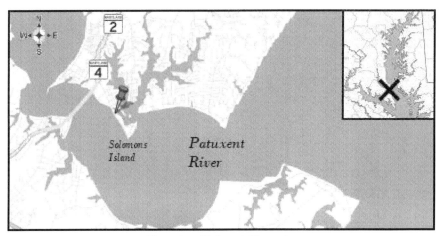

County: Calvert County
Open: Year Round
Latitude: N 38° 19' 22"   Longitude: W 76° 27' 35"
Body of Water: between The Narrows and the Patuxent River
Dockage: Yes
Picture Code: CR1 at www.crabdecksandtikibars.com/pix

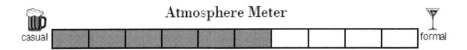

The music piped out to the street from Catamarans makes you turn your head to see what seems like a standard two-story clapboard house with a wrap-around porch.

But looks can be deceiving. This is no ordinary house, and it's full of pleasant surprises that are unveiled as you wander around the place.

The front patio is bordered with foliage that's tall enough to create a privacy screen from the street traffic but trimmed to the perfect height to not obstruct a fabulous view of the water flowing under Solomons Bridge.

The side porch leads to another patio in the back of the restaurant with wooden chairs and tables scattered about for easy mingling. Brightly colored vintage beer signs and tiki torches add a touch of cheer.

Inside the first floor is arguably one of the loveliest dining rooms in the area. The look is subtle urban chic: creamy lime walls highlighted with sheer white curtains and jet black chairs create a soothing sophisticated ambiance for dining.

But that's not all. Climbing upstairs reveals another deck that witnesses gorgeous sunsets over the Patuxent. Inside the second floor you'll find a bar/lounge area with beautiful high-vaulted windows. Comfy couches and deep cushioned chairs encircle a pool table with a Budweiser lamp glowing down on red felt.

It's tempting to hang out here all night and play billiards, but you might want to grab a bite as well. Catamarans recently hired chef Robert Hesse from the TV show *Hell's Kitchen,* and his cuisine pays tribute to local seafood and fresh regional ingredients.

The new menu showcases crabs, shrimp, oysters, and rockfish, but also caters to meat lovers with steaks, ribs, chicken, and sandwiches. Hesse prepares everything with an innovative flare and a dash of fun.

Stoney's Solomons Pier Seafood House

14757 Solomons Island Road South
Solomons, MD 20688
410-326-2424
www.stoneysseafoodhouse.com/solomons_pier.php

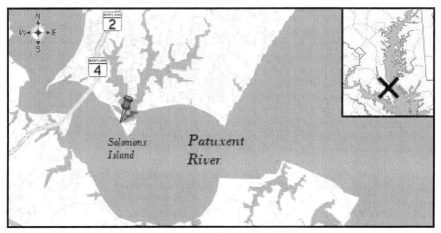

County: Calvert County
Open: Year Round
Latitude: N 38° 19' 14"   Longitude: W 76° 27' 32"
Body of Water: Patuxent River
Dockage: No
Picture Code: SSPSH at www.crabdecksandtikibars.com/pix

Atmosphere Meter

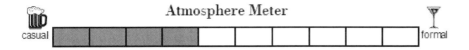

casual — formal

As you stroll along the river walk, you can't miss Solomons Pier jutting out into the water. Whether you grab a bite at the bar, out on the pier, or inside the dining room, you'll experience Southern Maryland's version of dinner and a show. The panoramic views of the Patuxent River are fun to watch any time of day or night. Patuxent Naval Air Station lies to the south; Thomas Johnson Bridge to the north, and all types of boats pass by before your very eyes.

Snacks, appetizers, and entrees represent the best of local seafood — jumbo lump crab cakes, pink steamed shrimp, little neck clams, and crispy crusted rockfish — to name a few.

There's even a seafood market next door if you haven't consumed enough and want to cook up some oysters or mussels at home later.

But you really shouldn't leave here without sampling the fresh oysters. After you've slurped down the first one, take a moment to inspect the shell, because oysters are a major player in Solomons' history.

When Isaac Solomon bought the land in 1865, it was little more than tobacco farms and grassy marshlands. Isaac built a cannery and housing for his workers, and a post office opened in 1870. Shipbuilding flourished, and by the late 1800s, the fishing industry boomed and seafood processing plants dotted the coastline.

Along came J.C. Lore, who opened a seafood processing house right down the street and expanded the island's size by building on top of thousands of tons of discarded oyster shells. The oyster house closed in 1978, but today if you walk to the back of this restaurant, you'll find a wall dedicated to Lore's oyster shuckers.

To learn even more, head over to the restored Lore Oyster House and Museum, which chronicles the story of the local seafood industry.

Calypso Bay Crab House

120 Charles Street
Solomons, MD 20688
443-404-5125
www.calypsobaycrabhouse.com

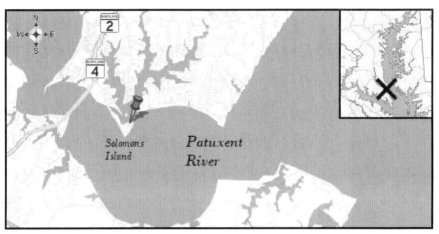

County: Calvert County
Open: Year Round
Latitude: N 38° 19' 12"   Longitude: W 76° 27' 16"
Body of Water: Back Creek off the Patuxent River
Dockage: Yes
Picture Code: CBCH at www.crabdecksandtikibars.com/pix

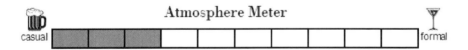

Calypso Bay is the kind of place that's easy to love.
It sits right on the water's edge at Harbor Island Marina in
Solomons Island.

The big gray clapboard building's main dash of color
comes from a huge orange and red surfboard sign ablaze
with the restaurant's name. Tall plastic palm trees and

plush tropical plants surrounding the outdoor patio bolster the island feel.

The upstairs deck, staged with wooden bar stools along open windows, gives a gull's eye view of the boats passing by. With a signature mai tai or orange crush in hand, you're quickly lulled into a state of relaxed bliss.

The casual inside decor hosts sea creatures, starfish, and coral to underscore its nautical roots. Big wooden ceiling fans keep the air moving to push away the summer heat.

An interesting mix of people kick back to enjoy upbeat music and fresh local food. Friendly waitresses carry trays laden with steamed crabs, steaks, seafood combos, sandwiches, and salads.

Specials like prime rib on Wednesdays and all-you-can-eat tacos on Thursdays make you want to come back often to enjoy good times at Calypso Bay.

The Tiki Bar
at Solomons Island

81 Charles Street
Solomons, MD 20688
410-326-4075
www.tikibarsolomons.com

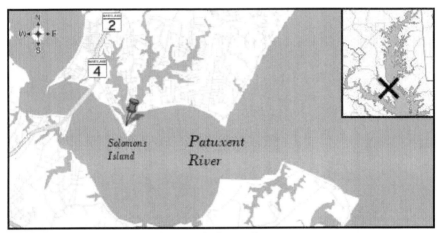

County: Calvert County
Open: Seasonal
Latitude: N 38° 19' 10"   Longitude: W 76° 27' 21"
Body of Water: Back Creek off the Patuxent River
Dockage: Yes
Picture Code: TTBSI at www.crabdecksandtikibars.com/pix

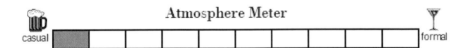

Brace yourself. When you visit The Tiki Bar at Solomons, you enter the Polynesian epicenter of the Bay. It's the Holy Grail of tropical island fun where people-watching can't be beat.

Bikers in black leather chaps buy beers for businessmen who loosen their ties, pleasure boaters and watermen share a smoke over tales of the sea, bikini-clad college girls gracefully skip past tourists in loud Hawaiian shirts — and everyone gets along just fine.

The Tiki Village is comprised of a huge bar, restaurant, gift shop, tobacco barn, and hotel. Bamboo walls are garnished with tiki wood carvings by California Polynesian pop artist Bosko Hrnjak, and massive Easter Island stone heads keep a steely eye on the crowd.

The thatched roof bar is decorated with tiki masks, fish, and erupting volcanoes. Big blue beach umbrellas cover picnic tables and chairs painted Key West green, blue, yellow, and orange.

Towering palm trees and sand are replaced each spring to keep the place looking fresh. Bands play Jimmy Buffett, Bob Marley — anything to top off the island ambiance.

Parties here are legendary, and when the 30th anniversary bash in 2010 attracted 20,000 guests, one had to wonder how they all fit on this tiny island.

So, if you're in a tiki state of mind, step inside and treat yourself to a signature mai tai, kokomo, or Cajun margarita and enjoy the wild tropical breeze blowing across the Bay.

The Dry Dock Restaurant

251 C Street
Solomons, MD 20688
410-326-4817
www.zahnisers.com/drydock.htm

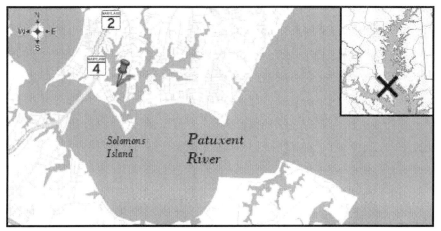

County: Calvert County
Open: Year Round
Latitude: N 38° 19' 43"   Longitude: W 76° 27' 31"
Body of Water: Back Creek off the Patuxent River
Dockage: Yes
Picture Code: TDDR at www.crabdecksandtikibars.com/pix

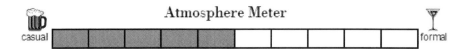

Atmosphere Meter

casual   formal

The name of the game at Dry Dock is easy living. It's part
of Zahnisers Yachting Center, which has committed decades
to helping folks enjoy life on the water.

The slate green building's upper balcony gives a
spectacular view of the marina where sail boats gently sway

with the waves. Children do cannonballs into the swimming pool, while parents relax with a cool beverage in hand.

The menu takes classic Chesapeake cuisine up a notch and promises "to use as much sustainable seafood and local produce as possible." You can jumpstart a meal with creamy crab soup, shrimp with Amaretto glaze, pecan-crusted sea scallops, or Oysters Rockefeller.

Seafood entrees include seared salmon with corn risotto cake, blackened rockfish in a béarnaise sauce, or coconut red curry sea bass.

Imaginative cooking also extends to land dishes: roasted chicken breast comes with gnocchi, filet mignon is blanketed in a port demiglaze, and braised lamb shank is flanked by a potato parsnip mash.

At Dry Dock, the dynamic combo of fine dining and phenomenal scenery is sure to make you want to come back as soon as possible.

The Captain's Table

275 Lore Road
Solomons, MD 20688
410-326-2772
www.massarosrestaurants.com/captainstable

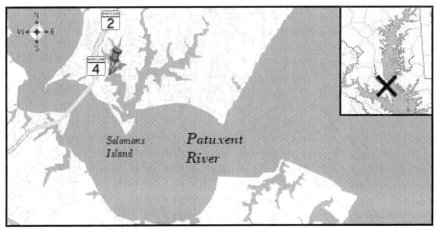

County: Calvert County
Open: Year Round
Latitude: N 38° 19' 56"   Longitude: W 76° 27' 40"
Body of Water: Back Creek off the Patuxent River
Dockage: Yes
Picture Code: TCT at www.crabdecksandtikibars.com/pix

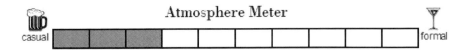

Don't be alarmed when you see a hotel chain next door to The Captain's Table. The two are separate. The family who owns the restaurant serves up hearty meals in the Chesapeake tradition. You can watch boats cruise by from the waterfront deck or take a seat on the tall-backed wooden benches in the air-conditioned dining area. Specials are based on what the local watermen bring to the cook that day. The menu begins with steamed mussels, portabellas stuffed with crab imperial, BBQ shrimp, and fresh sliced tomato and mozzarella salad. The Captain's Platter overflows with fried crab cakes, scallops, and oysters. Tender ribs, liver and onions, meatloaf, country fried steak, and a juicy New York strip can get any landlubber's mouth watering.

Be sure to notice the restaurant's logo, which pays tribute to an essential Bay tradition — three pirates slouch around a table while a surly wench serves their grog. During the early 17th Century, pirates roamed these waters and preyed upon ships crossing the Atlantic. They were tolerated, even courted, by colonists who wanted to thumb their noses at the British and buy black market goods.

A trio of privateers named Davis, Wafer and Hinson had stolen a king's fortune in the South Seas and then started wreaking havoc from the northern tip of the Bay southward. They were captured by Captain Rowe of the *Dumbarton* and thrown in the Jamestown jail for a year. The deal arranged for their release stated that their loot must be returned, and they had to pay an extra 300 pounds, which would eventually help establish the College of William and Mary.

The most infamous pirate to roam the local waters was Edward Teach (a.k.a. Blackbeard). He stood an imposing 6 feet 5 inches tall, and the beard that grew down to his chest was braided with ribbons. He liked to use the isolated necks of the Eastern Shore to ready his ships for sea and plundered local plantations and towns en route to the ocean. His pillaging days ended in 1718, when Navy Lieutenant Robert Maynard attacked Blackbeard's ship and fatally shot the pirate with his pistol. Maynard severed Blackbeard's head and mounted it on his ship's bow, then tossed the decapitated body into the water.

The Back Creek Bistro

14415 Dowell Road
Dowell, MD 20629
410-326-9900
www.backcreekbistro.com

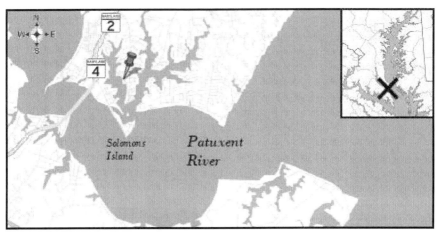

County: Calvert County
Open: Year Round
Latitude: N 38° 19' 56"   Longitude: W 76° 27' 22"
Body of Water: Back Creek off the Patuxent River
Dockage: No
Picture Code: TBCB at www.crabdecksandtikibars.com/pix

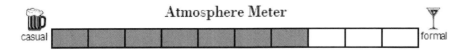

Take time and enjoy your visit to Back Creek Bistro. It's located at Calvert Marina on the second floor of a lovely red brick building with elegant green shutters.

The Thomas Johnson Bridge to Solomons Island provides the backdrop to an incredible view of the water and a quaint boating community.

Inside, exposed brick walls, oriental rugs, and plush couches create a soothing ambiance, and the staff is eager to please its guests with locally grown produce and seafood harvested from regional waters.

The menu presents a nice array of appetizers, salads, and sandwiches such as crab dip, calamari, lobster bisque, gorgonzola salad, and burgers made of certified Angus beef.

The kitchen kicks into high gear when preparing entrees: golden brown crab cakes, shrimp in a beurre blanc sauce, lobster smothered in Grand Marnier sauce, gnocchi tossed with jumbo crab meat in a vodka cream sauce, and chicken picatta dusted with capers.

The kids menu offers pasta, nuggets, and fries served quickly so the youngsters can goof around the gazebo outside while parents finish their meals at a more leisurely pace.

Music on Thursday and Saturday nights features local jazz and blues artists.

And if you need one more reason to like this restaurant, get this — the owners actively support charities and other community organizations such as Meals on Wheels, the fire department, Boys & Girls Club, Humane Society, and Chesapeake Bay Foundation.

Four Winds Café

14755 Dowell Road
Dowell, MD 20629
410-394-6373
www.fourwindscafe.net

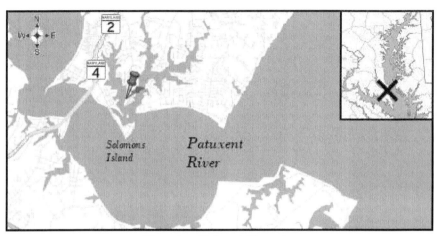

County: Calvert County
Open: Year Round
Latitude: N 38° 19' 41"   Longitude: W 76° 27' 19"
Body of Water: Back Creek off the Patuxent River
Dockage: Yes
Picture Code: FWC at www.crabdecksandtikibars.com/pix

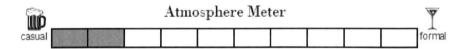

If you don't own a boat but still want that wonderful feeling of being on the water, head over to Four Winds Café.

It's a cozy little place that rests on pylons, juts out into Back Creek, and is surrounded by boats at Calvert Marina in the shadow of Solomons Bridge.

Boaters like it too, because docking is a breeze and the atmosphere is casual rustic. Sunsets are glorious, and the charter boat captain next door will gladly escort you to the Bay for a day of fishing.

Blue herons and sea gulls hover around looking for minnows, baby crabs, or French fries that topple overboard.

With such a small kitchen, it's understandable that the cook keeps the menu simple but does a bang-up job with local seafood. Creamy chowder with shrimp, scallops, and crab meat is irresistible. Crab cakes, blackened grouper, and fried flounder are cooked with a special blend of seasonings.

You can also opt for hot sandwiches (roast beef, turkey, or ham), cool salads, or pizza for the kids.

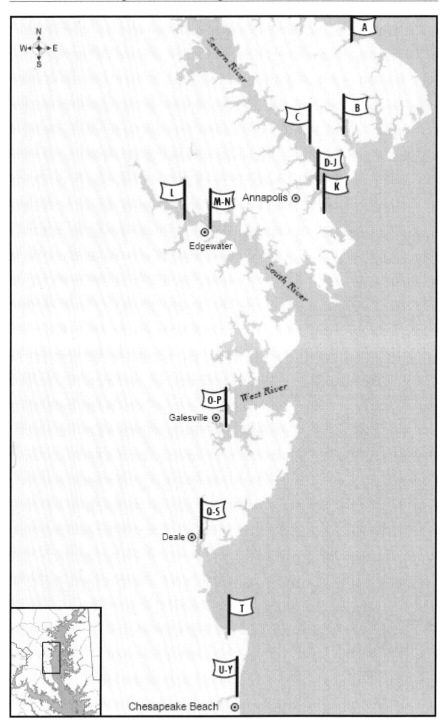

Annapolis to Chesapeake Beach

Deep Creek Restaurant

1050 Deep Creek Avenue
Arnold, MD 21012
410-974-1408 or 410-757-4045
www.thedeepcreekrestaurant.com

County: Anne Arundel County

Open: Year Round

Latitude: N 39° 2' 56"

Longitude: W 76° 27' 38"

Body of Water: Deep Creek off the Magothy River

Dockage: Yes

Picture Code: DCR at www.crabdecksandtikibars.com/pix

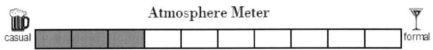

Atmosphere Meter

casual | | | | | | | | | | formal

From the first bite of crab bruschetta, you'll know you stumbled upon a special Chesapeake gem at Deep Creek Restaurant.

On a bed of greens, toasted Italian bread slices cradle garden-fresh diced tomatoes and basil, with chunks of delicate crab meat mounted on top.

The bruschetta — like every other dish cooked in this kitchen — shows Deep Creek cares about details and high-quality ingredients.

The menu features award-winning local seafood dishes of crabs, oysters, shrimp, and clams, yet makes room for other culinary preferences such as Cajun chicken, blackened beef tips, and roasted pork Cuban sandwich.

Family-owned since 1999, the cozy restaurant is tucked away in a small marina on the Magothy River where time seems to stand still on lazy summer afternoons. The beautiful waterfront view shows boats gracefully sailing by and children on the dock using chicken necks on a string to pull indignant crabs from the water.

Sunsets are picturesque. And when the work day is over, tiki torches are lit, a band begins to play, and cold beer is served to guests on the wooden deck outside.

It doesn't get much better than this.

Jimmy Cantler's Riverside Inn

458 Forest Beach Road
Annapolis, MD 21401
410-757-1311
www.cantlers.com

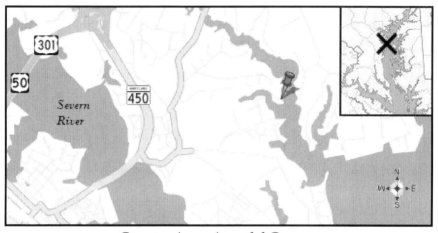

County: Anne Arundel County
Open: Year Round
Latitude: N 39° 0' 11"   Longitude: W 76° 27' 29"
Body of Water: Mill Creek off the Chesapeake Bay
Dockage: Yes
Picture Code: JCRI at www.crabdecksandtikibars.com/pix

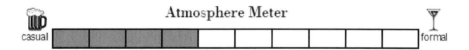

When you drive into Cantler's parking lot and come face-to-face with a giant Maryland blue crab painted on the side of a propane tank, think of it as a charming welcome committee of one. Then take a deep breath and let your nostrils fill with that unmistakable crab deck smell — the zing of Old Bay mixed with briny air and crabs steaming. The rhythmic sound of wooden hammers crushing crabs makes your stomach rumble with delight.

Cantler's wooden deck bustles with a mixed bag of local families, watermen, young couples, and businessmen enjoying the view of Mill Creek. With old oak trees holding down the banks and sail boats dutifully pointing their masts toward the sky, the scene is idyllic.

Once seated at a picnic table, you see plump steamed crabs piled high on black plastic trays. Cocktail sauce is squeezed out of 12-inch tall plastic bottles to accommodate mountains of pink shrimp. Men push back their Ravens caps to get a better view of their golf ball-sized steamed clams. Creamy coleslaw and crispy fries round out the meal.

When you've eaten your fill, don't miss a rare Bay treat. Walk down Cantler's steps and peek into the large metal tanks down by the docks. What are they? Crab shed tanks. When watermen come to Cantler's with crabs ready to molt (shed their shell), they sequester their catch in a tank filled with Bay water. The staff watches for clues that molting is near and quickly transfers those crabs into a shedding tank. They check the tanks several times a day for crabs that have outgrown their shells and place them in yet another tank.

Why all the fuss? Hard shell crabs are pretty aggressive and devour anything in sight. The molting process makes soft shell crabs more docile. Like medieval knights without armor, newly molted crabs hide in the Bay's grassy marshlands, laying low until new shells harden. Tanks lack places to hide, so humans need to step in and protect them – until they're ready to fry them up. Not every crab house can afford to run shed tanks. But after five generations in the seafood biz, Cantler's remains committed to the best traditions of the Bay.

Severn Inn

1993 Baltimore Annapolis Boulevard
Annapolis, MD 21409
410-349-4000
www.severninn.com

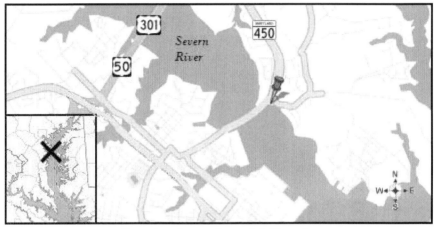

County: Anne Arundel County
Open: Year Round
Latitude: N 38° 59' 41"   Longitude: W 76° 28' 58"
Body of Water: Severn River
Dockage: Yes
Picture Code: SI3 at www.crabdecksandtikibars.com/pix

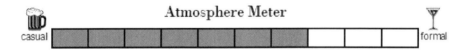

The view is so lovely at Severn Inn that it's tempting to spend all day on its waterfront decks watching boats sail by. Your eyes can't resist following the graceful lines of the bridge spanning the Severn River.

Directly across the water is a panoramic view of historic Annapolis and the U.S. Naval Academy that's been training officers to protect our shores since 1845.

Inside the restaurant, the atmosphere is a bit upscale, yet still cheery and inviting. Cherry wood chairs surround tables covered with white linens, and floor-to-ceiling windows ensure everyone gets a tremendous view of the water. On top of the dark wood bar, vintage oyster cans are piled high to salute the history of the Bay.

The menu is seafood-centric, fresh, and takes Chesapeake standards up a notch with innovative twists from around the globe. Snacks range from fried pickles to green bean tempura, and pub plates offer traditional fish-and-chips, as well as grilled cilantro-lime fish tacos.

For lunch, you can go with a crab cake sandwich, 8-ounce Angus burger, or quiche Florentine with crab. They pull out all the stops at dinner with choices like an Asian tapas plate, Salvadorian seafood stew, and tender veal tenderloin topped with prosciutto.

Afterward, you might want one last glance at the gorgeous river view before you head home. For a unique perspective, you could walk next door to Jonas Green Park (named after a printer who was Ben Franklin's cousin) to check out its sandy beach for boat launching and a wooden pier for fishing.

Hell Point Seafood

12 Dock Street
Annapolis, MD 21401
410-990-9888
www.hp-seafood.com

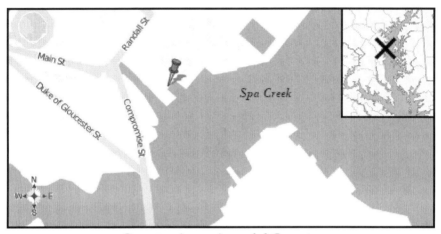

County: Anne Arundel County
Open: Year Round
Latitude: N 38° 58' 38"   Longitude: W 76° 29' 6"
Body of Water: Annapolis Harbor off Spa Creek off the Severn River
Dockage: No
Picture Code: HPS at www.crabdecksandtikibars.com/pix

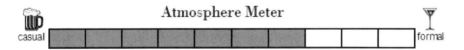

When award-winning chef, Bob Kinkead, decided to open a restaurant in downtown Annapolis in June 2009, he chose a spectacular location — right on the water overlooking Ego Alley (named after the owners of high-ticket yachts that crowd the piers).

The site was previously occupied by Harbor House and Phillips Seafood. "Hell Point" refers to this section of town that was little more than an unattractive mountain of oyster shells and a dingy gas station in the 1920s.

Well, things have changed, and the City Dock area is now the heart of Annapolis nightlife and a perfect home for this lovely dining establishment.

Just inside the arched brick entrance, you find a contemporary-style bar decorated with muted green and yellow colors, some nautical-themed paintings, and tall wood and chrome chairs.

The gracefully curved staircase leads you up to a spacious dining area, where ceiling-high windows reveal a dazzling harbor view.

Up one more flight of stairs, past a picture of a man steaming an industrial-sized bushel of crabs, and you reach the main dining room. Blue-and-white striped awnings and soft muted colors set the tone for casual, fine dining.

The food is fresh, seasonal, and pulled straight from the waters of the Chesapeake and Atlantic. Signature dishes include New England lobster roll, crab cakes with corn relish, bacon-wrapped swordfish with lentils, and Portuguese seafood stew.

Meals are so hearty and flavorful that you won't want to leave a drop on your plate. But you'll probably feel so full afterward that you'll want to stretch your legs and enjoy an evening stroll along the pier.

Middleton Tavern

2 Market Space
Annapolis, MD 21401
410-263-3323
www.middletontavern.com

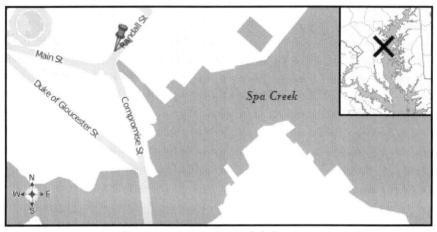

County: Anne Arundel County
Open: Year Round
Latitude: N 38° 58' 41"   Longitude: W 76° 29' 12"
Body of Water: Annapolis Harbor off Spa Creek off the Severn River
Dockage: No
Picture Code: MT at www.crabdecksandtikibars.com/pix

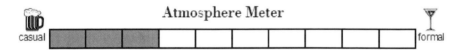

If you want to eat authentic Bay cuisine in a 250-year old building, then Middleton Tavern is the place for you. Established in 1750, this red Georgian-style building is located on Annapolis' City Dock area among a row of historic watering holes once frequented by the likes of George Washington, Thomas Jefferson, and Ben Franklin.

In the mid-1700s, the owner ran a ferry across to the Eastern Shore and managed his ship-building business from inside the tavern.

In tribute, early American artifacts now adorn the restaurant walls, where you see portraits of Revolutionary War heroes, Civil War muskets, and antique Naval Academy uniforms. Seats near an old wood and brick fireplace warm up winter visitors.

At the recently remodeled bar, you can order an array of light-fare treats such as oyster shooters, crab sliders, wings, or a bucket of mussels or little necks.

Traditional Chesapeake cooking dominates the dinner menu with shrimp steam pots, oyster loaf po boys, sea scallop sliders, crab cakes, and "naked" fish prepared just the way you like it. Meat lovers can choose garlic-roasted pork tenderloin, savory steaks, or juicy burgers.

During warm weather, the best seats in the house are outside on the covered deck, where you can gaze at the water and imagine how much Annapolis has changed since this tavern was built.

Hotels and upscale restaurants have replaced the oyster-packing plants and ship-building companies, but this vibrant town along the Bay somehow retains its historic charm.

Buddy's Crabs & Ribs

100 Main Street
Annapolis, MD 21401
410-626-1100
www.buddysannap.com

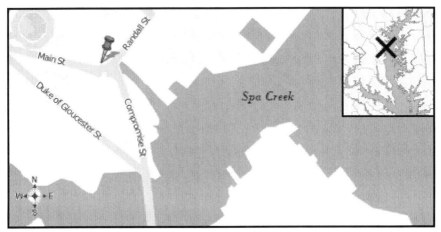

County: Anne Arundel County
Open: Year Round
Latitude: N 38° 58' 39"   Longitude: W 76° 29' 16"
Body of Water: Annapolis Harbor off Spa Creek off the Severn River
Dockage: No
Picture Code: BCR at www.crabdecksandtikibars.com/pix

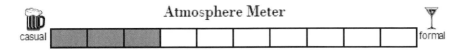

Of all the restaurants in the City Dock section of
Annapolis, Buddy's is by far the crabbiest. And in this neck
of the Bay, that's a real compliment.

Family-owned since 1988, it's a landmark in town with
just a few tables and a street sign out front. But once you

climb the stairs to the second floor, you reach the Mount Olympus of crab-eaters' heaven.

The restaurant is big and bustling with rows of wooden tables piled high with mountains of hot steamed crabs and baby back ribs.

Tall windows offer a bird's eye view of the harbor. Thirsty boaters, locals, and tourists crowd around the bar. Long, chrome buffet tables give you a steamy preview of what's in store for dinner.

The raw bar offers six-packs of oysters harvested from the Choptank River and other East Coast hot spots. Other starters include king crab legs, clam strips, steamed shrimp, Cajun crawfish, and Old Bay crab chips. The blooming onion is just plain fun.

Salads are mainly variations of mixed greens with crab or shrimp sprinkled on top. The sandwich board features soft shells, tuna steaks, beefy burgers, and chicken.

Some entrees are only meant for those with a Titan's appetite, namely the all-you-can-eat crab feast or the Royal Big Buddy, a one-pound monster-sized crab cake. Regular mortals can have their fill of local seafood or combo platters with tender ribs.

Children under 10 eat for free if adults order an entree, and a neon sign promises ice cream and crabs for dessert! It's the perfect combo from a place that aims to please crab eaters of every shape and size.

Pusser's Caribbean Grille

80 Compromise Street
Annapolis, MD 21401
410-626-0004
www.pussersusa.com/annapolis.shtml

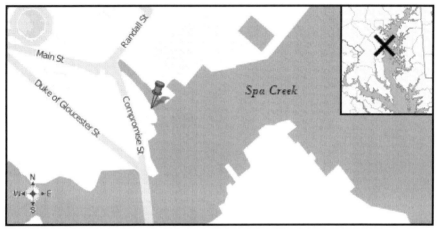

County: Anne Arundel County
Open: Year Round
Latitude: N 38° 58' 34"   Longitude: W 76° 29' 7"
Body of Water: Annapolis Harbor off Spa Creek off the Severn River
Dockage: No
Picture Code: PCG at www.crabdecksandtikibars.com/pix

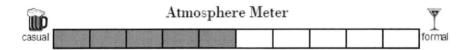

Even though America booted England from its ports during the War of 1812, Pusser's Caribbean Grille said they could come back if they agree to share their rum.

This expansive British pub is named after a 350-year old premium rum that "fueled" the British Royal Navy. From 1655 until 1970, every British sailor was allotted a daily ration of rum. Pusser is the corrupted version of the word "purser," who was the navy officer in charge of doling out that precious amber liquid to the men.

This maritime tradition continues at Pusser's with signature rum drinks like the Painkiller, Lavaflow, Dark & Stormy, and Jamaican Me Crazy.

The long dock-side restaurant is part of the Marriott Hotel and claims to occupy the most waterfront real estate in downtown Annapolis.

Inside you'll meet a wooden maidenhead dressed in 18th Century attire who silently ignores advances from sailors at the bar. Nautical artwork hangs on the walls, and white twinkling lights near the ceiling set a festive mood.

Music here combines acoustic with calypso, while the cuisine marries the Chesapeake with the Caribbean. Crab dip, coconut rum shrimp, oysters Rockefeller, and jerk chicken pineapple quesadillas are served as appetizers.

Specialty entrees include Olde English fish and chips, New England steamer pots, rasta pasta, Jamaican seafood stew, and jerk tuna steak.

On weekends or summer evenings, it can get a bit crowded and parking can get tricky, but it's still a great place to capture a little island fun.

Carrol's Creek
Waterfront Restaurant

410 Severn Avenue
Annapolis, MD 21403
410-263-8102
www.carrolscreek.com

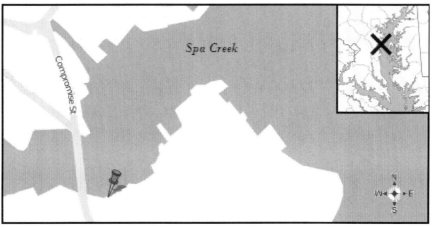

County: Anne Arundel County
Open: Year Round
Latitude: N 38° 58' 18"   Longitude: W 76° 29' 2"
Body of Water: Annapolis Harbor off Spa Creek off the Severn River
Dockage: No
Picture Code: CCWR at www.crabdecksandtikibars.com/pix

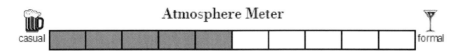

You're in for a triple-crown experience when you visit Carrol's Creek in Eastport — good food, an amazing view, and history dating back to the 1700s. Built in 1983, the dining area is casual/nice with an open airy feel. Nautical artwork brings color to tables covered with white linens.

The menu relies heavily on fresh seafood with innovative twists. House specialty Carrol's Creek Oysters are pulled from the Choptank River and then baked with horseradish, bacon, and cheddar. Tuna tartar and pepper-crusted beef carpaccio whet your appetite for the main dishes.

Must-try entrees include golden crab cakes, herbed rockfish, Mediterranean salmon, and chicken sautéed with sun-dried tomatoes and artichokes.

Out on the deck, the view keeps everyone busy while waiting for their food. An armada of sailboats, yachts, and water taxis drift along Spa Creek, almost close enough to touch. In the background lie Annapolis' capital dome, the Naval Academy, and the steeple on top of St. Anne's Church.

If the tall trees near the restaurant could talk, they'd tell tales of how Eastport played key roles in American history. Spa Creek was originally called Carrol's Creek, named after Charles Carroll — one of Maryland's favorite sons who signed the Declaration of Independence.

During the Revolutionary War, the area was an encampment for Lafayette's troops while en route to defeat the British in Yorktown. Later, it was the site of Fort Horn, which protected Annapolis during the War of 1812.

From around 1913 to 1974, Eastport hummed with the sounds of wooden boat building. Companies like John Trumpy & Sons crafted high-quality yachts with the famous "golden T" on the bow, and Chance Marine Construction build sub-chasers and PT boats for the U.S. Navy during World War II. With all this in one location, it's hard to resist visiting Carrol's Creek.

O'Leary's Seafood Restaurant

310 Third Street
Annapolis, MD 21403
410-263-0884
www.olearysseafood.com

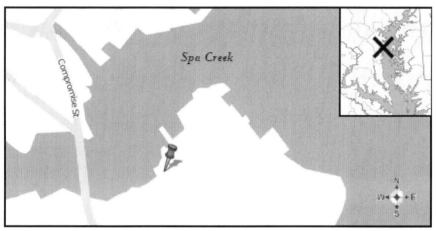

County: Anne Arundel County
Open: Year Round
Latitude: N 38° 58' 20"   Longitude: W 76° 28' 54"
Body of Water: Annapolis Harbor off Spa Creek off the Severn River
Dockage: No
Picture Code: OLSR at www.crabdecksandtikibars.com/pix

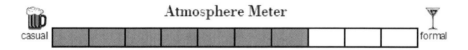

O'Learys Restaurant might be small in size, but it's big in commitment to fresh seafood — today and for future generations.

Protecting the marine environment is paramount for the chef, who evaluates species, fisheries, and methods of harvest before any ingredients appear on his plates.

As a result, your conscience is clear to enjoy a fine-dining experience rich in robust flavors that are prepared in a creative and responsible fashion.

Stand-out starters include sea scallops in phyllo with pesto, crispy fried Virginia oysters with pineapple mango chutney, and Belgian mussels bathed in lager beer with leeks, chorizo, and tomato.

Entrees run the gamut from classic Chesapeake crab cakes to a zarzuela fish stew laden with lobster, shrimp, and other fruits of the sea.

The atmosphere reflects the spirit of Annapolis — warm, sophisticated, and welcoming. Soft, mustard-colored walls are covered with vibrant abstract artwork painted by the owner himself. Black linen tablecloths are accented with plush burgundy back cushions in the booths.

Behind the rounded wooden bar is a collection of fine wines from California, France, and around the globe. Put it all together, and you get a wonderful little gem of the Bay.

Chart House Restaurant

300 Second Street
Annapolis, MD 21403
410-268-7166
www.chart-house.com

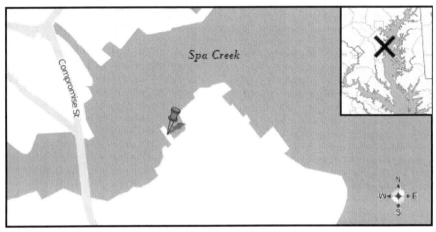

County: Anne Arundel County
Open: Year Round
Latitude: N 38° 58' 25"   Longitude: W 76° 28' 53"
Body of Water: Annapolis Harbor off Spa Creek off the Severn River
Dockage: No
Picture Code: CHR at www.crabdecksandtikibars.com/pix

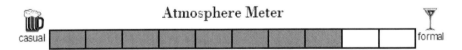

It's only fair to warn you right from the get-go that Chart House is part of a chain owned by Landry's Restaurants, with locations from Malibu to Miami specializing in seafood.

The paradox is, it doesn't feel like a chain. In fact, it's lovely, and it sits out on the water overlooking Annapolis Harbor with the capital dome in the distance.

It's located in an old boat-building warehouse, and the outrageously tall vaulted ceilings are supported by thick wooden beams that look like the interior of an old ship.

Tall windows running from the carpet to the top of the walls allow golden rays of sunlight to pour in and create a spacious, open feel. Browns and earth tones are accented with just a stroke of blue.

A stand-alone copper fireplace surrounded by leather couches creates a comfy lounge to wait for your table or meet friends for happy hour.

Nautical decor celebrates Maryland's maritime history with framed boat specs, paintings of skipjacks, miniature sailboat hulls, and models of old schooners. Glass panels etched into waves are placed around the booths.

The menu's daily catch covers all the Bay standards of crab, shrimp, oysters, and rockfish. A salad bar back by the kitchen lets you get your meal started while watching the cooks do their stuff. They also added some turf to the surf with prime rib, steaks, and chicken.

Decadent desserts, like Hot Chocolate Lava Cake and raspberry soufflé, are big enough to share and add the finishing touch to a pleasant meal along the water.

Sam's on the Waterfront

2020 Chesapeake Harbour Drive East
Annapolis, MD 21403
410-263-3600
www.samsonthewaterfront.com

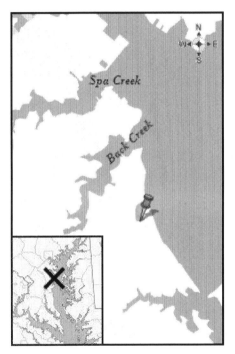

County: Anne Arundel County

Open: Sam's year-round;
Proud Mary's seasonal

Latitude: N 38° 57' 26"

Longitude: W 76° 28' 27"

Body of Water: Chesapeake
Harbour off the
Chesapeake Bay

Dockage: Yes

Picture Code: SW at
www.crabdecksandtikibars.com/
pix

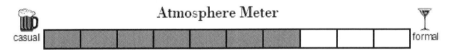

Atmosphere Meter

casual ████████████ formal

Back in the mid-1800s, screw-pile lighthouses dotted the coastline of the Chesapeake. Their spider-legged design with iron pikes drilled into the soft sand or muddy sea bottoms were ideal for the region.

Cottages within the structures housed lighthouse keepers who lived in isolation through scorching summer heat and icy winter winds.

Only a few of these lighthouses survived the past century, so in 1986, the owners of Sam's on the Waterfront built its restaurant to look like a screw-pile lighthouse as a tribute to Chesapeake maritime history.

Instead of hovering over marshy grasslands, it's nestled along the waterfront of a new residential development. Mustard-colored walls and white linen tablecloths create an elegant and romantic setting.

The chef uses fresh seafood and ingredients bought from local Maryland farmers to create a modern American cuisine with regional influences and an Asian flair.

For starters, the menu presents a classic cream of crab soup, as well as Thai steamed mussels and crab shiitake spring rolls. Traditional entrees like poached rockfish and jumbo lump crab cakes share the spotlight with braised short ribs, pasta with lamb bolognese, and a tender hanger steak with savory truffle fries.

And if you're in the mood for an after-dinner mojita or a crisp chardonnay, stop at Proud Mary's Dock Bar near the water and watch the boats parade along Back Creek.

Mike's Restaurant & Crab House

3030 Riva Road
Riva, MD 21140
410-956-2784
www.mikescrabhouse.com

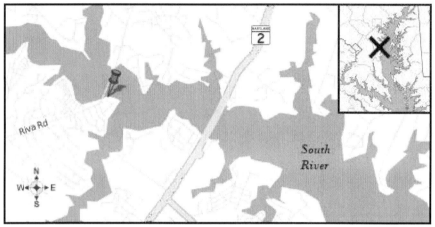

County: Anne Arundel County
Open: Year Round
Latitude: N 38° 57' 14"   Longitude: W 76° 34' 26"
Body of Water: South River
Dockage: Yes
Picture Code: MRCH at www.crabdecksandtikibars.com/pix

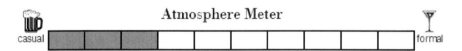

If you want to know what "peelers, keepers, and doublers" are, then you should go to Mike's web site for a full tutorial on Maryland blue crabs. But if you want to know what they taste like, you have to visit the restaurant.

Mike's has been around since 1958, and it's such a classic that it regularly wins awards for best crab house, crab cakes, and crab soup, and you envy locals who can eat there any time they want.

The big outdoor deck sits on top of the water giving diners a panoramic view of boaters navigating and recreating on the South River. The two-lane bridge in the background catches the amber light of sunset just right.

Inside the restaurant, casual dining continues with tables covered by brown paper and shakers filled with Old Bay. Your nose might dictate what you order when it gets a whiff of fresh crabs steaming in the kitchen.

You can't go wrong if you stick with traditional Bay cuisine: crab cakes, steamed shrimp, fried oysters, broiled rockfish, and Chesapeake fried chicken. Steaks, pork chops, BBQ ribs, and burgers accommodate the carnivores in the crowd.

Also on site is a country store that sells bait, beer, ice, and snacks — everything you need for a water adventure on the Bay.

In case you're still wondering, "peelers" are crabs that are ready to molt their outer shell; "keepers" are crabs that have grown to at least 5 inches from tip-to-tip and are big enough to catch, and "doublers" are two mating crabs swimming together, with the male above gently protecting his female below.

Yellowfin Steak & Fish House

2840 Solomons Island Road
Edgewater, MD 21037
410-573-1333
www.yellowfinrestaurant.com

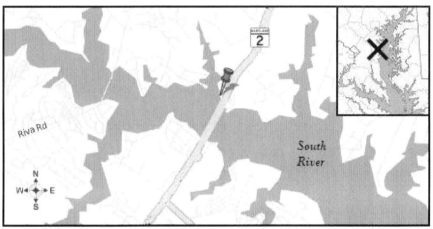

County: Anne Arundel County
Open: Year Round
Latitude: N 38° 57' 17"   Longitude: W 76° 33' 13"
Body of Water: South River
Dockage: Yes
Picture Code: YSFH at www.crabdecksandtikibars.com/pix

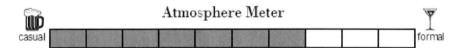

If you can cast aside the standard crab house image of an old clapboard building surrounded by a rickety wooden deck, then you might like Yellowfin.

An architectural firm from Annapolis did extensive renovations of a 10,000 square foot 50-year old restaurant using "aquatic metaphors." The result is Yellowfin's nouvelle nautical modern decor featuring a huge yellow sail stretched over the entrance, walls of blue canvass waves, and giant fish shapes all over the place. It's owned by Land & Sea Group, who also manages Buddy's Crabs & Ribs, Big Fish Grill, and Red Sky Steak & Fish House.

Yellowfin's dining area and lower deck present a lovely waterfront view, especially at sunset. The marble and chrome bar wraps around a show kitchen where you can watch cooks prepare your meal. The ambiance fluctuates between casual and fine dining, because patrons wear everything from T-shirts to ties.

The cuisine is innovative, but not outlandish, and is very seafood-centric. Sushi takes the top spot on the menu, offering rolls, tempura, tuna tartar, and seaweed salad.

Other starters add a creative twist to their Bay roots: rockfish tacos, "shrimptini" cocktail, and crab dip with artichokes and garlic. Entrees cover all the bases with a Maryland seafood trio of crab cake, pan-fried rockfish, and sautéed shrimp. The seafood theme continues with seared scallops, paella, and lobster tails. Pasta, poultry, certified Angus steaks, and gourmet sandwiches complete the menu.

Crab Decks & Tiki Bars of the Chesapeake Bay

Coconut Joe's
Hawaiian Bar & Grill

48 South River Road
Edgewater, MD 21037
443-837-6057
www.coconutjoesusa.com

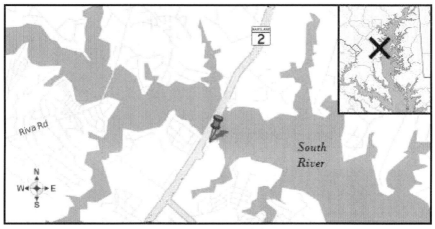

County: Anne Arundel County
Open: Year Round
Latitude: N 38° 56' 53"   Longitude: W 76° 33' 21"
Body of Water: South River
Dockage: Yes
Picture Code: CJHBG at www.crabdecksandtikibars.com/pix

Atmosphere Meter

casual | | | | | | | | | | formal

It doesn't matter what time of year you come to Coconut Joe's. It's a great place for every season. This "totally tiki" spot can melt away the chill of a dreary winter day.

When you walk through the bamboo-and-thatch entrance, past the heated cage for a bearded dragon lizard, you enter "Hawaiian Paradise."

Warm red and green accent lights and brightly colored surf boards cover the bar's wood and pressed tin walls. Palm trees, coconut candle holders, and Polynesian signs set the mood for fun.

The indoor dining area has a vintage 1950s tiki grace. Smooth wooden tables are covered with old photos and postcards from exotic tropical destinations. Fantastic carved tiki masks are mounted on big banana leaves and woven palm mats.

Some seafood is cooked with an island influence — coconut shrimp, pan-seared mahi-mahi, and macadamia nut encrusted salmon. Traditionalists gobble up the local steamed crabs, rockfish, and crab cakes. Grilled steaks, pulled BBQ pork sandwiches, waikiki chicken, and pasta dishes make everyone happy to be hungry.

In the spring, when full tiki regalia unfolds, it's time to move outside. Kids climb around a boat in the sandy playground area, while adults hit two-levels of decks with bars overlooking the South River.

Coconut Joe's kicks off the warm weather on the decks with a blow-out Hawaiian luau complete with a pig roast, dancing hula girls in grass skirts, fire eaters, and live bands.

And if you're looking for one more reason to visit this place — it's owned by a local family that also runs Mango's at North Beach and Calypso Bay restaurants in Solomons and Tracys Landing.

Pirate's Cove Restaurant

4817 Riverside Drive
Galesville, MD 20765
410-867-2300, 410-269-1345 or 301-261-5050
www.piratescovemd.com

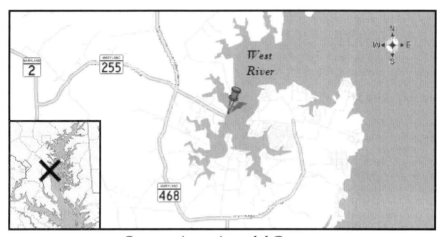

County: Anne Arundel County
Open: Year Round
Latitude: N 38° 50' 35"   Longitude: W 76° 32' 20"
Body of Water: West River
Dockage: Yes
Picture Code: PCR at www.crabdecksandtikibars.com/pix

Restaurant
Atmosphere Meter

casual | formal

Dock Bar
Atmosphere Meter

casual | formal

Everybody likes choices, and you've got three good options for things to match your mood at Pirate's Cove.

First of all, you can enjoy a lovely waterfront meal at the restaurant, which could be considered "Fresh-Shirt Casual" (toss an article of clothing over your bathing suit or switch a clean shirt for one's that's stained with suntan oil or bait drippings).

The raw bar offers a nice selection of fresh local seafood ranging from Oysters Rockefeller to smoked bluefish. Appetizers and entrees focus on daily catch from the Bay, but also indulge carnivores with prime rib, filet mignon, and chicken dishes.

Second choice: you could hang out at Big Mary's Dock Bar. It's a "Flip-Flop Casual" place that brings a splash of tropical fun to the Chesapeake. Light fare of crab dip, nachos, wings, chicken tenders, soups, and salads are served under bright blue and yellow umbrellas and palm trees.

At Big Mary's from April to September, you can watch sailboat races every Wednesday or hear a live band on Friday and Saturday nights.

Your third option is the Inn at Pirate's Cove, which could be considered "Don't Wanna Leave Casual," because it offers pleasant accommodations for folks who simply aren't ready to go home.

A bonus option: Take a walk around the quaint historic town of Galesville. This 350-year old village (one of the oldest in the United States.) takes you back to a simpler time when people picked up mail at the local post office or went for picnics after church on Sunday.

Thursday's Steak & Crabhouse

4851 Riverside Drive
Galesville, MD 20765
410-867-7200
www.thursdaysrestaurant.com

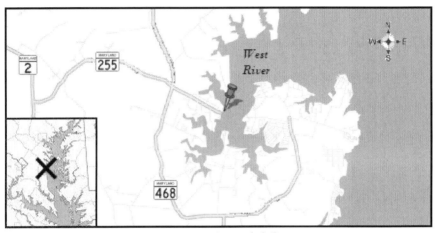

County: Anne Arundel County
Open: Year Round
Latitude: N 38° 50' 27"   Longitude: W 76° 32' 22"
Body of Water: West River
Dockage: Yes
Picture Code: TSC at www.crabdecksandtikibars.com/pix

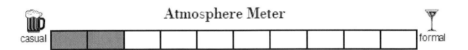

Boaters never have to step on shore and landlubbers get a 360-degree view of the water when they visit Thursday's. Located at the end of a pier, this one-story rustic building is like an island of merriment, surrounded by long wooden decks.

Deep blue awnings and brightly colored umbrellas cast welcome shade upon rows of picnic tables laden with fruits of the sea. Boats of every size, shape, and pedigree unload people who come here for fun, food, and sun. The outside bartenders keep drinks flowing and guests well hydrated in the relentless August heat.

Cooks dish out traditional Bay cuisine at a reasonable price. Steamed crabs, shrimp, and mussels are the menu's centerpiece. Crab soup and south-of-the-border chili team well with salads topped with your choice of grilled chicken, steak, or tuna.

Chicken alfredo and shrimp scampi are leaders in the pasta category, while Steak Neptune (covered with shrimp, scallops, and crab meat in a cream sauce) gets high marks among the meat dishes. Ribs are slow-roasted until they almost fall off the bone.

After the last crab is picked and you want to stretch your legs after a pleasant meal, head for the shoreline of historic Galesville. The waterfront village was founded in 1652 and is currently home to about 600 residents.

It was a hub for Quaker settlement in the 1600s and is named after Richard Gale, a prominent Quaker planter. It grew into a port-of-entry for the shipping trade, and from the 1800s until the early 20th Century, the steamboat *Emma Giles* used to run through Galesville, Baltimore, and Annapolis to shuttle wares.

If you want to learn more, the Galesville Heritage Museum up the hill on Main Street gladly provides more details about this charming little town.

Calypso Bay Boatyard
Bar & Grill

421 Deale Road
Tracy's Landing , MD 20779
410-867-9787
www.calypsobayusa.com

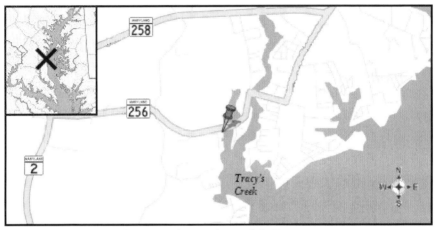

County: Anne Arundel County
Open: Year Round
Latitude: N 38° 46' 39"   Longitude: W 76° 33' 52"
Body of Water: Tracy's Creek off Rockhold Creek off Herring Bay
Dockage: Yes
Picture Code: CBBBG at www.crabdecksandtikibars.com/pix

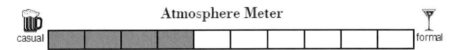

Where can you find three tiki treats in one unexpected location? At Calypso Bay in Tracy's Landing. The outside is a tiki deluxe paradise. A pair of massive 15-foot tall elephant tusks arch their tips together to form an inviting entrance to this tropical escape, complete with palm trees and sand.

The thatched roof bar that overlooks the water soothes you with reggae music while dishing out signature rum drinks and icy cold beer.

Carved wooden tiki heads and masks stand guard while guests lounge under bright red umbrellas and watch the boats sail along Tracy's Creek.

Inside the dining area, tiki decor gets tuned down and Chesapeake cuisine gets turned up. Nautical artifacts, seascape paintings, and an occasional stuffed parrot garnish the walls.

A stone fireplace crackles with warmth in the off-season. Tables covered with ivory linens are laden with silky cream of crab soup, fresh oysters, local rockfish, overstuffed sandwiches, and first-rate jumbo lump crab cakes.

During one late November visit, the chef graciously accommodated a request for fried oysters, even though they didn't appear on the menu. The staff is warm, friendly, and eager to please.

Tiki Part III is in the sports bar where murals are painted with a mixed tribute to Caribbean sunsets and Chesapeake oystermen and crabbers. Big-screen TVs, a blond-wood pool table, and video games entice you to come in, have some fun, and forget about the daily grind.

Happy Harbor
Waterfront Restaurant & Bar

533 Deale Road
Deale, MD 20751
410-867-0949

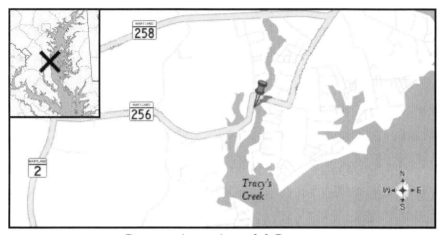

County: Anne Arundel County
Open: Year Round
Latitude: N 38° 46' 55" Longitude: W 76° 33' 35"
Body of Water: Rockhold Creek off Herring Bay
Dockage: Yes
Picture Code: HHWRB at www.crabdecksandtikibars.com/pix

Atmosphere Meter

casual ▮▮▮▮▯▯▯▯▯▯▯▯ formal

Slow down as you drive east on Route 256 right before you reach the Deale Bridge or you'll miss a slice of good old Maryland.

It doesn't get much more authentic than Happy Harbor Restaurant. This popular spot has served local watermen and landlubbers alike since 1933, and it plans to continue unless "One of them big storms comes up the Bay and blows us into the water," chuckled one of the employees.

The no-frills menu of steamed seafood, standard pub fare, sandwiches, baskets with fries, and salads is reasonably priced and fresh.

You can eat inside in casual comfort or enjoy the outdoor wooden deck where charter boats line up along the docks and fishermen crowd three-deep at the bar.

Mousetraps are thoughtfully screwed into the unfinished-pine bar top, so you can clamp down your dollar bills and stop the easterly winds from blowing them away.

Bright blue, red, green, and yellow bar stools, a string of white lights, and a lone palm tree add a touch of cheer to the bustling waterfront deck.

Skipper's Pier
Restaurant & Dock Bar

6158 Drum Point Road
Deale, MD 20751
410-867-7110
www.skipperspier.com

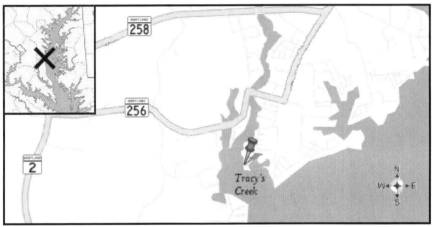

County: Anne Arundel County
Open: Year Round
Latitude: N 38° 46' 21"   Longitude: W 76° 33' 38"
Body of Water: Rockhold Creek off Herring Bay
Dockage: Yes
Picture Code: SPRDB at www.crabdecksandtikibars.com/pix

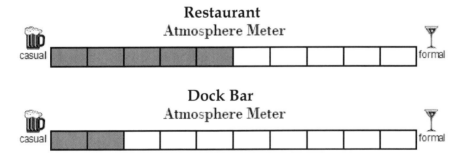

Good times are in store for everyone who visits Skippers Pier. About 80 years ago, the building was a clam-shucking shack. Today it's a casual restaurant with a focus on fresh ingredients and local seafood.

Dishes are prepared home-style, encouraging you to share plentiful servings with family and friends. Many folks come here for steamed crabs, but the local fish, shrimp, and clams are also first-rate.

Juicy prime rib and oyster shooters are savory house specialties. If you want, you can also pile your plate high at the seafood buffet.

When the temperatures drop, patrons dine inside next to an old stone fireplace. Summer breezes might tempt you to sit at the outside deck where you can watch boats cruise across Rockhold Creek or toss some left-over French fries to ducks paddling below.

Children who grow impatient with the slowed-down pace of a waterfront meal can walk the plank in a young pirate's play area. The kids crawl around a sturdy old wooden boat or dig in the sand while parents get to finish their meal or tell one last story.

But that's not all at Skippers Pier. If you tie up or stroll out on the pier, you'll find the legendary Barnacles Dock Bar resting upon the water.

A 10-foot tall green plastic parrot welcomes you onboard the two-story deck and bar building, where sounds of laughter and the clink of glasses echo across the waves.

Mango's Bar & Grill

7153 Lake Shore Drive
Rose Haven, MD 20758
410-257-0095
www.mangosonthebay.com

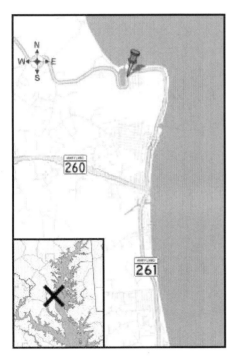

County: Anne Arundel County

Open: Year Round

Latitude: N 38° 43' 35"

Longitude: W 76° 32' 27"

Body of Water: Herrington Harbour off Herring Bay

Dockage: Yes

Picture Code: MBG at www.crabdecksandtikibars.com/pix

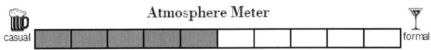

Atmosphere Meter

casual _____ formal

When you enter Mango's, it feels like a tropical breeze blew up the Bay and left behind a touch of the islands at Herrington Harbor Marina.

Built in 2004 with a "tasteful tiki" décor, this place is casual, vibrant, and fun. At the bar, a three-foot tall red parrot dressed in a Hawaiian shirt and beach hat stands watch over an extensive wine collection.

Bartenders pour crisp martinis from glistening silver shakers and mix specialty drinks like Mango Mai Tai, Pain Killer, and Herrington Hurricane.

A tall stone fireplace is in a corner by the dimly-lit dance floor. A bamboo and etched glass screen marks the entrance to the circular-shaped dining room.

Fans with wooden banana leaf blades gently spin above ficus plants that are strategically placed around the windows so they don't obstruct the lovely view of the water. Tables are set with red and gold floral prints covered with glass.

The menu creatively combines fresh local ingredients with Caribbean flavors. Traditional appetizers like crab balls and steamed mussels compete for attention with Coco-Bongo shrimp and cabbage rolls stuffed with garlic mashed potatoes and corned beef.

Show-stopping entrees include Mango Crab Explosion, Caribbean chicken, and Siracha aioli lobster mac and cheese. Sandwiches, salads, and pasta round out the lighter fare.

The Cabana Bar out back provides an ideal spot to enjoy an after-dinner nightcap and the gorgeous view of Herrington Harbor. Burnt orange umbrellas open up next to green palm trees and tiny black tiki heads.

When boats pull up at the dock and the night sky starts to twinkle, you realize you've found a slice of tropical paradise right on the Bay.

Crooked I
Sports Bar & Grill

8323 Bayside Road
Chesapeake Beach, MD 20732
410-257-7999
www.crookedibar.com

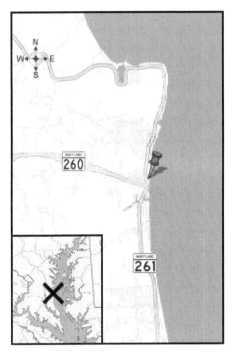

County: Calvert County

Open: Year Round; Bayside Tiki Bar is open during late Spring through early Fall

Latitude: N 38° 41' 49"

Longitude: W 76° 32' 1"

Body of Water: directly on the Chesapeake Bay

Dockage: No

Picture Code: CISBG at www.crabdecksandtikibars.com/pix

Atmosphere Meter

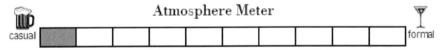

casual | | | | | | | | | | formal

The Crooked I has a vintage feel with red-and-white linoleum tiles on the floor and cushioned black vinyl stools lined up at the bar.

Big-screen TVs mounted on the walls broadcast sporting events, and pool tables glow with light cast down from rectangular lamps colored with beer company logos. Multiple rows of keno machines flash and beep and are ready for you to test your luck.

If you wade through the gamblers absorbed in their bets, you'll find a wall with old photos and newspaper clippings telling the story of a local boxer named Dale Staley, who almost made the big time.

Nightly entertainment options include beer bingo, karaoke, DJ dance parties, and live bands. You can also head outside for a cool cocktail at the Bayfront Tiki Bar that provides a pleasant outdoor alternative to the crowded sports bar climate inside.

Raucous games of horseshoes, wooden picnic tables, a long grassy lawn, and glorious views of the water make it a popular local hangout.

If all this works up an appetite, the menu offers decent pub fare: spicy chicken wings, bacon and cheddar or chili cheese fries, nachos, standard salads, burgers, wraps, and extra-cheesy pizza.

When you're at Crooked I Sports Bar, it's all about easy living and good times at the Bay.

Abner's Crab House

3748 Harbor Road
Chesapeake Beach, MD 20732
410-257-3689 or 301-855-6705
www.abnerscrabhouse.com

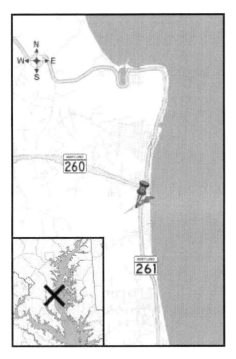

County: Calvert County

Open: Year Round

Latitude: N 38° 41' 23"

Longitude: W 76° 32' 17"

Body of Water: Fishing Creek
off the Chesapeake Bay

Dockage: Yes

Picture Code: ACH at
www.crabdecksandtikibars.com/
pix

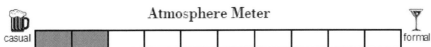

Since the 1950s, the Abner family has hauled crabs from the Bay and been major players in the regional seafood industry.

Bobby Abner owns 10 acres of land at Fishing Creek Marina and 600 crab pots that supplement the local fishermen's catch for his restaurant.

Generations of Abners work at this classic Chesapeake crab house serving dozens of rosy steamed crabs on long paper-covered tables.

The outside deck affords a waterfront view of local fishermen delivering fresh crabs, shrimp, oysters, clams, mussels, and rockfish for the raw bar and seafood platters inside.

Jumbo lump crab cakes are made with only a whisper of filler and fried to golden perfection. On the menu, a handful of meat dishes interrupt this seafood celebration — surf and turf, chicken breasts, pork BBQ, and burgers.

Poker leagues meet on Tuesday and Thursday nights, karaoke contests on Saturdays are lively enough to scare away seagulls, and a new game room is packed with folks determined to win their first million at the keno machines.

Sharky's Tiki Bar

3800 Harbor Road
Chesapeake Beach, MD 20732
443-964-8433

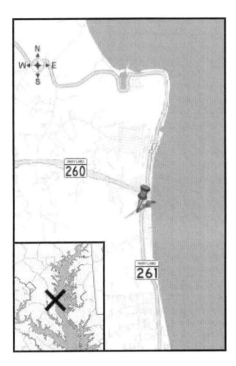

County: Calvert County

Open: Year Round

Latitude: N 38° 41' 24"

Longitude: W 76° 32' 15"

Body of Water: Fishing Creek off the Chesapeake Bay

Dockage: No

Picture Code: STB at www.crabdecksandtikibars.com/pix

Atmosphere Meter

casual ▮▯▯▯▯▯▯▯▯▯ formal

There's nothing fancy about Sharky's, but it can be a lot of fun. When you walk inside its unassuming tall brown building, you'll notice right away that the walls are painted burgundy and gold for Redskins fans.

A few locals put back some cold ones over a game of pool, and the DJ or rock band turns up the volume on weekends.

Stairs lead up to a two-tier wooden tiki deck decorated with bright blue umbrellas, potted plants, surf boards painted with tropical scenes, and a big yellow-orange mask of the sun.

Tall bar stools let you sit and take in the expansive view. To the east, you'll see boats docked in the marina at Fishing Creek and mounds of crab pots eager to get tossed into the Bay. To the west, the sun sets over rows of new housing developments encroaching on the tiny crabs and minnows that hide in the grassy marshlands.

Sharky's kitchen is best known for its award-winning cream of crab soup and brick oven pizza, but it also cooks up crabs and shrimp delivered daily by local watermen.

The rest of the menu is decent pub fare including spicy wings, mozzarella sticks, steak and cheese sandwiches, burgers, and salads.

And there's always plenty of cold beer on hand to wash down your meal or make a toast to life on the Bay.

Smokey Joe's Grill

4165 Mears Avenue
Chesapeake Beach, MD 20732
301-855-3089 or 410-257-2427
www.chesapeakebeachresortspa.com/smokey-joes-grill.htm

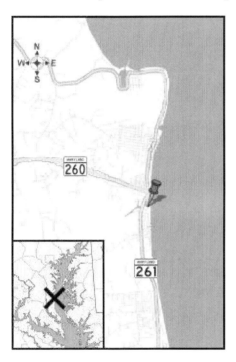

County: Calvert County

Open: Year Round

Latitude: N 38° 41' 26"

Longitude: W 76° 32' 1"

Body of Water: Fishing Creek off the Chesapeake Bay

Dockage: Yes

Picture Code: SJG at www.crabdecksandtikibars.com/pix

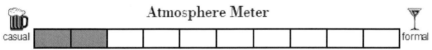

Atmosphere Meter

casual | | | | | | | | | | formal

At Chesapeake Beach Resort & Spa, Smokey Joe's offers a casual, family-friendly alternative to the more upscale dining at Rod 'N' Reel Restaurant.

Since 1990, hearty Southern Maryland cuisine has been served up all day long. For breakfast, you can bust your daily calorie quota with steak and eggs, biscuits with sausage gravy, a stack of pancakes, and omelettes with grits or toast.

Later on, you can enjoy starters such as an onion bloom, nachos, steamed shrimp, or potato skins. Signature entrees include local crab cakes, fall-off-the-bone BBQ ribs, Chesapeake seafood platter, and country fried steak smothered with gravy.

If you feel like the button on your pants is about to pop, you can head across the street and test the water slides and lazy river at the Chesapeake Beach Water Park. It's open from Memorial Day to Labor Day.

Or take a quick ride south on Route 261 to Bayfront Park, where you can play in the surf, examine the dramatic sea-carved cliffs, and dig in the sand for real shark's teeth.

A word of warning: Bring two items along with you. First, grab some zip lock sandwich bags for storing your collection of tiny shark teeth.

Second, have meat tenderizer or vinegar on hand during the peak summer months when jellyfish are abundant in the Bay waters.

If you do get nailed by a stinging nettle, first scrape the inflamed area with a credit card, apply ice until numb, and then add your meat tenderizer. Medicinal cold beers are recommended for adults.

Rod 'N' Reel Restaurant

4165 Mears Avenue
Chesapeake Beach, MD 20732
410-257-2735 or 301-855-8351
www.chesapeakebeachresortspa.com/rodnreel.htm

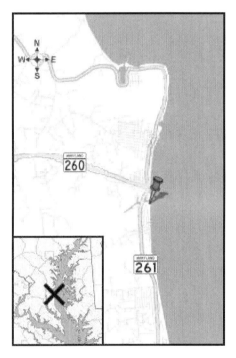

County: Calvert County

Open: Year Round

Latitude: N 38° 41' 26"

Longitude: W 76° 31' 59"

Body of Water: directly on the Chesapeake Bay

Dockage: Yes

Picture Code: RNRR at www.crabdecksandtikibars.com/pix

Atmosphere Meter

casual | | | | | | | | | | formal

The Rod 'N' Reel has been around since 1946. Over the years, it's evolved from a simple crab house to its new incarnation as the centerpiece of fine dining at Chesapeake Beach Resort and Spa.

This upscale, yet comfortable, facility has banquet rooms that are ideal for weddings and corporate retreats. You can pamper yourself with a massage at the spa or take a dip in the heated indoor pool. All 72 rooms overlook the Bay and Calvert Cliffs.

The tavern is separated from the dining area by etched glass panels carved with scenes of Chesapeake aquatic life and habitat. At happy hour, you can grab a stool at the bar and snack on rockfish bites, Buffalo chicken sliders, or popcorn shrimp.

In the dining room, you can gaze out the wall of windows and enjoy a lovely waterfront view. Appetizers present variations on fried, steamed, or raw oysters, clams, shrimp, and crabs.

Entrees focus on fresh seafood (local and imported) with dishes such as macadamia-crusted tilapia, Maine lobster, and salmon stuffed with shrimp, brie, and spinach. Plump crab cakes are ranked among the best along the Bay.

New York strip, filet mignon, and chicken breast are on call for meat lovers. Sunday breakfast and brunch buffets are legendary for opulent presentations of eggs, sausages, pastries, and fresh fruit

If you want to stretch your legs after a hearty meal, check out the Railway Museum on the grounds nearby or take a leisurely stroll along the boardwalk and admire the beauty of the Bay.

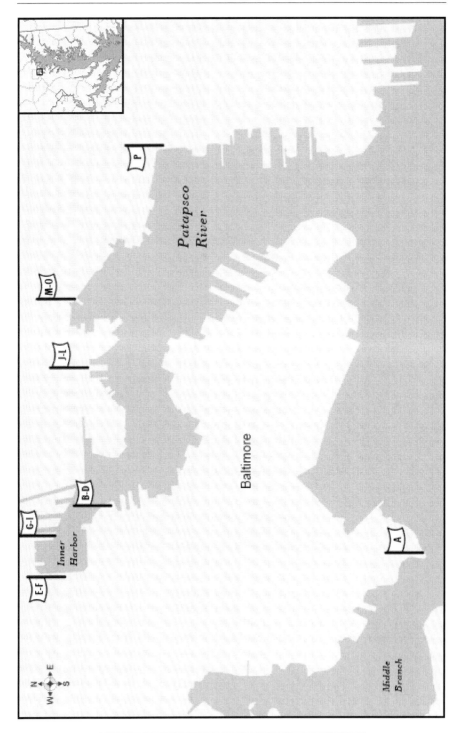

Baltimore Downtown

Nick's Fish House

2600 Insulator Drive
Baltimore, MD 21230
410-347-4123
www.nicksfishhouse.com

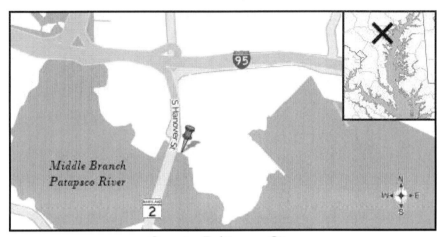

County: Baltimore City
Open: Year Round
Latitude: N 39° 15' 38"   Longitude: W 76° 36' 48"
Body of Water: Middle Branch Patapsco River
Dockage: Yes
Picture Code: NFH at www.crabdecksandtikibars.com/pix

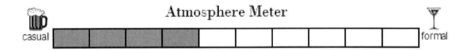

The only time you'll feel sad at Nick's is when it's time to leave. It's a perfectly comfortable place — not too fancy, not too rowdy — and the staff pulls out all the stops to make sure everyone has a good time.

It's located in Baltimore's industrial Locust Point, where brick and steel warehouses and factories provide a backdrop to sailboats gliding along the Middle Branch of the Patapsco River.

Grab a cold one at the bar on Nick's long wooden deck and listen to the band or take in a fabulous view of the Hanover Street Bridge. Built in 1916, its graceful arches meet in the middle to support a drawbridge surrounded by four tall towers. Pink and salmon hues at sunset accentuate its design.

At Nick's you can take a peak inside the banana yellow shack where crabs get steamed with special spices or admire the mural showing a seagull soaring over Neptune as he offers a massive gray half shell to a lovely lady.

Inside you'll find a tribute to Baltimore traditions in both the decor and cuisine. Vintage signs, boats, and crab pots pay homage to the Bay, while the menu is heavily influenced by seafood caught nearby.

The food is terrific, and the raw bar and sushi are fresh and flavorful. Plump fried oysters on top of on crispy French fries, half-pound broiled crab cakes with goat cheese grits, and beer-battered fish and chips guarantee you won't leave hungry. East Baltimore style steak-and-cheese and char-broiled Angus burgers make meat lovers smile.

When you're finished eating, pause for a moment outside and listen for the ghosts of Captain John Smith and his crew. In 1608, he sailed the length of the Patapsco in an unsuccessful attempt to find the Pacific Ocean. Some say late at night you can hear Smith's men shouting and the ship's floorboards mysteriously creaking.

By the way, you're more likely to succeed at ghost-spotting if you take along one of Nick's tasty rum punches, served in a convenient little bucket with a handle.

Tiki Barge

500 Harborview Drive
Baltimore, MD 21230
800-867-5309

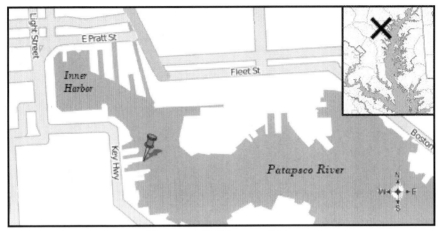

County: Baltimore City
Open: Seasonal
Latitude: N 39° 16' 34"   Longitude: W 76° 36' 3"
Body of Water: Baltimore Inner Harbor off the Patapsco River
Dockage: Yes
Picture Code: TB at www.crabdecksandtikibars.com/pix

Atmosphere Meter

casual | | | | | | | | | | formal

Whoever came up with the idea of plopping a tiki bar on the end of a pier in the middle of Baltimore's Inner Harbor was a genius. Actually it's more of a Tiki Barge, and it's become Charm City's party central for fun on the water.

It looks like a happy misfit with its bright orange and turquoise walls contrasting with the grays of the old industrial plants and corporate skyscrapers standing nearby.

On top of the two-story vessel rests a massive thatched roof with a wooden deck and railings, and colorful lights are strung from pole to pole. Pirate signs and ship flags hang above the bamboo bar.

Down below on the ground level, another thatched-roof bar serves up cool beverages next to a swimming pool that's surrounded by beach chairs facing the sun. Swaying palm trees encircle the deck.

Food isn't really essential to life on the Tiki Barge. D'Grill cranks out extremely casual fare of hot dogs, burgers, and fries. But specialty rum drinks with fruit juices provide enough vitamin C to ward off scurvy.

The best part about the Tiki Barge is the 360-degree view of the water. The former Domino Sugar factory and Inner Harbor city skyline shape the background, while sailboats, power boats, cruise ships, and barges glide past before your eyes.

Docked beside the Tiki Barge is a relic of local history — the *Maryland Independence*. Originally built as a submarine chaser in 1944, it was converted into a luxury yacht in the 1970s. Governor Hughes bought it in the 1980s to court dignitaries and business executives.

In a grand gesture of fiscal responsibility, Governor Bob Ehrlich auctioned it off on eBay in 2003. Now in private hands and newly restored, *Maryland Independence* is available for parties or inspection of the curious passing by.

Tabrizi's Restaurant & Catering

500 Harborview Drive
Baltimore, MD 21230
410-727-3663
www.tabrizis.com

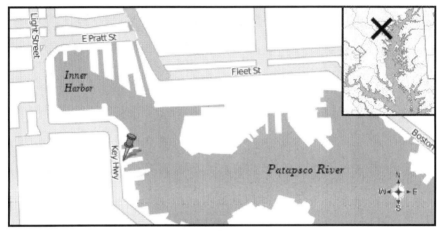

County: Baltimore City
Open: Year Round
Latitude: N 39° 16' 34"   Longitude: W 76° 36' 15"
Body of Water: Baltimore Inner Harbor off the Patapsco River
Dockage: Yes
Picture Code: TRC at www.crabdecksandtikibars.com/pix

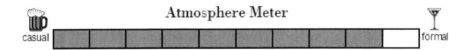

Atmosphere Meter

casual | | | | | | | | | | | formal

At Tabrizi's, the Mediterranean meets the Bay in a culinary marriage that presents the best of both worlds. It's located at the Harborview Marina on the "secret" side of Baltimore's Inner Harbor where people come to escape the mayhem of the crowds and tourists.

The ambiance is casually sophisticated with a soothing Tuscan feel. The L-shaped dining room glows in soft gold and brown colors, with an open kitchen for observing the chef at work. A long blond wood bar topped with black marble beckons you to take a seat and sip chilled cocktails.

A baby grand piano in the middle sets a relaxing yet lively tone. The upstairs banquet room's graceful decor makes it a popular venue for weddings and special gatherings.

The menu dresses up Chesapeake seafood with fresh Italian spices and ingredients. For starters, crab meat is nestled in an avocado and sprinkled with aioli emulsion and caviar, and shrimp is sautéed with garlic and bell peppers. Stuffed grape leaves, grilled sardines, and baba ghanoush are reminders of the cook's Mediterranean roots.

Entree standouts include pan-seared sea bass encrusted with sesame seeds, Moroccan-style cornish hen, and New Zealand lamb kabobs with hummus. For dessert, you can cool down with Gifford's ice cream or warm up with baklava drizzled with honey and pistachio nuts.

All summer long on Friday nights, live jazz music plays outside on the deck, while diners relish an unforgettable waterfront view of the stars coming out above the scenic city skyline.

The Rusty Scupper Restaurant

402 Key Highway
Baltimore, MD 21230
410-727-3678
www.selectrestaurants.com/rusty

County: Baltimore City
Open: Year Round
Latitude: N 39° 16' 55"   Longitude: W 76° 36' 26"
Body of Water: Baltimore Inner Harbor off the Patapsco River
Dockage: Yes
Picture Code: TRSR at www.crabdecksandtikibars.com/pix

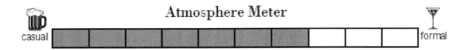

casual — Atmosphere Meter — formal

Rusty Scupper would be a handsome restaurant regardless of where it stood, but the panoramic view of Baltimore's Inner Harbor raises the dining experience to a whole new level. On the roof deck, the debate rages on about the best time of day to gaze across the water. Sunsets seem to garner the most votes with the heavens streaked in rose and salmon.

But evenings get their share of approving nods when the lights in the tall office buildings blend into the velvety darkness of a starry night. During the day, the skyline feels like it's closer, revealing details on every structure from the Legg Mason building to the Intercontinental Hotel.

Inside the restaurant, every seat has a spectacular vantage point. The ambiance is contemporary and urban, but nautical artwork and exposed-wood rafters and beams soften the decor. Cobalt blue wine glasses echo the waters of the Bay.

It's a large place — 270 seats in the dining room and 75 stools at the bar. Live jazz piano and the famous Sunday brunch make it a popular destination for special events, so reservations are recommended.

Seafood dominates the menu, with selections such as a fresh oyster sampler, Maryland lump crab cakes, and Kent Island crab-stuffed shrimp. Options that aren't pulled from the sea include New York strip steaks and lemon garlic chicken.

Rusty Scupper has been a Charm City icon for years, but it's now owned by Select Restaurants out of Cleveland. Bay purists shouldn't turn up their noses at the idea of dining at a chain restaurant, because Rusty Scupper buys its seafood from local oyster growers and fishermen. As a good neighbor, it joined the Chesapeake Bay Oyster Recovery Partnership (ORP), an alliance of Maryland, D.C., and Virginia eateries that recycle used oyster shells. As a result, ORP collected almost 60,000 bushels of used shells last year and planted more than 450 million baby oysters onto 316 acres of land along the Bay.

Phillips Harborplace

301 Light Street
Baltimore, MD 21202
410-685-6600
www.phillipsseafood.com

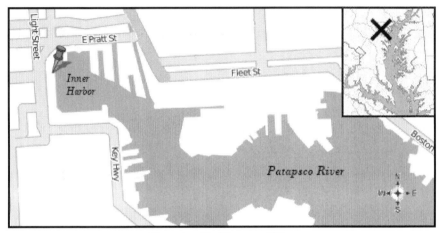

County: Baltimore City
Open: Year Round
Latitude: N 39° 17' 5"   Longitude: W 76° 36' 43"
Body of Water: Baltimore Inner Harbor off the Patapsco River
Dockage: No
Picture Code: PH at www.crabdecksandtikibars.com/pix

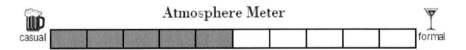

Even though Phillips Harborplace is nestled among
Baltimore's tourist attractions and towering skyscrapers, its
history dates back to 1914 when A.E. Phillips started a
crab processing plant on remote Hoopers Island in
Dorchester County.

The next generation of Maryland's "first family of crab" moved to Ocean City, MD, and opened a tiny take-out joint to sell excess crabs from the processing plant. They only sold their wares in the summer, using Shirley Phillips' recipes for steamed crabs.

The business flourished, expanding to full-service seafood restaurants in Ocean City, Atlantic City, Philadelphia, and Washington, D.C. In 1980, Phillips joined the urban renewal efforts at Baltimore's Inner Harbor.

Today, Phillips is the world's largest manufacturer of blue crab meat, spices, and related products with 13 processing plants in the United States and abroad and its headquarters in Baltimore.

The family is still deeply entrenched in the business, guaranteeing each of the seven main locations and multiple satellite eateries serve the freshest ingredients possible.

Phillips Harborplace is known for its casual environment, a welcoming bar, comfortable indoor dining, and an outside deck sitting on the edge of the water.

The raw bar of freshly shucked oysters and clams, colossal shrimp, and steamed mussels provides an ideal start to a seafood feast. Creamy crab soup and crab cakes regularly win blue ribbon awards around the region.

Seafood platters (broiled or fried) and the clam bake for two evoke memories of summer cookouts along the shore. Steaks and chicken elbowed their way on the menu to keep meat-eaters happy. In fact, everyone seems to leave Phillips happy to have experienced this long-standing Bay tradition.

J. Paul's Restaurant

301 Light Street
Baltimore, MD 21202
410-659-1889
j-pauls.capitalrestaurants.com/harbor

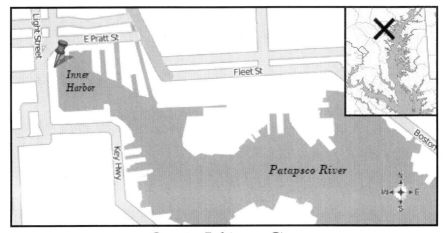

County: Baltimore City
Open: Year Round
Latitude: N 39° 17' 6"   Longitude: W 76° 36' 43"
Body of Water: Baltimore Inner Harbor off the Patapsco River
Dockage: No
Picture Code: JPR at www.crabdecksandtikibars.com/pix

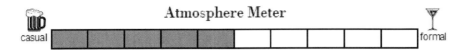

After a long day of exploring the Maryland Science Center
and other Inner Harbor attractions, J. Paul's offers a pleasant
place for weary travelers to kick back and rest their aching
feet. Its decor resurrects the charm of turn-of-the-century
saloons that were popular watering holes along the Baltimore
waterfront. The grand old wooden bar is surrounded by

brown leather booths and tables covered with white linens and paper for doodling. In the Crab Room, generally used for large parties, a mural of a lady with flowing golden locks delicately holds a wooden hammer above three unsuspecting steamed crabs.

If the name rings a bell, that's because it's owned by Capital Restaurant Concepts, parent company of J. Paul's in Washington, D.C. They opened this location in 1997, with the hope of sharing their American pub fare infused with locally grown ingredients.

Maryland crab soups, steamed mussels, and crab cake sliders appear on the menu along side fried green tomatoes, buffalo wings, and nachos. Seafood favorites include bacon-wrapped Cajun scallops, grilled salmon, and crispy fried shrimp. Steaks, pulled pork, burgers, and sandwiches come with fries and coleslaw. You can wash down these dishes with the restaurant's award-winning Amber Ale, made from Loudon County spring water.

Green umbrellas over a red brick patio invite you to step outside and check out the sites around the harbor. To the south rises Federal Hill, which got its name in 1789 for being the end of a parade and the beginning of celebrations over ratifying the new U.S. Federal Constitution.

That famous hill also played a key role in the Civil War. After the Baltimore Riots in 1861, Northern officials became concerned about Confederate sympathizers taking control of the city. So, late one night, Union troops occupied the hill and erected a fort on top. Baltimore citizens awoke to cannons pointing down at their waterfront businesses, threatening to let loose their fury if Baltimore joined Southern secessionists in breaking apart the Union. In this case, the forced allegiance worked, and Maryland remained with the North.

M & S Grill

201 East Pratt Street
Baltimore, MD 21202
410-547-9333
www.mccormickandschmicks.com/Locations/
maryland/baltimore-maryland/prattstreet.aspx

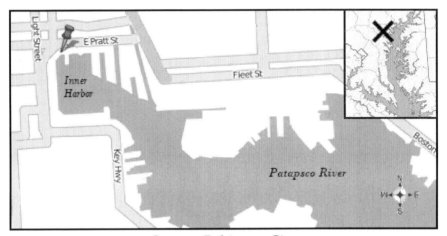

County: Baltimore City
Open: Year Round
Latitude: N 39° 17' 9"   Longitude: W 76° 36' 42"
Body of Water: Baltimore Inner Harbor off the Patapsco River
Dockage: No
Picture Code: MSG at www.crabdecksandtikibars.com/pix

Atmosphere Meter

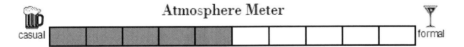

M&S Grill is like the cute little brother of its big sister restaurant, McCormick & Schmick's. It's just not as large or expensive, and you can't beat the location. M&S Grill sits at the crown of Baltimore's Inner Harbor, just blocks away from Camden Yards and M&T Bank Stadium.

Right in front of the outdoor patio floats the
U.S.S. Constellation, which was built in 1854 as the last all-sail warship. It's the final Civil War vessel still afloat, and you can climb aboard to imagine life as a 19th Century sailor.

Or you could walk over to the Baltimore World Trade Center. Its floor-to-ceiling windows present a glorious 360-degree view of downtown and the water.

With all this to see outside, why go inside M&S Grill? The decor is made cozy and casual with lots of warm cherry wood and vintage stained glass.

Around the oval-shaped bar hang colorful pennants of baseball teams. Deep wooden booths with soft green cushions encircle the dining room, while contemporary nautical art hangs on the walls.

The chef concentrates on delivering fresh ingredients at the peak of their season, and a "Fresh List" highlights the daily catch. The Seafood Bar tempts you with items caught all along the Atlantic seaboard. Sushi and sashimi, custom-aged steaks, and honey glazed chicken are regular crowd pleasers.

There's seafood aplenty with plump crab cakes, shrimp scampi, and parmesan-encrusted flounder. The Sunday Brunch, featuring regional fare, is simply Delmarvelous.

The kitchen also shows its compassionate side by offering wallet-friendly specials. The lunch menu lists 10 items for $10, and happy hour pleases budget-conscious patrons with half-price cheeseburgers and steamed mussels.

Dick's Last Resort

621 East Pratt Street
Baltimore, MD 21202
443-453-5961
www.dickslastresort.com/domains/Baltimore

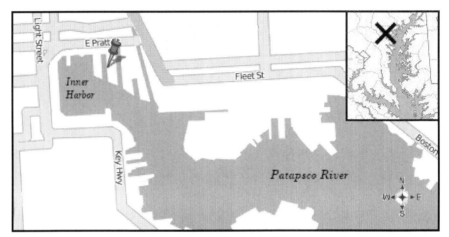

County: Baltimore City
Open: Year Round
Latitude: N 39° 17' 9"   Longitude: W 76° 36' 25"
Body of Water: Baltimore Inner Harbor off the Patapsco River
Dockage: No
Picture Code: DLR at www.crabdecksandtikibars.com/pix

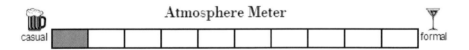

When you walk outside Baltimore's National Aquarium across the pedestrian bridge over the water, you'll come face-to-face with a tall mannequin of a grumpy old man dressed in a blue crab-print Hawaiian shirt holding a frosty beer. That would be Dick, and this is his last resort.

He's part of a chain of several Dick's owned by Triton Pacific Capital Partners with other locations in Dallas, San Antonio, San Diego, Chicago, Boston, Las Vegas, and Myrtle Beach, S.C.

The patio outside caters to waterfront fans, and inside is a cacophony of visual and audio mayhem. The busy decor has touches of tiki with palm trees, wooden rum barrels, fish nets, tiki masks, and a massive mural packed with all sorts of sea creatures, mermaids, boats, and rusty buckets.

On the dining room walls hang anything from bras to motorcycles, T-shirts, and vintage signs. Classic rock bands play nightly without a cover charge, but most of the noise comes from the surly, high-energy wait staff who's trained to banter with patrons.

The atmosphere strives to "make everyone feel like they're temporarily breaking all the rules ... and getting away with it." Most the time it's fun; sometimes not so much, so be sure to bring along your sense of humor.

Snarling coconut heads hold match boxes at the bar, which mixes up a long list of specialty drinks and offers a variety of domestic, imported, and local beers on tap.

Food is served in plastic baskets or metal buckets lined with paper and is mostly fried. Menus nailed upon the walls include ribs, chicken, seafood, and steaks, priced a tad high for what you get.

But what the heck, Dick's is like a quirky three-ring circus, worth the price of admission for many fun seekers.

McCormick & Schmick's Seafood Restaurant

711 Eastern Avenue
Baltimore, MD 21202
410-234-1300 or 1-888-226-6212 toll free
www.mccormickandschmicks.com

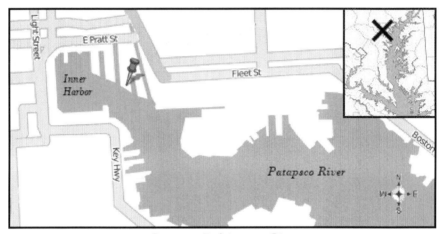

County: Baltimore City
Open: Year Round
Latitude: N 39° 17' 2"   Longitude: W 76° 36' 21"
Body of Water: Baltimore Inner Harbor off the Patapsco River
Dockage: Yes
Picture Code: MSSR at www.crabdecksandtikibars.com/pix

Atmosphere Meter

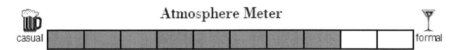

McCormick & Schmick's menu offers 30 types of seafood daily. That's a boatload of fish, but with 95 locations around the country and a headquarters in Portland, OR, the company has developed effective systems for bringing great ingredients to its restaurants. And somehow the chef manages to retain quality and freshness.

Standing near the long galley kitchen with its shiny chrome pick-up station, you can watch how smoothly dishes move from range top to table top.

Oysters, catfish, shrimp, crabs, salmon, and scallops are pulled from Atlantic waters and prepared with a contemporary twist. Aged steaks, tender chicken, savory soups, and crisp salads complete the culinary options. McCormick & Schmick's calls itself "affordable upscale, with a warm, sophisticated atmosphere."

The two-story waterfront building is shaped like a lighthouse and located near the Pier Six Pavilion. Stools with black leather seats are stationed along the graceful wooden bar and stained glass lights overhead create an old, established feeling. Sailboats, fish, and pictures of oysters garnish the dark wood paneling.

The dining room's floor-to-ceiling windows give everyone a lovely view.   Blue and green umbrellas on the patio tempt you to come outside, take a seat, and watch the bustling Inner Harbor.

The background is lined with boats and buildings, and in the foreground stands the red and black Seven Foot Knoll Lighthouse. It was built in 1855 and is the oldest screw pile lighthouse in Maryland.

The lighthouse originally warned ships of danger at the mouth of the Patapsco River but was moved to Pier 5 in 1988 to become part of the Baltimore Maritime Museum. Go ahead and climb inside to get a unique glimpse of the Bay's nautical past.

Shuckers Restaurant & Bar

1629 Thames Street
Baltimore, MD 21231
410-522-5820
www.shuckersoffellspoint.com

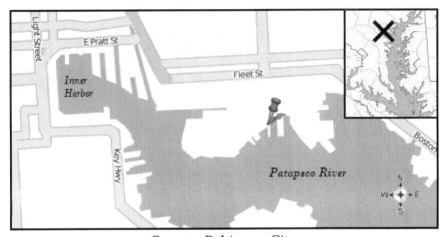

County: Baltimore City
Open: Year Round
Latitude: N 39° 16' 52"   Longitude: W 76° 35' 35"
Body of Water: Patapsco River
Dockage: No
Picture Code: SRB at www.crabdecksandtikibars.com/pix

Atmosphere Meter

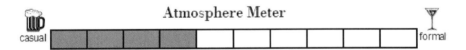

casual — formal

Oyster lovers simply smile when they look up at the sign in front of Shuckers. That name and the opened pair of oyster shells promise that somebody else will do the hard work while you sit back and savor the Chesapeake's most famous bivalve.

The place is casual and friendly, with a small outdoor patio just steps away from Baltimore's busy harbor and a mixed nautical/sports theme inside. Sports fans are spoiled with 40 flat-screen TVs, and a special bar area has overstuffed black leather sofas for watching games with that in-your-buddy's-basement feel.

The large fish tank at the entrance shows that Shuckers is serious about local seafood. The raw bar presents a variety of oysters, mussels, and clams from around the mid-Atlantic region. Crab cakes, shrimp, and fried rockfish have a just-caught freshness. Burgers, steaks, and BBQ chicken provide options to meat lovers.

Daily specials save a few bucks on drinks and snacks, and they even take 20% off the tab if you bring your dog to Wednesday happy hour when the patio is open.

The cobblestone street outside reminds you that oysters have been a staple in this area for a very long time. In fact, the word Chesapeake comes from the Algonquian phrase "Great Shellfish Bay." Archaeological evidence shows that Native American started eating oysters around 4,500 years ago.

European explorers in the early 1600s marveled at the size and quantity of oysters in the Bay — some measuring up to 13 inches long, laying in beds so large that ships had to avoid wrecking into them.

During the golden era of oystering in the 1880s, over 20 million bushels of Chesapeake oysters were harvested and shipped around the country as a coveted delicacy. It's hard to imagine a more popular culinary treat. So go ahead and order up your own dozen on the half shell and offer a toast to this sumptuous little bivalve.

Woody's Rum Bar & Island Grill

1700 Thames Street
Baltimore, MD 21231
410-563-6600
www.woodysrumbar.com

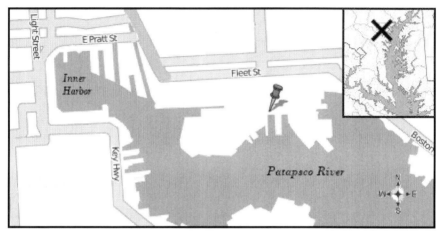

County: Baltimore City
Open: Year Round
Latitude: N 39° 16' 55"   Longitude: W 76° 35' 33"
Body of Water: Patapsco River
Dockage: No
Picture Code: WRBIG at www.crabdecksandtikibars.com/pix

Atmosphere Meter

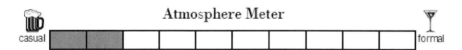

casual ▢ formal

When someone says Fels Point, tiki and Caribbean music don't usually come to mind. Most people think of old taverns, cobblestone streets, and rows of houses that date back to the early 1700s.

But just as palm trees and thatched roofs are popping up all around the Bay, another tiki stronghold has taken root in Fels Point.

Woody's Rum Bar is oddly located above an ice cream parlor. It's easy to miss the side entrance, even though the door's painted with tropical flowers and a parrot. So, keep an eye out for the pirate flags with black-and-white skulls and crossbones waving from the third floor deck.

Once you climb the stairs, you're rewarded with island-inspired murals, split bamboo, and tables made of hand-painted steel drums.

In 2009, it won awards for Best View Overlooking the Harbor and Best Bar to get Day Drunk, but there's more to Woody's than just pretty scenery and potent rum drinks.

Its Caribbean-style food mixes fresh seafood with island flavors, creating standouts like coconut shrimp bathed in grilled pineapple sauce, jerk chicken wraps, and mahi-mahi fish tacos. The menu accommodates more traditional palates with juicy burgers, crab cakes, and tangy wings.

The thatched-roof bar serves specialty drinks, including the rum runner, dark & stormy, hurricane, and mai tai. After the first sip, you'll feel the breeze, relax, and make a toast to celebrate island influences on the Bay.

Riptide by the Bay
Restaurant & Bar

1718 Thames Street
Baltimore, MD 21231
410-732-4585
www.riptidebythebay.net

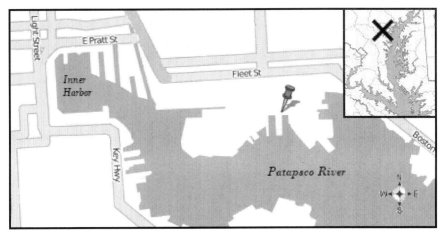

County: Baltimore City
Open: Year Round
Latitude: N 39° 16' 55"   Longitude: W 76° 35' 30"
Body of Water: Patapsco River
Dockage: No
Picture Code: RBRB at www.crabdecksandtikibars.com/pix

Atmosphere Meter

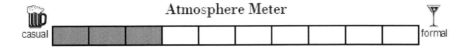

casual ← → formal

Riptide's is located inside one of those beautiful old
red-brick row houses that harkens back to Fels Point's
beginning in the early 18th Century. A handful of tables out
front provide a street-level view of water taxis and boats
pulling into the harbor. To the right of the front doors is the

Riptide Crab Room. Its rustic wooden doors lead you into an open-air covered seating area with hand-painted murals depicting Chesapeake sailboats, light houses, and wildlife. Inside the dining area, wooden booths and seafoam-green walls showcase pictures of schooners and nautical artifacts.

The menu kicks off with Bay classics, such as crab dip and grilled oysters, then mixes things up with inland-influenced appetizers like jerk chicken wings and a coconut shrimp and strawberry martini. Light fare treats include shark taco, crab cake sandwich, and baby back ribs. Steamed crabs and peel-and-eat shrimp pay homage to regional cuisine.

Best of all, Riptide's has a charming neighborhood feel. During a recent visit, a local waterman told tales about life in taverns like this during the oyster heyday of the 1800s. Local wealth was created through ship building and seafood processing, which attracted men from around the globe looking for riches and opportunity.

A Wild West boom-time atmosphere developed with saloons and brothels growing around the docks. Gunfights broke out between Maryland and Virginia boat crews competing for lucrative oyster beds. Dredging for oysters was rough work in the coldest months of the year, and many men didn't want to do it. But captains needed able hands to work their ships, so they'd come to Fels Point taverns seeking recruits. Often targeting new immigrants and strong young men, captains would get them drunk, drag them to the docks, and shanghai them to work on their ships. Some workers got paid, but many were tossed overboard without a penny in their pocket. So the next time you order oysters in a Fels Point bar, watch your back to make sure an unscrupulous sea captain isn't lurking in the shadows, waiting to take you aboard his ship.

Captain James Crabhouse & Restaurant

2127 Boston Street
Baltimore, MD 21231
Landing Restaurant: 410-327-8600
Crab House & Carry Out: 410-675-1819;
www.captainjameslanding.com

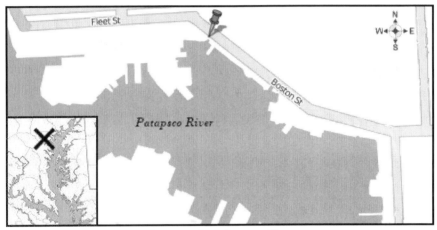

County: Baltimore City
Open: Year Round
Latitude: N 39° 17' 2"   Longitude: W 76° 35' 10"
Body of Water: Patapsco River
Dockage: Yes
Picture Code: CJCR at www.crabdecksandtikibars.com/pix

Restaurant
Atmosphere Meter

casual | formal

Crab House
Atmosphere Meter

casual | formal

As you cruise down Boston Street, don't be surprised to see a building that looks like a huge ship anchored at the curb. It's Captain James Landing — Baltimore's only dining establishment shaped like a merchant vessel.

Four brothers built the restaurant in 1978, and it's been a local landmark ever since. The dining room's circular wooden bar with a brass railing and O-shaped windows create the impression of being on board a cruise ship. Berry-red table cloths with white linen covers set the tone for fine dining.

The menu's classic Chesapeake cuisine showcases seafood specialties, such as golden brown crab cakes, shrimp stuffed with crab imperial, pan-fried soft shells, and flounder filet.

If you're in the mood for more casual fare, walk across the street to Captain James Crabhouse, where crabs and cold beer take center stage. Located right on the water overlooking Baltimore Harbor, the blue and white roof atop a weathered wooden deck draws boaters and seafood lovers from miles around.

All-you-can-eat steamed crabs head the menu's line-up, followed by little neck clams, mussels, calamari, and shrimp. Hush puppies, corn-on-the-cob, and boardwalk fries are served on the side.

To make sure everyone can partake in the sport of crab picking, a 101 tutorial lesson on the menu offers an 8-step program for releasing the tender meat from the shell.

Tiki Bay Frozen drinks for dessert quench crab eaters' thirst and take the edge off a hot summer night.

Bo Brooks Crab House

2780-A Lighthouse Point
Baltimore, MD 21224
410-558-0202
www.bobrooks.com

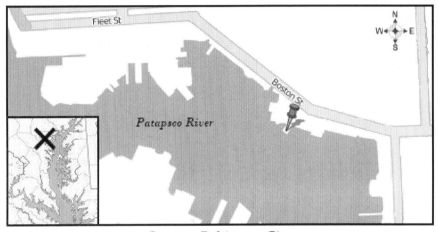

County: Baltimore City
Open: Year Round
Latitude: N 39° 16' 38"   Longitude: W 76° 34' 43"
Body of Water: Patapsco River
Dockage: Yes
Picture Code: BBCH at www.crabdecksandtikibars.com/pix

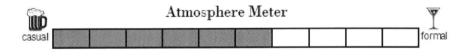

Bo Brooks opened its doors in 1964 in the Gardenville section of East Baltimore. When it moved to the Canton Waterfront in 2000, owners refused to change their traditional Maryland style of cooking.

Rather than boiler-steaming mass amounts of crabs and letting them sit around for hours, each meal is made to order to maximize flavor and texture. The secret spice blend has been delighting taste buds for more than 45 years.

Plus the atmosphere is hard to beat. Strolling past a gorgeous antique oak bar leads you to the dining area, where you can slide into a high-backed booth for privacy during picking or spread out at a wooden table for more elbow room.

Understated contemporary decor with wall-to-wall windows and an occasional map of the Chesapeake prove a fantastic Bay view needs no distractions.

When waiters deliver plastic trays piled high with hot steamed crabs, you see patrons' faces light up, anticipating Baltimore's favorite culinary treats.

The Half-and-Half irreverently swirls together tomato-based and cream crab soups, and the appetizer sampler gives you a nibble of calamari, fried shrimp, and jerk chicken skewers. Salads and sandwiches are innovative and fresh.

Showstopping entrees include seafood pot pie, sesame tuna steak, and chicken Chesapeake topped with lump crab and imperial sauce.

Outside at the foot of Bo Brooks' towering black-and-white striped lighthouse, you can toss back rum drinks at the thatched-roof Tiki Hut while listening to local bands or simply watching the bustle in Baltimore Harbor.

And if you have time, check out the *Black Eyed Susan* next door. This turn-of-the-century paddle-wheel boat (available for private parties or public cruises) showcases classic Victorian craftsmanship with nine-foot ceilings, brass sconces, and Tiffany ceiling fixtures.

The Bay Café

2809 Boston Street
Baltimore, MD 21224
410-522-3377
www.baycafeusa.com

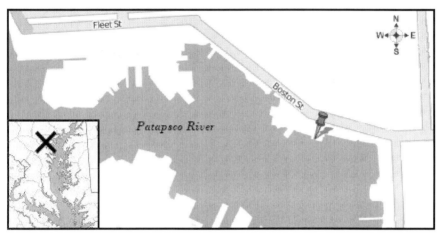

County: Baltimore City
Open: Year Round
Latitude: N 39° 16' 37"   Longitude: W 76° 34' 35"
Body of Water: Patapsco River
Dockage: Yes
Picture Code: TBC at www.crabdecksandtikibars.com/pix

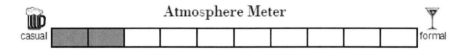

Bay Café wants to transport you — away from work woes, family stress, the doldrums, or whatever is chipping away at your life sparkle — to a place that can rejuvenate your spirit.

They converted the energy plant from an old factory into a tropical get-away with perhaps the best beach in Baltimore.

It features plush green foliage, swaying palm trees, flaming tiki torches, aged wooden decks, and enough sand to bury your feet ankle-deep.

The towering brick smokestack overlooks a long tin roof with a huge Red Stripe label and touches of rust that suggest a quick jaunt to Jamaica.

If that's not enough to wash away the blues, Bay Café can lighten your mood with live music, bikini contests, bongo beach parties, visits from Ravens cheerleaders, and massive windows offering an exceptional view of the Bay.

Good times and good food go hand-in-hand here. The diverse and reasonably priced menu presents sandwiches overstuffed with local seafood, jerk chicken with an island flare, handmade pizza, thick juicy burgers, delicate crab cakes, fresh fish du jour, and delectable steaks.

Plus, Bay Café's extensive list of beer, wine, and specialty rum or tequila drinks should help put the spring back in your step.

Hamilton's Canton Dockside

3301 Boston Street
Baltimore, MD 21224
410-276-8900
www.cantondockside.com

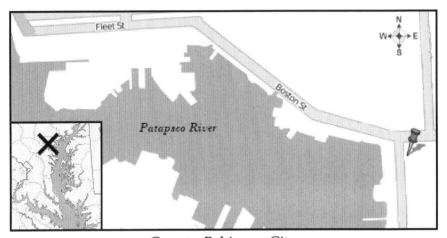

County: Baltimore City
Open: Year Round
Latitude: N 39° 16' 35"   Longitude: W 76° 34' 8"
Body of Water: Patapsco River
Dockage: No
Picture Code: HCD at www.crabdecksandtikibars.com/pix

Atmosphere Meter

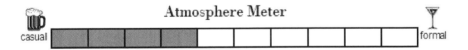

casual — formal

When you come to Canton Dockside, you better be serious about Maryland seafood. They are.

Sure, you can order chicken, steak, or burgers, and you won't leave disappointed. But sticking to what they do best almost guarantees a terrific evening. The Harrison family deals directly with local watermen to ensure they serve the best of the daily catch.

Everything is cooked to order — authentic Bay style and homemade. The menu offers a cornucopia of seafood options.

And at the risk of sounding like Forest Gump with his shrimp litany, Canton seems to have unlimited imagination for crab dishes: crab balls, crab pretzel, crab dip, crab cakes, crab soup, crab imperial, crab fluffs, crab alfredo, and crab marinara. You name it, they make it … with crabs.

Eating outside on the expansive wooden deck next to a tall neon palm tree lets you feel the warm breezes drift in from the Bay.

Dining inside offers a visual tribute to Maryland history and nautical tradition, where murals depicting oystermen and crab pots, Baltimore and Annapolis landmark buildings, and local sports legends brighten the walls.

Wherever you sit, the energy, bustle, and personable staff will make you want to return to Canton over and over again.

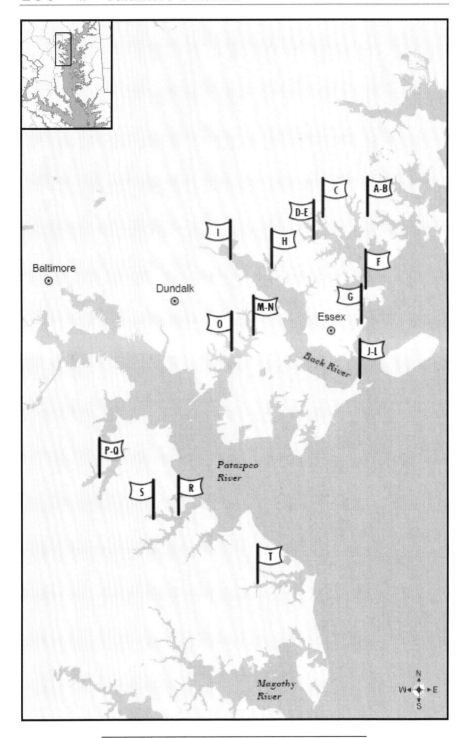

Baltimore

Dundalk

Essex

D-E

C

A-B

I

H

F

G

M-N

O

J-L

Back River

Pataspco River

P-Q

S

R

T

Magothy River

N
W ← ◆ → E
S

Baltimore Outskirts

Long Beach
Restaurant & Tavern

818 Bowley's Quarters Road
Middle River, MD 21220
410-335-9444
www.longbeachrestaurant.net

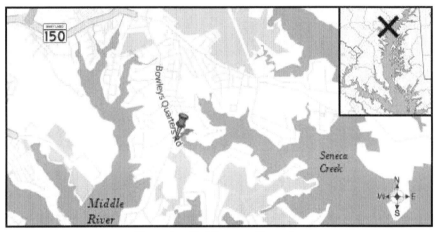

County: Baltimore County
Open: Year Round
Latitude: N 39° 19' 16"   Longitude: W 76° 23' 33"
Body of Water: Seneca Creek off the Chesapeake Bay
Dockage: No
Picture Code: LBRT at www.crabdecksandtikibars.com/pix

Atmosphere Meter

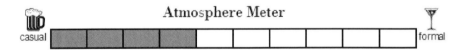

casual   formal

You feel a sense of neighborhood pride when you enter
Long Beach Restaurant. It serves up down-home food in a
casual setting where family and friends gather for a hearty
meal at a reasonable price.

The menu offers something for everyone. Crowd-pleasing appetizers include potato skins topped with crab and shrimp, crispy Texas onion petals, and steamed mussels.

Brave diners with robust appetites can try to tackle a 30-count mountain of spicy chicken wings. On a bone-chilling rainy day, it's tough to decide between a steaming bowl of homemade chili or Maryland crab soup.

The kitchen cooks a mean meatloaf with brown gravy and fork-tender rack of ribs. Local ingredients are showcased in the golden-brown crab cakes, creamy seafood alfredo, and fried shrimp and rib eye combo.

The Utter Bar helps take the edge off your work day with a cold beer, good music, and a game of foosball. Between the bar and restaurant, the open deck gives a nice view of boats pulling into the marina.

So what makes this little spot feel special? Maybe it's the community spirit in the Bowleys Quarters area. It's named after Daniel Bowley, a sea captain who bought about 2,000 acres around Baltimore in the mid-1700s and housed his slaves in the "quarters."

Years later, the land was converted to a game preserve where presidents, local politicians, and even Babe Ruth came for duck hunting. The steel and manufacturing heyday of the 1900s brought blue-collar families to the area.

More recently, floods from Hurricane Isabel wreaked havoc on Bowleys Quarters, knocking out hundreds of homes. But these hard-working folks continue to rebuild and welcome visitors to their home along the Bay.

The Wild Duck Café

3408 Red Rose Farm Road
Middle River, MD 21220
410-335-2121
www.thewildduckcafe.com

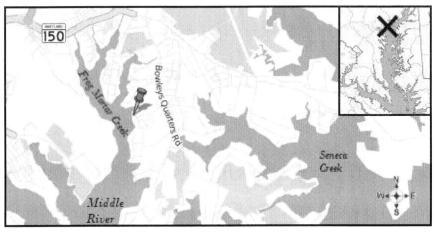

County: Baltimore County
Open: Year Round
Latitude: N 39° 19' 26" Longitude: W 76° 23' 58"
Body of Water: Frog Mortar Creek off the Middle River
Dockage: Yes
Picture Code: TWDC at www.crabdecksandtikibars.com/pix

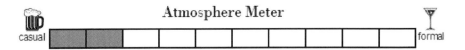

Wild Duck Café is the type of place that makes you want to call in sick on a warm summer day. It tempts you out of the office with beach parties, classic rock bands, and casual dining in a terrific location.

T-shirts, flip-flops, and denim shorts work just fine, because people come here to kick back and soak up the sun.

Nestled among the trees on the banks of Frog Mortar Creek, Wild Duck offers three areas for fun. On the indoor dining room walls, flat-screen TVs play Orioles or Ravens games.

The elevated deck is covered with a green awning that allows diners to enjoy the scenery of the marina where boats tie up to a 300-foot floating pier.

Down on the beach, the thatched bar shakes things up with orange crushes and icy beers. Tiki lanterns cast a warm light along the water's edge. You can dig your toes in the sand while checking out the menu and daily specials.

You could start with steamer pots packed with shrimp, clams, mussels, or veggies, or nibble on standard pub fare of wings, nachos, and mozzarella sticks. Soups, salads, and sandwiches are available for light meals.

Dinner entrees feature fresh local seafood, crab cakes, and steaks. Put it all together and you get a hassle-free locale that shows how life can be better at the Bay.

Carson's Creekside

1110 Beech Drive
Middle River, MD 21220
410-238-0080
www.carsonscreekside.com

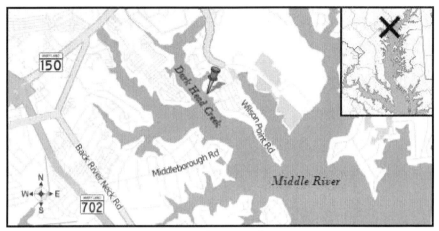

County: Baltimore County
Open: Year Round
Latitude: N 39° 19' 16"   Longitude: W 76° 25' 35"
Body of Water: Dark Head Creek off the Middle River
Dockage: Yes
Picture Code: CC at www.crabdecksandtikibars.com/pix

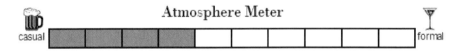

You wouldn't expect to find a Chesapeake gem so close to a busy state airport, but that's where you'll discover Carson's Creekside.

Its one-story red brick building shares a parking lot with Austin's Alehouse, Carson's Market, and Taylor's Treats of

Sweets. A flat green sailboat serving as a planter holds up the restaurant's sign.

An antique wooden fish, crab pots, and buoys decorating the outside suggest that Bay culinary traditions and laid-back lifestyle are cherished inside.

A fireplace warms the air in winter, and the dazzling view of Dark Head Creek pulls your attention outside in the summer. To combat cool weather, heaters are thoughtfully placed on the covered deck for alfresco fans.

As proof that it's a favorite local watering hole, happy hour in the lounge runs from 11:00 a.m. to 7:00 p.m. during the week, and karaoke or DJs get the party started on weekends. Children feed ducks down by the water.

Classic American steaks and regional seafood take center stage on the menu, serving patrons from lunch to late-night bites. Light fare includes creative salads and sandwich specialties such as French dip, seafood wrap, open-faced hot turkey, and Carolina pulled pork.

Bay-influenced entrees, such as crab cakes, shrimp stuffed with crab imperial, and bouillabaisse with crusty bread, are complimented by meat-lovers' prime rib, chicken marsala, and baby-back ribs.

The River Watch Restaurant

207 Nanticoke Road
Essex, MD 21221
410-687-1422
www.riverwatchrestaurant.com

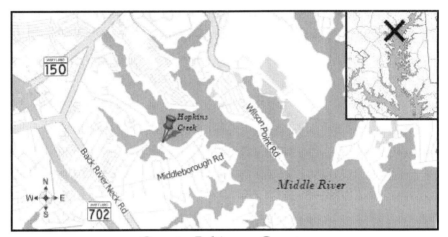

County: Baltimore County
Open: Year Round
Latitude: N 39° 18' 42"   Longitude: W 76° 25' 56"
Body of Water: Hopkins Creek off the Middle River
Dockage: Yes
Picture Code: TRWR at www.crabdecksandtikibars.com/pix

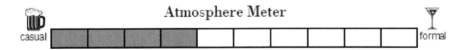

Atmosphere Meter

casual   formal

Some people like the calm solitude of the Bay in winter.
They hunker down in places with stone fireplaces and
steaming bowls of crab soup that offer a respite to the
bitter winds.

Others prefer the livelier pulse of summer, where bikinis, boats, and beer rule in the sun. River Watch finds a way to accommodate both seasons and temperaments.

The dining room's cozy romantic atmosphere can melt away the worst case of the cold February blues. Rows of beautifully etched glass panels depict the region's nautical heritage through schooners and sailboats — and remind you that winter will eventually end and you'll soon be back out on the water.

When the weather breaks, people pack away their bulky sweaters, pull on a T-shirt and shorts, and head for River Watch. The huge outdoor deck is big enough to fit everyone who's emerging from hibernation.

A covered deck with a bar runs the entire length of the building. A lower-level patio, with bars on both ends, sparkles from a string of white lights overhead. Boaters tie up at the marina, ready for action. A band starts to play, and the party begins.

The food is fresh, picking the best of what's in season, and the kitchen skillfully blends Chesapeake cuisine with classic American fare. Salads are crisp, sandwiches are filling, and steaks are juicy and tender.

Noteworthy entrees include slow-cooked prime rib, creamy crab imperial, and seafood decceco (sautéed shrimp and scallops with artichokes, mushrooms, and tomatoes).

You can end the night with a rum-infused specialty drink — the River Watch Sunset — while you listen to the band and watch the stars come out over the water.

Marli's Dockside Grill
& Crabhouse

203 Nanticoke Road
Essex, MD 21221
410-574-6275
www.marlisdockside.com

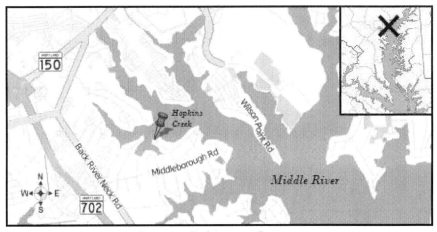

County: Baltimore County
Open: Year Round
Latitude: N 39° 18' 41"   Longitude: W 76° 25' 58"
Body of Water: Hopkins Creek off the Middle River
Dockage: Yes
Picture Code: MDGC at www.crabdecksandtikibars.com/pix

Atmosphere Meter

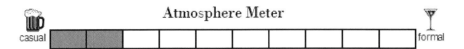

Marli's claims that its seafood is so fresh that only the ice is frozen. A statement that bold makes you want to investigate.

Well, the location is right. It sits on the water's edge where Middle River and Hopkins Creek converge.

One of the partners owns a charter boat that cruises for fish between here and the Atlantic.

When the restaurant opened in July 2010, the walls were painted bright Caribbean turquoise, orange, and yellow, with a few palm trees adding to the tropical island feel.

Even the logo sports a marlin bursting out of the waves and a crab hoping to avoid the steam pot. A second-story deck lets you feel the summer breeze and check out boats in the marina below.

But what about the food? The kitchen offers a few savory beef and chicken dishes, with items such as St. Louis-style BBQ ribs, flat iron steaks, chicken marsala, and prime rib on special nights.

Most of the menu is a tribute to the sweet bites of a Maryland summer. Mountains of hot steamed crabs and shrimp are ready for you to pick. Flounder is stuffed with crab imperial and served over red pepper aioli.

Grilled scallops are wrapped in bacon, and potato skins are topped with shrimp, scallops, and jumbo lump crab. They even serve pizza with seafood baked into four bubbling cheeses.

Then it's confirmed. If you want fish fresh from the Bay, head straight over to Marli's.

Sue Island Crab House & Dock Bar

900 Baltimore Yacht Club Drive
Essex, MD 21221
443-460-0092

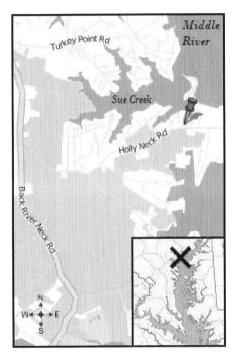

County: Baltimore County

Open: Year Round

Latitude: N 39° 17' 3"

Longitude: W 76° 23' 43"

Body of Water: Sue Creek off the Middle River

Dockage: Yes

Picture Code: SICHDB at www.crabdecksandtikibars.com/pix

Atmosphere Meter

casual ▮▮▮□□□□□□□□□ formal

It's perfectly fine to serve crabs and beer at a marina dock bar. But once you add a touch or two of tiki, people start to smile ... and relax ... and have a little more fun.

That's what's happening at Sue Island. Nestled among the boats at Sue Creek, this charming little place offers a fabulous view of the water. The rustic tiki bar brings a dash of color with strings of hibiscus flowers, a mermaid piñata, a few plastic sharks, and a palm tree made of lights.

Under the covered pavilion outside, picnic tables are lined up with families in T-shirts and bathing suits, and tiki torches cast an amber glow along the white picket fence.

A sign above the doorway to the dining room, "Friends Gather Here," simple states that friends, neighbors, and guests are always welcome. The walls are covered with hand-painted pictures of power and fishing boats with names of the beloved captains and vessels that cruise the local waters.

Hot steamed crabs, shrimp, and corn-on-the-cob are presented on blue plastic trays with wooden hammers for whacking shells. Oysters in season are sumptuous.

At Sue Island, it's all about Chesapeake summertime.

Island View Waterfront Café

2542 Island View Road
Essex, MD 21221
410-687-9799
www.islandviewwaterfrontcafe.com

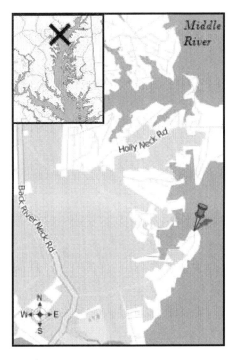

County: Baltimore County

Open: Seasonal

Latitude: N 39° 16' 8"

Longitude: W 76° 23' 45"

Body of Water: directly on the Chesapeake Bay

Dockage: Yes

Picture Code: IVWC at www.crabdecksandtikibars.com/pix

Atmosphere Meter

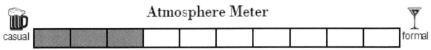

casual   formal

Island View makes you feel like you've stepped back in time. When this quaint Chesapeake gem was built in 1928, the house served as a dance hall, tavern, and picnic grove.

Even in the remote necks of the Bay, jazz and blues had permeated the radio waves, and Prohibition rules were beginning to crumble. Just imagine women dressed in their

Saturday night best testing the latest dance moves with men who took an occasional sip from a silver flask tucked inside their jackets.

As time passed, it became a restaurant, and in 1968, the Laing family bought the property. They handed it down for three generations to family members who added upgrades but maintain a down-home, old-fashioned feel.

The calm blue walls are decorated with duck decoys, paintings of waterfowl, and antique memorabilia. On the outside deck, you're treated to a beautiful waterfront scene of picnic tables on a grassy lawn, families playing horse shoes, and boats tied up to a long wooden pier.

The home-style food reminds you of what was served in your grandmother's kitchen. Crab cakes, pot roast, fried chicken, stuffed pork chops, and seafood marinara are dished out in hefty portions. One April Sunday, pierogies and stuffed cabbage were the daily special. Eggs, bacon, and chipped beef with gravy are highlights on the weekend breakfast menu.

When you're at Island View, take a moment to check out the gun ceremoniously hung on the door frame leading to the bar. It's a replica of an old punt gun that makes today's environmentalists cringe. These cannon-like shotguns were used in the 1800s around the Bay to hunt flocks of waterfowl.

The gun's recoil was so strong that hunters had to mount them on flat-bottom boats called "punts." After packing punt guns with up to a pound of shot, they'd fire with a deafening roar and kill up to 50 ducks with one powerful blast. Working together, groups of hunters could take out 500 birds in a day. Obviously, this decimated the waterfowl population, and Federal laws banned the use of punt guns by 1920.

Brewers Landing Bar & Grill

801 Woodrow Avenue
Essex, MD 21221
443-231-5037
www.brewerslanding.net

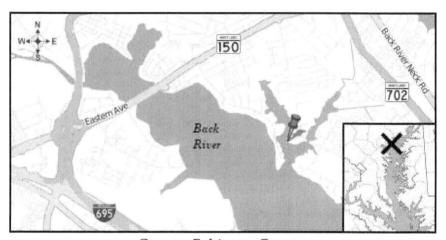

County: Baltimore County
Open: Year Round
Latitude: N 39° 17' 45"   Longitude: W 76° 27' 49"
Body of Water: Duck Creek off Deep Creek off Back River
Dockage: Yes
Picture Code: BLBG at www.crabdecksandtikibars.com/pix

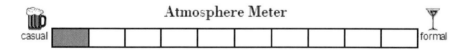

Atmosphere Meter

casual | | | | | | | | | | formal

There's always something going on at Brewer's Landing. You'll find a band or DJ getting things moving on the dance floor each weekend, along with Ravens or Oriole fans glued to flat-screened TVs.

They've got pool tables, Texas Hold 'em tournaments, darts leagues, and even keno machines if you're feeling lucky.

Crabs painted with each NFL team logo are hung on a wall to track each team's progress during the football season.

If you can drag yourself away from this indoor fun, you'll discover plenty to do outside. Under the awning, long lines of wooden tables and chairs offer a lovely view of Duck Creek.

Picnic tables scattered about the grassy area bring you closer to the water's edge. Tiki lights mounted on the wooden fence cast a festive light while people take turns tossing horse shoes.

The menu gives early birds the choice of eggs, pancakes, creamed chipped beef with gravy, or crispy fried scrapple for breakfast. Daily specials offer good prices for a pound of steamed shrimp, spaghetti and meatballs, or a steak and crab cake dinner.

The regular menu starts with standard pub favorites of nachos, spicy chicken wings, crab dip, and cheesy waffle fries. Burgers, wraps, salads, and quesadillas round out the casual fare, while steamers, crab cakes, and batter-fried fish give a nod to old-school Chesapeake cooking.

Juicy steaks, chicken breasts, and pork chops appeal to meat-lovers in the crowd. So eat, drink, and be merry at Brewers Landing Bar & Grill.

Bluefins Seafood
Restaurant & Bar

8247 Eastern Avenue
Baltimore, MD 21224
410-282-5050

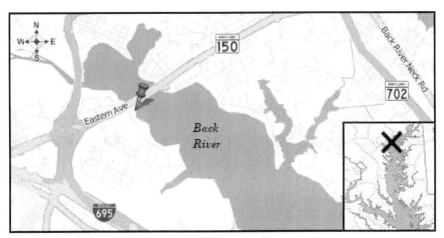

County: Baltimore County
Open: Year Round
Latitude: N 39° 18' 1"   Longitude: W 76° 29' 26"
Body of Water: Back River
Dockage: No
Picture Code: BSRB at www.crabdecksandtikibars.com/pix

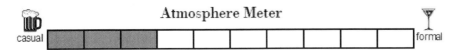

Atmosphere Meter

casual   formal

As you drive west out of Essex on Route 150 and cross the bridge over Back River, it's hard to miss Bluefins. Mounted on top of a 20-foot tall pole is a giant blue swordfish sign that serves as a beacon to the restaurant below.

The top of the building is trimmed with a row of neon blue waves cresting toward a pair of lighthouses on the front corners.

The inside dining area provides a comfortable atmosphere for enjoying your fill of good local seafood, steak, chicken, and assorted munchies at a reasonable price.

Outside, green glowing palms trees are lined up along a white lattice fence to mark the spot where music and laughter are top priorities.

Flaming tiki torches cast a gentle amber light along the water's edge, and the view is delightful. Wooden picnic tables are packed with patrons listening to a live band or working their way through a dozen fresh steamed crabs.

At the bar, another large blue swordfish trapped in a Tommy Bahama Rum box holds glasses for the Crush Station, where tropicolada, melonball, and orange crushes are ready to quench your thirst.

Islander Inn & Catering

9008 Cuckold Point Road
Sparrows Point, MD 21219
410-388-0713
www.islanderinnandcatering.com

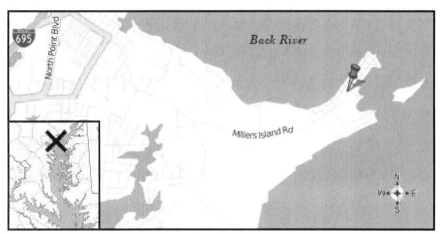

County: Baltimore County
Open: Year Round
Latitude: N 39° 14' 0"   Longitude: W 76° 24' 13"
Body of Water: between the Back River and the Chesapeake Bay
Dockage: No
Picture Code: IIC at www.crabdecksandtikibars.com/pix

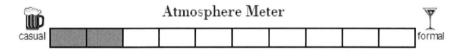

When Hurricane Isabel came barreling up the East Coast
in 2003, her damage to the Bay was catastrophic. She was
especially harsh to Millers Island, dumping 3.2 tons of debris
on residents' front lawns and destroying more than
300 buildings.

But as you look at the neighborhoods near Islander's Inn, you see new homes, defiantly built up high and to code to withstand nature's next tempest.

Islander Inn has a timeless sturdiness that makes you believe it can survive anything. The blue dining room walls are trimmed with a border of red and white lighthouses, and a nautical theme plays throughout.

Crabs, fishing poles, blue marlins, pictures of boats, and even a six-pack of Bud caught in a net decorate the dining area. Duck decoys and fishing gear garnish the top of the wood and pressed-tin bar. Ravens fans gather around a dimly lit pool table to discuss strategies for whooping their rival in Pittsburgh.

The food is classic Chesapeake cuisine: crabs are simmered in a smooth creamy dip, tucked into soft pretzels, pressed into cakes, fried soft, or simply steamed fresh and hot.

Pork is pulled into tender BBQ bites, and prime rib is slow-cooked to mouth-watering perfection. It's home of the $1 crabs from April to November, and free purple shooters are awarded for Ravens' touchdowns.

It's hard to skip a place as authentic as this.

Rowboat Willie's Dock Bar

9033 Cuckold Point Road
Sparrows Point, MD 21219
410-477-5137 or 410-388-1091

County: Baltimore County
Open: Seasonal
Latitude: N 39° 14' 2"   Longitude: W 76° 24' 5"
Body of Water: directly on the Chesapeake Bay
Dockage: Yes
Picture Code: RWDB at www.crabdecksandtikibars.com/pix

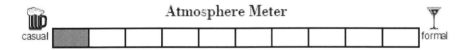

Atmosphere Meter

casual ▢▢▢▢▢▢▢▢▢ formal

It's a simple two-story structure — more wooden deck than building — with a few palm trees, colorful umbrellas, and tables scattered around.

But what makes Rowboat Willie's special is the spectacular location. It's at the tip of Millers Island where the Back River flows into the Chesapeake, and you'd be hard pressed to find a more expansive view of the Bay.

With music playing gently in the background, you can kick back on the upper deck, grab a cold beer or frozen drink, and watch the boats arrive at Bill's Yacht Basin Marina. If you're hungry, you can grab a bite to eat at Dock of the Bay next door.

You can gaze out a bit farther to check out the Craighill Lighthouse and Hart-Miller Island State Park, a 244-acre preserve that's only accessible by boat.

It used to be three islands — Hart, Miller and Pleasure — but the spaces in between are getting filled in with dredge materials. In the 1940s, Pleasure Island was developed as an amusement park, connected to the mainland by a wooden bridge, but storms knocked out the bridge in the 1960s.

Now the island's main visitors are waterfowl, migrating birds, and adventure-seeking boaters who come ashore to wade along its sandy beaches or enjoy a scenic picnic lunch.

Dock of the Bay Restaurant

9025 Cuckold Point Road
Sparrows Point, MD 21219
410-477-8100
www.dockofthebay.net

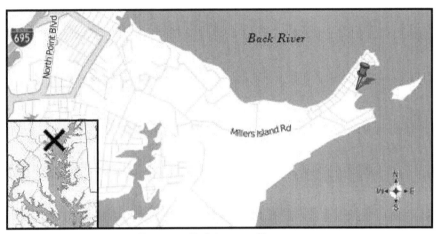

County: Baltimore County
Open: Year Round
Latitude: N 39° 14' 0"   Longitude: W 76° 24' 6"
Body of Water: directly on the Chesapeake Bay
Dockage: Yes
Picture Code: DBR at www.crabdecksandtikibars.com/pix

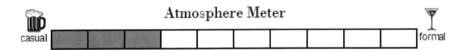

Dock of the Bay is a landmark on this neck of the Chesapeake. "I've been coming here picking crabs since I was just a little girl. I can't imagine a time when it wasn't part of our lives," the bartender says and smiles.

She points to a photo of flood damage from Hurricane Isabel and talks about all the hard work needed to rebuild.

Renovations were completed in December 2003, resulting in an 80-foot long bar with 10 beers on tap and seven wide-screen TVs mounted on the walls.

A big green awning stretches over the patio and matching umbrellas shield patrons from the summer sun on 6,500 square feet of outdoor seating.

Kayla's Cove, a sandy play area, tempts children to crawl around a wooden pirate ship and imagine a swashbuckler's life on the seas.

Boaters like the free docking on the 105-foot long pier, where sets of comfy Adirondack chairs are thoughtfully placed, encouraging you to take a moment and enjoy the view.

And what a sight you'll see. Surrounded by glistening waters stands the historic Craighill Lighthouse, built in 1875. At 105 feet, it's the tallest lighthouse in Maryland. Its red and white, four-sided pyramid design was constructed with a granite base and an iron and wood structure.

The only thing that could drag you away from this spectacular sight is the smell of crabs steaming and steaks sizzling. The menu runs the gamut of fresh seafood delivered each morning by local watermen.

Fried, steamed, or broiled — whatever you want; cooked however you like. Burgers, chicken, and a little pirate's menu ensure everyone gets his fill.

When dinner's done, feel free to linger a while, listen to the band, and watch the stars come out over one of the nicest dock bars on the Bay.

Seahorse Inn

710 Wise Avenue
Dundalk, MD 21222
410-388-1150

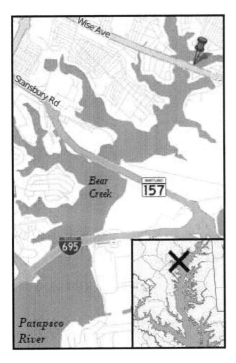

County: Baltimore County

Open: Year Round

Latitude: N 39° 15' 38"

Longitude: W 76° 28' 29"

Body of Water: Oakleigh Cove off Bear Creek off the Patapsco River

Dockage: Yes

Picture Code: SI2 at www.crabdecksandtikibars.com/ pix

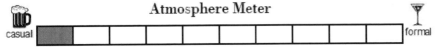

Atmosphere Meter

casual   formal

    Seahorse Inn is located in a Dundalk neighborhood that makes anyone who grew up in an industrial Northeast town feel a sense of nostalgia, if not a little homesick.

    Streets are lined with red brick ramblers built for working class families by steel mills and shipbuilding companies. It harkens back to the day when churches, union halls, and corner bars created a holy trinity of social life in tight-knit, blue-collar communities.

The outside of Seahorse's two-story cinder block and brick building has a fresh coat of tan paint, but its former name, Oakleigh Tavern, bleeds through the front awning, reminding you that the view of Oakleigh Cove on Bear Creek remains lovely.

The inside walls and ceiling are cluttered with a collection of stuff that shows a nautical theme blended with an assortment of things left behind.

Plastic fish, blue crabs, rusty anchors, over-sized fishing lures, and yellow water skis are tacked up next to Budweiser beer steins, a Hulk Hogan action figure, a stuffed raven, and best of all, a two-foot long baby doll's leg that gets a fresh sock to commemorate special holidays.

When you walk outside to the deck, your eyes are treated to chairs and tables painted a rainbow of cheerful Caribbean colors. Down below by the water, the view of wooden docks and tree-lined river banks only gets better.

Boaters come ashore ready for a game or two of horseshoes, and families gather around picnic tables munching on platters of nachos, chicken wings, pizza, hot crabs, seafood steamers, and burgers.

Sunsets over the water make it difficult to go home.

The Seasoned Mariner

601 Wise Avenue
Dundalk, MD 21222
443-242-7190
www.seasonedmariner.com

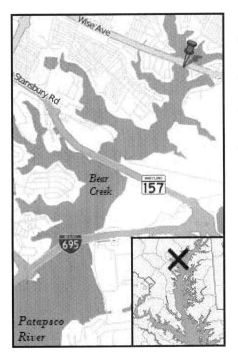

County: Baltimore County

Open: Year Round

Latitude: N 39° 15' 37"

Longitude: W 76° 28' 35"

Body of Water: Bear Creek off the Patapsco River

Dockage: Yes

Picture Code: TSM at www.crabdecksandtikibars.com/pix

 Atmosphere Meter

casual | | | | | | | | | formal

Over the years, it's been called Beach House, Bahama Mama's, Dick's on the Dock, and Bear Creek Inn, but as of June 2010, the sign out front reads the Seasoned Mariner.

Despite all its name changes, the location remains spectacular. Views of the neighboring bridge over Bear Creek and the tree-lined banks of the river form a lovely backdrop for waterfront dining and crab deck fun.

Swaying palm trees, a sandy beach, a children's play area, a busy outside bar, and brightly colored umbrellas create an upbeat island feel.

The new owners spruced up the place inside "to give diners a pleasant environment to enjoy a nice meal." They painted the walls creamy gold and earthy sage and stood tropical plants in the corners.

A subtle nautical theme uses hand-painted fish to brighten the decor. A little porcelain mermaid wearing a bikini top made of turtle shells keeps an eye on the dining room. A ceiling-to-floor, two-sided indoor waterfall lulls you into a relaxed state of mind.

The menu leans toward fresh seafood, making the most of local watermen's daily catch. House specialties include a piping hot Smith Island Stew, horseradish encrusted rockfish, mountains of hot steamed crabs, and a hearty seafood sub that lines crab cakes, shrimp, scallops, and fried fish on a fresh-baked hoagie roll.

Cream of crab soup is thick, velvety, and laced with nice chunks of crab. Chicken Chesapeake and seafood stew are fresh and irresistible.

The Hard Yacht Café

8500 Cove Road
Dundalk, MD 21222
443-407-0038
www.hardyacht.com

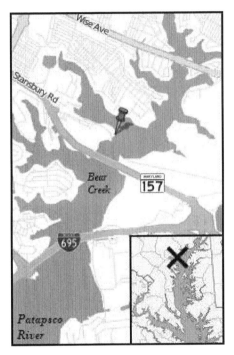

County: Baltimore County

Open: Year Round

Latitude: N 39° 15' 3"

Longitude: W 76° 29' 19"

Body of Water: Bear Creek off the Patapsco River

Dockage: Yes

Picture Code: THYC at www.crabdecksandtikibars.com/pix

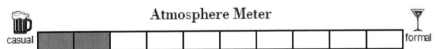

Atmosphere Meter

casual | | | | | | | | formal

Some of the best restaurants around the Bay tell stories of their humble beginnings — an oyster shucking plant or a spot at the local marina with a few beach chairs and a cooler.

The birth of Hard Yacht Café follows this admirable tradition. In the 1980s, the property was "nothing more than a trash pile for debris that was pulled from the rest of the dump-like marina." They built a deck, added some picnic tables, and put up a cover as shelter from bad weather. After walls were built, it became the Crab Shack.

Over the years came heat, refrigerators, coffee pots, a stove, and other amenities until it eventually evolved into a beloved local hangout and a testament to what friends and family can accomplish after a few beers and a lot of sweat equity.

Today, Hard Yacht Cafe is a visual cornucopia of stuff collected and tacked up on the walls. Palm trees sprout from the deck, a ship's bridge serves as the deck cover, and the tiki bar sign is painted on an overturned row boat.

Surf boards, rusty crab pots, tiki heads, license plates, Ravens banners, nautical flags, fish nets, electric guitars, framed photos, and more fill every nook and corner of the place. Even a motorcycle and deer's head hang from the rafters.

The food is hearty and homey. Breakfast of eggs, sausage, scrapple, and pancakes is served daily. Oyster po boys, crab cakes, fried shrimp, wings, burgers, conch fritters, and chili fill diners' bellies later in the day. At night, the place rocks with music, cold beer, and merriment.

One cautionary note: It's not easy to find, so pay close attention to directions. If you get lost, you'll wind through areas with run-down buildings and rusty warehouses that represent Baltimore's industrial heritage — a time when local steel mills made girders for the Golden Gate Bridge and ship-building was in its heyday.

Reckless Ric's Bar & Grill

1702 Furnace Drive
Glen Burnie, MD 21060
410-590-2280
www.recklessrics.com

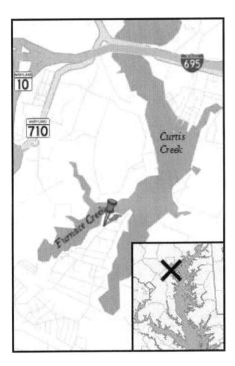

County: Anne Arundel County

Open: Year Round

Latitude: N 39° 11' 0"

Longitude: W 76° 35' 8"

Body of Water: Furnace Creek off Curtis Creek off the Patapsco River

Dockage: Yes

Picture Code: RRBG at www.crabdecksandtikibars.com/pix

Atmosphere Meter

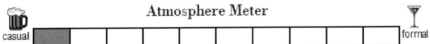

casual ▮▮▮▮▮▮▮▮▮▮ formal

If you follow the roaring thunder of a Harley passing through Glen Burnie, you might end up at Reckless Ric's. Bikers, boaters, and locals are welcomed into this self-described "Redneck Yacht Club" by a big red sign out front.

A mural in blue tones along the side wall depicts the dreamy side of motorcycle living through babes, beaches, and bikes. Patrons are reminded to be on their best behavior with messages stating, "Respect the neighborhood, will ya. Show your class and not your ass."

Not a bad idea, because everyone should get a chance to enjoy this high-energy locale. The centerpiece of the waterfront beach area is a massive tree trunk detailed with ominous-looking tiki masks on two sides.

Palm trees stand out in contrast to the maples and oaks of the working-class neighborhood. Inside is a collage of leather, chrome, tattoos, tank tops, and pool tables. Billiards leagues and bike shows attract a colorful crowd.

The menu is hearty casual, with appetizers like crab dip, steamed shrimp, jerk chicken, and hot wings. Crab soup, chili, and gumbo take the edge off a cold wintry ride.

Salads and wraps help cool you down in the summer. Entrees include crab cakes, steaks, burgers, chicken, and pizza. It's all classic Americana, with an extra dash of freedom.

Point Pleasant Beach Tavern

1750 Marley Avenue
Glen Burnie, MD 21060
410-553-0600

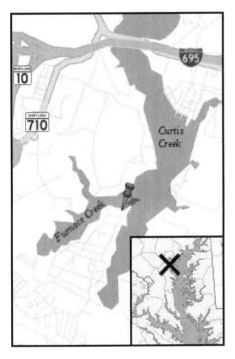

County: Anne Arundel County

Open: Seasonal

Latitude: N 39° 11' 6"

Longitude: W 76° 34' 55"

Body of Water: Curtis Creek
off the Patapsco River

Dockage: No

Picture Code: PPBT at
www.crabdecksandtikibars.com/
pix

Atmosphere Meter

casual | | | | | | | | | | | formal

Point Pleasant Tavern's one-story red building has a low-key, unassuming feel. Even the restaurant's name gets second billing to the Pepsi logo on the sign out front.

No matter. Folks around Glenn Burnie know it's there. Neighborhood watering holes like this are the backbone of working class communities, along with churches, schools, and family-owned shops.

The restaurant doesn't have many windows out front. Instead, it saves the view for the tables that face the river and boats tied up at the dock.

It sits right on the water's edge — so close that you might wonder how it has survived the storms and floods that hit these waters far too often.

The beach area is packed with picnic tables and children who don't dare traipse inside if their bathing suit is dripping wet.

The down-home food is simple, filling, and connected to the fresh seafood of the Bay. And the casual hospitality ensures that everyone gets what they want at Point Pleasant.

Need proof? Someone even lifted up the bottom of a chain-link fence so ducks can take an easier route to the water. Now, that's home-town hospitality.

Stoney Creek
Inn & Restaurant

8238 Fort Smallwood Road
Greenland Beach, MD 21226
410-439-3123
www.stoneycreekinnrestaurant.com

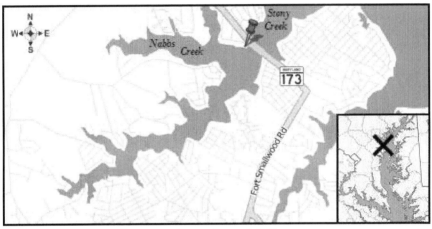

County: Anne Arundel County
Open: Year Round
Latitude: N 39° 9' 48"   Longitude: W 76° 31' 37"
Body of Water: Stony Creek off the Patapsco River
Dockage: Yes
Picture Code: SCIR at www.crabdecksandtikibars.com/pix

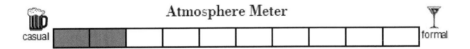

Atmosphere Meter
casual ———— formal

Being at Stoney Creek Inn might remind you of having a home-cooked meal at your favorite aunt's house.

It started out as Bill's Seafood Carry-Out & Crabs in 1998 and moved to its current location in 2001, but it feels like this classic crab shack has been around forever. The exterior walls of the one-story building are made of faux-stone cement blocks that prove you're just south of Baltimore.

Those walls worked so well on the outside that they used them inside as well, softened with old-fashion white lace curtains, light blue table cloths, and honey-brown linoleum floors.

Decorative crabs that are wood-carved, painted red, or glorified in photos show the owners take great pride in serving up the best fruits of the Bay. A special blend of seasonings and unshucked ears of corn cover crabs while they steam for exactly 25 minutes.

Shrimp and scallops come wrapped in bacon, and oysters are fried to a crispy golden bliss. The "Bawlmer Special" deep-fries a large hard crab that's stuffed with a crab cake and coated in batter.

All entrees, including chicken and steak, arrive with tasty sides such as creamy cole slaw, hush puppies, and a refreshing cucumber salad pickled with white vinegar, sugar, and sweet white onions.

You can order all these treats inside the charming restaurant or out back on the wooden deck while enjoying views of the marina, Stony Creek Bridge, and fabulous sunsets on the water.

Warning: Stoney Creek has limited seating, so you might want to call ahead if you're bringing a large group.

Nabb's Creek
Dock Bar & Grille

864 Nabbs Creek Road
Glen Burnie, MD 21060
410-437-3737
www.nabbscreekdockbar.com

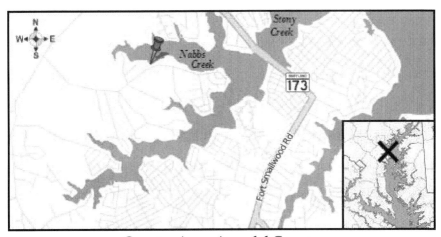

County: Anne Arundel County
Open: Year Round
Latitude: N 39° 9' 43"   Longitude: W 76° 32' 42"
Body of Water: Nabbs Creek off Stony Creek off the Patapsco River
Dockage: Yes
Picture Code: NCDBG at www.crabdecksandtikibars.com/pix

Atmosphere Meter

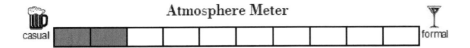

casual   formal

Two features make Nabb's Creek stand out among other
waterfront places — its huge A-frame building and an
exceptionally large wooden deck. New owners took
over in June 2010, renovating and upgrading a terrific
marina location.

The brown building houses a reasonably priced restaurant on the first level with a bar, pool table, fireplace, and flat-screen TVs.

Murals depicting herons in marshy grasslands and an eerie mermaid with a lantern give the space a nice Chesapeake touch. The staff is so proud of the improvements that you'd think they did it themselves.

The second floor has a spacious room for parties or bands and a deck for keeping an eye on the activities below — and there's a lot to watch down near the water.

That's home to Dolphin Dan's Tiki Bar, where boaters, bikers, and beach lovers mingle among thatched umbrellas, wooden picnic tables, and tiki torches. Cold beer, icy rum drinks, and live music keep the party hopping.

Inside and out, you'll find plenty of good casual fare served in baskets. Appetizers range from Bay favorites like crab dip and steamed shrimp to mozzarella sticks and fries topped with gravy or nacho cheese.

Burgers weigh in with a half-pound of ground beef, and wraps envelope blackened chicken with a soft tortilla. Entrees feature crab, shrimp, tuna, and steak.

All in all, it's a lively place to make some summer fun.

Cheshire Crab Restaurant

1701 Poplar Ridge Road
Pasadena, MD 21122
410-360-2220
www.cheshirecrab.com

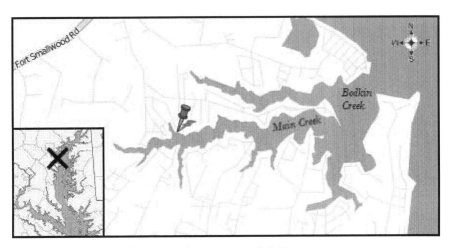

County: Anne Arundel County
Open: Year Round
Latitude: N 39° 7' 38"   Longitude: W 76° 28' 23"
Body of Water: Main Creek off Bodkin Creek off the Chesapeake
Bay
Dockage: Yes
Picture Code: CCR at www.crabdecksandtikibars.com/pix

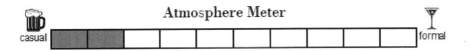

Atmosphere Meter

casual | | | | | | | | | | formal

If you haven't been to the Cheshire Crab in a while, you're in for a big surprise. Literally. Right beside the restaurant now stands an astonishingly gigantic structure recently built by the owners of Pleasure Cove Marina.

This canary yellow and white striped monster of a building offers parking for anything up to 45 feet tall, with enough space for mega-yachts, souped-up pleasure crafts, and maybe even the Queen Mary.

Somehow the Cheshire Crab holds its own next to this behemoth neighbor. The sign's red crab still grins its toothy grin and holds a sudsy beer.

The waterfront wooden deck continues to creak under the weight of folks enjoying a meal or singing along with a live band.

Thanks to new management, the indoor dining room areas have undergone renovations to accommodate the growing summertime crowds.

The menu's gotten a face lift as well, but the cook still dishes out fresh steamed crabs, beer-battered rockfish, shrimp sprinkled with Old Bay, and other fresh seafood.

In addition to those Bay standards, dining options have expanded to include wings, jerk chicken sticks, burgers, pulled pork or Cuban sandwiches, pasta, steaks, and ribs.

The view is beautiful, and the drinks are frosty cold — so why not give the new and improved Cheshire Crab a try?

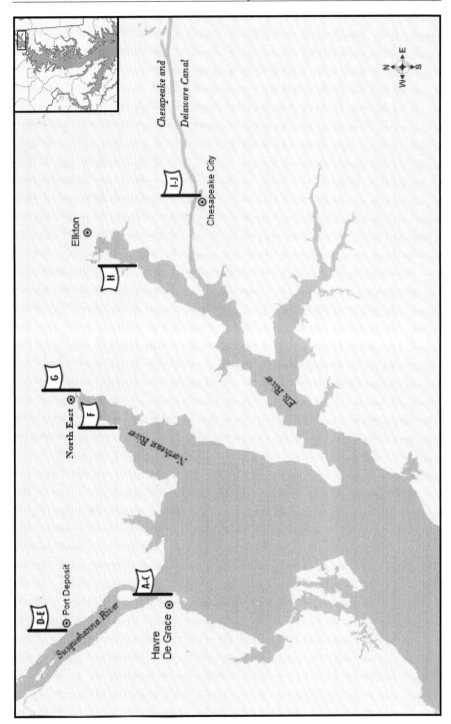

Headwaters of the Bay

Tidewater Grille

300 Franklin Street
Havre de Grace, MD 21078
410-939-3313 or 410-575-7045
www.thetidewatergrille.com

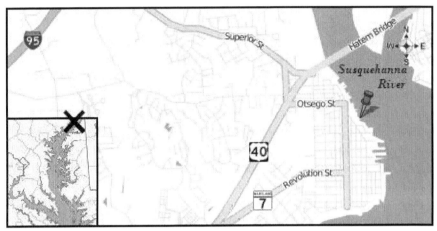

County: Harford County
Open: Year Round
Latitude: N 39° 33' 2" Longitude: W 76° 5' 22"
Body of Water: Susquehanna River
Dockage: Yes
Picture Code: TG at www.crabdecksandtikibars.com/pix

Atmosphere Meter

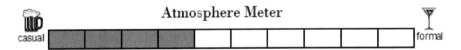

casual .... formal

It's hard to beat the location of Tidewater Grille. It sits along a river bank where the Susquehanna meets the headwaters of the Bay.

Out on the deck, a cool breeze comes off the river while you watch trains chug across the Amtrak Bridge or inspect the boats tied up at the 90-foot long dock. Listening to bands at sunset is a special summer treat.

If stormy weather chases you inside, you won't miss anything. The open design and walls of windows guarantee a good view no matter where you sit.

Dark oak floors and creamy white walls are accented with stained glass pictures that salute Chesapeake heritage with renderings of sailboats, lighthouses, waterfowl, and fishermen.

You'll need to take your eyes off the view for a moment to glance at the menu. It's a thoughtful marriage of fine dining and casual fare, and the choices are so extensive that if you can't find something you like, then maybe you're not hungry.

They offer everything from seafood to sandwiches, ribs, chicken, steaks, burgers, and salads — all cooked fresh with local ingredients. Standouts include crab and shrimp bruschetta, coconut lime tilapia, char-grilled flat iron steaks with melted bleu cheese crumbles, and Tidewater jambalaya.

Another bonus to visiting Tidewater is its hometown location. Take a stroll around the charming streets of Havre de Grace, and you'll discover antique stores, gifts shops, a duck decoy museum, and buildings that date back to the early 1800s.

The town got its name in 1782. In a letter to George Washington, the Marquis de Lafayette noted that this "graceful harbor" reminded him of a lovely French seaport called Le Havre. Centuries later, the town still lives up to its name.

MacGregor's Restaurant

331 St. John Street
Havre de Grace, MD 21078
410-939-3003
www.macgregorsrestaurant.com

County: Harford County
Open: Year Round
Latitude: N 39° 33' 2" Longitude: W 76° 5' 25"
Body of Water: Susquehanna River
Dockage: No
Picture Code: MR at www.crabdecksandtikibars.com/pix

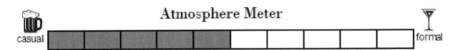

MacGregor's offers four options for people seeking a pleasant waterfront experience in a quaint historic town. Its main restaurant spans two-tiers, with exposed brick, dark wood, soft lighting, and tall windows creating a lovely ambiance.

Extensive menus accommodate appetites for lunch, dinner, and champagne brunch. Fresh local seafood leads the pack with jumbo crab cakes, wasabi ahi tuna, and a broiled Atlantic seafood platter. Surf is followed by turf with favorites such as flat iron steaks, Santa Fe chicken and rib platter, and chicken tortellini.

If you're in a more casual mood, head for the Tavern, where Scottish pub charm gets a modern upgrade with plasma TVs playing Ravens or Orioles games. Light fare is served here: mainly appetizers, spicy wings, cheesy nachos, fresh salads, juicy burgers, and sandwiches.

When you're ready to step outside for a gorgeous view of the Susquehanna River and Amtrak Bridge, mosey out to the Deck Bar. The wooden floor, black outdoor furniture, and strings of colorful beer signs set the tone for casual fun. Plans are underway to expand for more elbow room.

And if you want a space for corporate meetings or family gatherings, the Banquet Room will meet your needs, equipped with multimedia systems and catering.

While admiring the Gaelic influence at MacGregor's, keep in mind that other natives of the Emerald Isle have left their mark on Havre de Grace.

During the War of 1812, it was attacked by 15 barges of British soldiers. A local militiaman named John O'Neil tried to defend the town, but was injured by the recoil of his own cannon. He was captured and sentenced to death by hanging, but his young daughter bravely rowed out to the English admiral and pleaded for her father's life. O'Neil was spared, but the torch-happy British burned the city to the ground anyway.

Price's Seafood Restaurant

650 Water Street
Havre de Grace, MD 21078
410-939-2782
www.pricesseafood.com

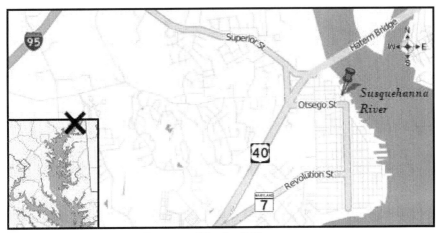

County: Harford County
Open: Year Round
Latitude: N 39° 33' 14"   Longitude: W 76° 5' 33"
Body of Water: Susquehanna River
Dockage: No
Picture Code: PSR2 at www.crabdecksandtikibars.com/pix

Atmosphere Meter

casual ▮▮▮ formal

If the image of old wood paneling decorated with fish nets, crabs, and striped bass doesn't hook you, then the briny aroma of steamed crabs will.

At Price's, you'll experience an authentic Maryland crab house that has upheld Chesapeake traditions since 1944. Located on the shore where the Susquehanna River meets the

Upper Bay, it's the kind of place where both adults and children wear protective bibs while wrestling tender chunks of crab meat from the shells.

Boys who grow restless from the slow pace of picking whack each other with crab hammers, and local fishermen toast the day's favorable weather. Silver buckets are placed on tables for discarded shells and empty beer bottles.

Like many waterfront restaurants, Price's added an outside deck, lit by orange and lime green paper lantern balls and strings of Christmas lights that spell out the restaurant's name. Wooden picnic tables are painted purple, blue, and green to add extra cheer.

Inside and out, the food is reasonably priced and well cooked. You can choose between Price's signature seasoning and Old Bay on crabs and shrimp, and mussels are tossed with melted butter and garlic.

A half pound of beef is wedged inside a hamburger bun, while chicken breasts are smothered with BBQ sauce, bacon, tomato, and cheese.

Whatever you pick for dinner, it's a delightful, homey place to enjoy a summer breeze and catch the sunset over the bridges.

Susky River Grille

600 Rowland Drive
Port Deposit, MD 21904
410-378-4600
www.suskyrivergrille.com

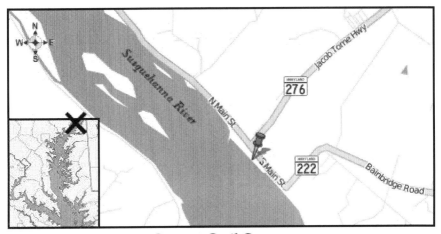

County: Cecil County
Open: Year Round
Latitude: N 39° 36' 15"   Longitude: W 76° 6' 58"
Body of Water: Susquehanna River
Dockage: Yes
Picture Code: SRG at www.crabdecksandtikibars.com/pix

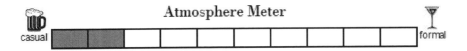

Atmosphere Meter

casual | | | | | | | | | | | formal

Wait a minute! Who said you're allowed to mix crabs with comedy? The Susky River Grille did.

In 2009, Baltimore native Bill Herold rolled into Port Deposit and set up his dream restaurant with a comedy club and a Key West, happy-go-lucky attitude. Called the

Laff Lounge, the club attracts national-class acts and fun-seekers from as far away as Philly.

Add some big-screen TVs for watching Ravens games, and you've got good times waiting to happen. The room's pale green walls are brightened by arched windows topped with painted palm trees.

Out on the waterfront deck, you will find a thatched roof-and-bamboo tiki bar serving cold drinks to hot patrons. Picnic tables anchored into the sand present a fabulous view of the Susquehanna River and a conga-line of bridges leading out to the Bay.

And don't forget about the crabs. They come in soups, cakes, or on top of Chicken Chesapeake. Easy fare includes spicy wings, cheese sticks, and crisp salads. Pounds of shrimp, mussels, and clams are fresh out of the local waters. Steaks, pasta, burgers, and wraps round out your choices of entrees.

Backfin Blues Bar & Grill

19 South Main Street
Port Deposit, MD 21904
410-378-2722
www.backfinblues.com

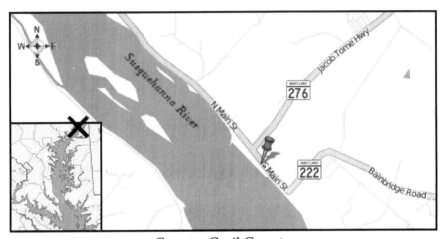

County: Cecil County
Open: Year Round
Latitude: N 39° 36' 15"   Longitude: W 76° 6' 53"
Body of Water: Susquehanna River
Dockage: No
Picture Code: BBBG at www.crabdecksandtikibars.com/pix

Back in the 1800s, Port Deposit served as a junction point for floating lumber, grain, coal, whiskey, and tobacco down the Susquehanna River.

It was so small that it didn't even catch the attention of the invading British in 1813, who skipped over the town and burned down a warehouse across the river instead. So, who'd expect to find a top-notch restaurant right on Main Street today?

Since 2004, Backfin Blues has served innovative dishes in a casual environment. Service is excellent, and the chef takes risks, giving fresh ingredients a new lease on life.

Seafood plays a prominent role on the menu, where you find scallops dusted with porcini and tomato relish, salmon finished with tzatziki sauce, and shrimp wrapped in wontons with sweet chili sauce.

Crab cakes are massive and tender. Rib-eye steaks are rubbed with coffee and chocolate then grilled, and chicken breasts are stuffed with spinach, crab, and feta.

The intimate dining area's exposed brick walls are decorated with crabs and fish, and the cozy bar shakes up cool smooth martinis.

Out on the deck, a yellow cover casts a warm glow on guests catching a splendid sunset over the river. Okay, so you have to look over the railroad tracks to get a glimpse of the water, but it's still a lovely view.

And you won't regret taking a walk around this charming little town that's eager to show off its gorgeous Victorian houses, quaint shops, and stunning scenery.

The Wellwood Restaurant

523 Water Street
Charlestown, MD 21914
410-287-6666
www.wellwoodclub.com

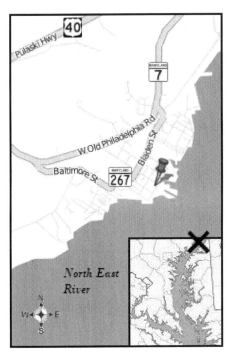

County: Cecil County

Open: Year Round

Latitude: N 39° 34' 22"

Longitude: W 75° 58' 20"

Body of Water: North East River

Dockage: Yes

Picture Code: TWR at www.crabdecksandtikibars.com/pix

Restaurant
Atmosphere Meter

casual | formal

River Shack
Atmosphere Meter

casual | formal

In Cecil County you can discover some of the most beautiful old buildings along the water, and Wellwood is no exception. Built in 1901, it originally housed a private hunting and fishing club that aimed "to reduce the friction of life to a minimum and increase the pleasure of existence to the maximum."

Later it was turned into a country and yacht club with a nine-hole golf course, duck pond, gardens, and swimming pool. Noteworthy guests included Teddy Roosevelt and Calvin Coolidge.

From 1958 to the present, Wellwood has been owned by the Metz family, who host everything from a romantic dinner for two to a big family wedding.

In the dining room, white linen tablecloths, candle light, and a crackling fireplace create a soothing ambiance for fine regional cuisine that showcases oysters, duck, crabs, and rockfish, as well as beef dishes. Iceberg wedge salads and oyster samplers lead into entrees such as Boursin-stuffed chicken, crab cakes, fried oyster dinners, pasta primavera, and flounder stuffed with shrimp, scallops, and crab.

While there, take a moment to look at the collection of antiques: a bust of George Washington, a lithograph of Lincoln, and a hand-carved eagle donated by President Roosevelt after his visit.

The Club Room encourages more casual dining with cozy seating and a big-screen TV. The teak wood furniture on the outdoor patio gives you a front-row seat for watching the boats sail along the North East River or listening to a band.

Around back awaits the River Shack, where its rustic tiki flare, wooden picnic tables, and sandy beach create the idea spot for all-you-can-eat crabs and Wellwood's legendary bucket of Maryland fried chicken.

Nauti-Goose Restaurant

200 West Cherry Street
North East, MD 21901
410-287-7880
www.nautigoose.net

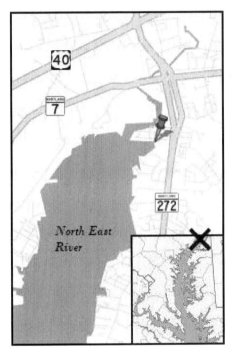

County: Cecil County

Open: Seasonal

Latitude: N 39° 35' 34"

Longitude: W 75° 56' 41"

Body of Water: North East River

Dockage: Yes

Picture Code: NGR at www.crabdecksandtikibars.com/pix

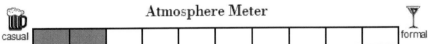

Atmosphere Meter

casual | | | | | | | | | | formal

When you explore the headwaters of the Chesapeake, Nauti-Goose should top your list of fun places to visit with family and friends.

Docking is easy with four long piers to accommodate 50 boats, and a marina is conveniently located next door. Parents can let children run amok in the spacious park and playground nearby before settling down to a hearty waterfront meal.

The restaurant is best known for its prime rib and seafood buffet, and the chef recently designed a new menu featuring local ingredients and fresh fruits of the Bay.

Hot steamed crabs and shrimp, juicy burgers, and thick steaks — there's something for everyone here.

The upbeat, casual atmosphere flows outdoors to two massive decks that span the length of the slate-blue building and offer dazzling views of the water, especially at sunset. Its five bars and live bands on weekends keep the energy level high.

If that's not enough, you can find plenty to see and do in this neck of the woods. Elk Neck State Park has sandy beaches, camp sites, excellent fishing spots, and wooded bluffs that overlook the river.

You can hike out to Turkey Point Lighthouse (built in 1833) and climb 35 feet to the top to catch an unparalleled view of the water.

Or you can check out the Upper Bay Museum that celebrates the heritage of local watermen, waterfowl hunting, and art of decoy carving.

Triton Bar & Grill

285 Plum Point Road
Elkton, MD 21921
410-620-3060 or 443-350-9943
www.tritonmarina.com

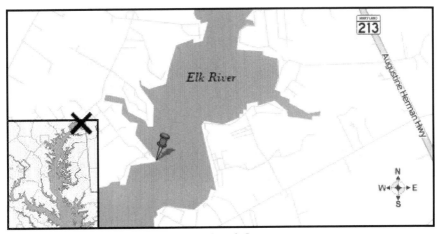

County: Cecil County
Open: Year Round
Latitude: N 39° 33' 39"   Longitude: W 75° 51' 26"
Body of Water: Elk River
Dockage: Yes
Picture Code: TBG2 at www.crabdecksandtikibars.com/pix

Atmosphere Meter

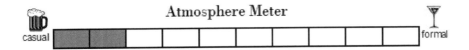

Triton is the kind of place that makes you want to buy a boat (or be glad you have one). It represents the celebration of life on the water that's unique to the Bay and its tributaries.

Restaurants like this and their marinas are the central hub of rural communities — the Chesapeake equivalent to granges in land-locked regions. Parents gather at picnic tables picking crabs, while still keeping a watchful eye as their children splash in the water. Boaters pull up pink-faced from the sun, opening coolers to show off the day's catch of blues or rockfish.

The focal point at Triton is the restaurant — a beautiful old gray-and-tan stone building where steamed crabs, fried shrimp, and fresh local seafood is served along with icy pitchers of beer. Casual fare of sandwiches and burgers perfectly matches the laid back atmosphere.

Ancient oak trees cast shade on the wrap-around deck that gives a gorgeous view of the water or the firework display on July 4th. Friends toss horseshoes or listen to a band on weekends, while their dogs chase squirrels across the wide grassy lawn.

The full-service marina claims eight acres of land with three sandy beaches along the Elk River, and its High & Dry Boatel has room for boats up to 47 feet long.

In a nutshell, whether you arrive by land or sea, you'll be glad you came to Triton Bar & Grill.

Bayard House

11 Bohemia Avenue
Chesapeake City, MD 21915
410-885-5040 or 877-582-4049
www.bayardhouse.com

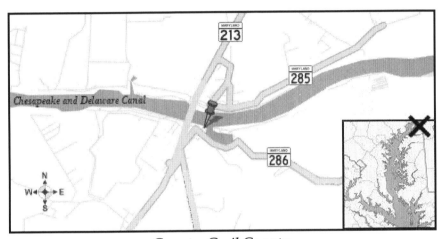

County: Cecil County
Open: Year Round
Latitude: N 39° 31' 39"   Longitude: W 75° 48' 43"
Body of Water: Chesapeake and Delaware Canal
Dockage: No
Picture Code: BH at www.crabdecksandtikibars.com/pix

Atmosphere Meter

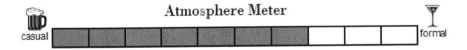

casual   formal

    Bayard House is the oldest building in Chesapeake City, MD. Built around 1780 when the town was still called Village of Bohemia, the house was converted to a pub called Chick's Tavern in 1829.

    By 1911, it was christened Harriot Hotel, and its dubious claim to fame was the Hole in the Wall Bar, so named because of a hole in the back where "blacks would be served by reaching their hands in to receive a drink."

Allaire DuPont restored the building in 1983 with a meticulous eye to authenticity, recreating details right down to the locks on the doors.

Bayard's visitors today can feast their eyes on the suspension arch bridge over the C&D Canal and watch the commercial and recreational boats passing by.

You can unwind in the warm, friendly atmosphere of the Hole in the Wall Bar downstairs or relax on the brick patio overlooking the water.

The window-lined dining room pays homage to its architectural and culinary heritage by adding an elegant Old World twist to Chesapeake traditions.

Crab cakes are topped with a lemon buerre blanc sauce, filet mignon is served with roasted cremini mushrooms and rosemary demi-glaze, and Anaheim peppers are stuffed with lobster, crab, and shrimp. Soups, salads, and sandwiches are fresh and filling.

When your meal is over, take some time to traipse around this charming town. Its restored Victorian homes, galleries, antique stores, craft shops, boat tours, and summer concerts create an idyllic spot for a weekend get-away.

Chesapeake Inn Restaurant

605 Second Street
Chesapeake City, MD 21915
410-885-2040
www.martuscelliandsons.com/ci

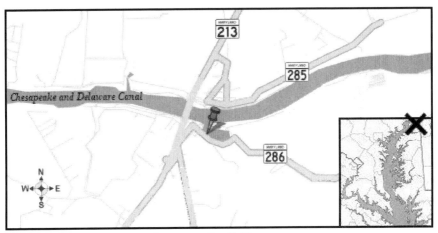

County: Cecil County
Open: Year Round
Latitude: N 39° 31' 34"   Longitude: W 75° 48' 38"
Body of Water: Chesapeake and Delaware Canal
Dockage: Yes
Picture Code: CIR at www.crabdecksandtikibars.com/pix

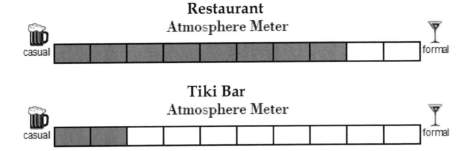

You never know what could happen when you mix traditional Bay with tiki, but at the Chesapeake Inn, they seem to pull it off without a hitch. Its upscale, yet comfortable, dining room puts you at ease with cream-colored linens on the tables, soft subtle lighting, and a piano player on weekends. An antique maidenhead is mounted above a fish tank.

The fine cuisine blends classic Bay dishes with a Mediterranean touch. Outside on the veranda, you can enjoy crab cakes, steak, or pasta, garnished with a gentle summer breeze. The Inn's banquet room is a popular locale for weddings, graduation dinners, and corporate retreats.

The bar downstairs sports a more rustic nautical theme with vibrant flags, old boat oars, and model ships accenting the wood and exposed brick walls.

Evenings get kicked up a notch at the tiki bar on the deck. Giant tiki masks are nailed into palm trees lit with strings of lights. A plastic shark's head chews its way through the roof of a full-service bamboo bar. A band cranks up the tunes, and the party shifts into high gear.

What makes all this work in one setting? Perhaps the common thread is the waterfront. Young and old alike can't resist gazing out at the beautiful backdrop of the C&D Canal.

History buffs know that it's not your run-of-the-mill waterway. When it opened it 1829, the canal had a monumental impact on the mid-Atlantic region by creating a quicker way to transport goods between the Chesapeake Bay and the Delaware River.

It's only 14 miles long, but by taking a direct path, the canal reduces the route between Baltimore and Philadelphia by 300 miles. It's the third busiest canal in the world, so when you visit Chesapeake Inn, enjoy the parade of cargo ships, tankers, barges, and sailboats traveling upon its waters.

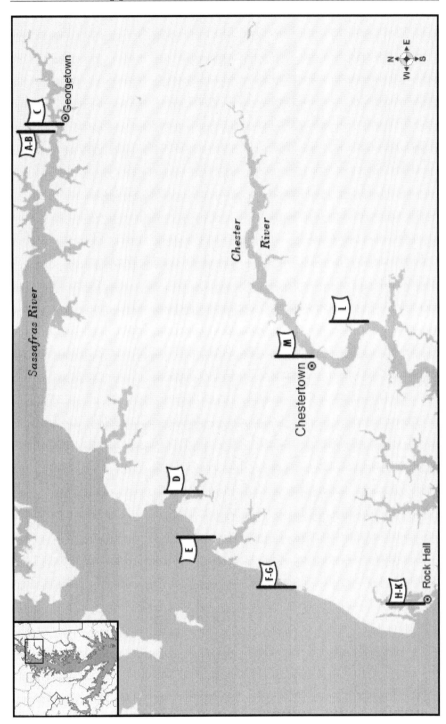

Upper Eastern Shore

Signals Restaurant

150 Skipjack Road
Georgetown, MD 21930
410-275-2122
www.skipjackcove.com/restaurant.php

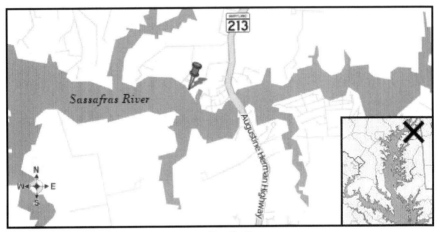

County: Cecil County
Open: Seasonal
Latitude: N 39° 22' 1"   Longitude: W 75° 53' 28"
Body of Water: Sassafras River
Dockage: Yes
Picture Code: SR2 at www.crabdecksandtikibars.com/pix

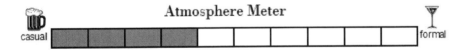

When you sit on the wooden deck on top of the hill at Signals, you can't help but feel a sense of awe for the fleets of boaters who love cruising around this part of the Bay and its tributary rivers.

And who could blame them? The Sassafras River is famous for its hidden coves and beaches with fresh water for swimming without fear of jellyfish.

The 365-slip marina below bustles with every imaginable type of water vessel, and families leave stress behind to build memories together. Children are begrudgingly stuffed into puffy life vests, and parents patiently untangle fishing lines.

Whether you're a boater or landlubber, you can begin your day with Signal's breakfast of eggs, bacon, and hot cakes. Or you can grab some salads and sandwiches for a picnic lunch along the water's edge.

The blue and white, six-sided building has a casual, relaxing feel. Friends gather for happy hour on the deck to watch the sun set over the river and Cecil County farmland.

Once you work up an appetite, you can enjoy classic Chesapeake dishes. The kitchen turns out an array of sumptuous treats: award-winning crab cakes, juicy steaks and potatoes, tender baby back ribs, shrimp fried to a golden brown, and chicken topped with tender crab meat.

Then, when the day is done and little eyelids get heavy, you can start planning your next Chesapeake adventure at Signal's Restaurant.

The Granary Restaurant & Sassafras Grill

100 George Street
Georgetown, MD 21930
410-275-1603
www.granary.biz

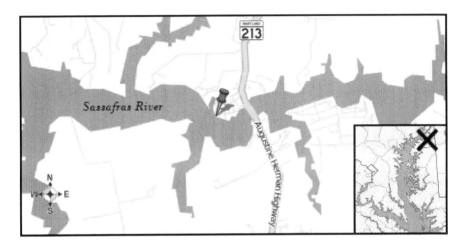

County: Kent County
Open: Seasonal
Latitude: N 39° 21' 49"   Longitude: W 75° 53' 17"
Body of Water: Sassafras River
Dockage: Yes
Picture Code: TGR at www.crabdecksandtikibars.com/pix

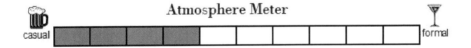

The Granary is located on one of the many spots where the British wreaked havoc during the War of 1812. Local residents had built Fort Duffy on this site, but the invading

Brits burned it to the ground in 1813 along with neighboring Fredericktown and Georgetown (both ironically named after King George's sons).

In 1876, a warehouse was erected to store corn and grain slated for shipment to Baltimore. Years later, it housed the Tockwogh Yacht Club, and in the 1940s it was turned into a restaurant that was destroyed by fire in 1985. Some of the original hand-hewn beams were saved and used to construct the restaurant that stands here today.

The Granary's formidable two-story building has wrap-around decks on both levels that overlook the Sassafras River and boats tied up in the marina.

Picnic tables on the lower deck rest on crushed clam shells bleached white by the sun. A statue of a goose in flight and a real osprey nest on top of a pole remind diners of the abundant waterfowl in the area.

The main dining room is spacious yet comfortable for brunch, lunch, and dinner. The menu shows off the culinary riches of the region with sautéed soft shell crabs and shellfish scampi in a roasted garlic-champagne sauce. You have a variety of other dining choices ranging widely from sandwiches and fajitas to steak and ribs.

On the ground level, a thatched roof entrance leads into the Sassafras Grill with a more casual feel and fare, including steamed seafood platters, Old Bay spiced shrimp, fried oysters, Eastern Shore crab cake sandwiches, hot dogs, and pizza.

Water taxis are available to take you home or across the river, but when the band warms up on a summer eve, you won't want to leave this lovely place.

Kitty Knight House
Inn & Restaurant

14028 Augustine Herman Highway
Georgetown, MD 21930
410-648-5200
www.kittyknight.com

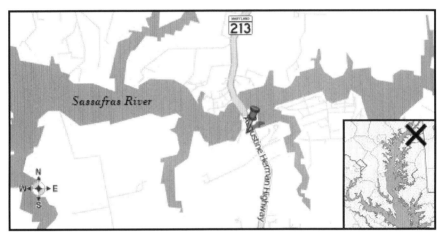

County: Kent County
Open: Restaurant open year-round;
deck open Memorial Day to Labor Day
Latitude: N 39° 21' 39"   Longitude: W 75° 52' 49"
Body of Water: Sassafras River
Dockage: No
Picture Code: KKHIR at www.crabdecksandtikibars.com/pix

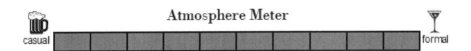

The tale of Kitty Knight's fearless efforts to save a piece of
Georgetown ranks among the favorites on the Eastern Shore.

During the War of 1812, the British burned down towns along the Chesapeake shoreline to curb local resistance against their invading soldiers. After torching Fredericktown and a good portion of Georgetown, British troops set their sights on two brick houses on the hill above the Sassafras River.

But their plans for further destruction were squelched by a defiant Kitty Knight. She came from an upper-class family and neither of the brick homes belonged to her, but she knew that an elderly woman who lived in one house was too sick to flee.

When Kitty arrived on the scene, the Brits had already lit the house on fire, but she stomped out the flames and appealed to the commanding officer. He stopped his soldiers on the first house but allowed them to ignite the second. Again, Kitty doused the fires and pleaded to stop the carnage. The officer begrudgingly agreed and ordered his troops back to the ship, sparing the houses and a church nearby.

Those houses bear Kitty Knight's name as tribute to her heroism and continue to stand watch on the hill over Georgetown Harbor. The view is spectacular, and the decor is Old World elegance at its best.

The dining room's crisp white linens, gentle candle light, and pristine oak floors set the stage for upscale regional cuisine. Guinness-marinated fried oysters, jumbo shrimp stuffed with crab imperial, Miss Catherine's seafood jambalaya, and chicken gruyere are show-stoppers. Gourmet sandwiches, burgers, and salads provide more casual fare on the deck.

Bottom line: It's a perfect blend of history, location, and fine dining.

Harbor House Restaurant

23145 Buck Neck Road
Chestertown, MD 21620
410-778-0669
www.harborhousewcm.com

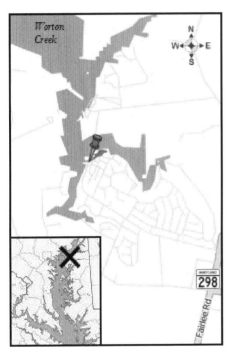

County: Kent County

Open: Year Round

Latitude: N 39° 16' 31"

Longitude: W 76° 10' 3"

Body of Water: Worton Creek
off the Chesapeake Bay

Dockage: Yes

Picture Code: HHR at
www.crabdecksandtikibars.com/
pix

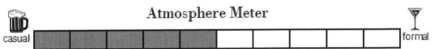

Atmosphere Meter

casual | | | | | | | | | | formal

Buy locally; think globally. That's the name of the game in
the kitchen at Harbor House at Worton Creek Marina.

The menu changes constantly, because the chef scours
farmers markets and fishing docks to gather the freshest
ingredients in the region and follow the harvest of the

seasons. Dishes are even paired with the top wines of Maryland vintners.

His efforts pay off royally. Mixing Eastern Shore cuisine with modern influences from around the world result in delicious specialties such as chicken fried soft-shell crab, sesame Asian flat-iron steak, scallops pan-seared in truffle oil, and slow-roasted BBQ pork.

The location underscores the magnificence of the Chesapeake Bay's scores of backwaters. Tall oak trees surround the quaint gray stone building that overlooks boats sailing across the water.

The bar's wood-panel walls are covered with photos of historic Bay lighthouses. A fireplace crackles in the winter, and windows are opened in the spring to let a soft breeze drift in from the river.

It's simply a treat to visit any time of year.

Great Oak Landing

22170 Great Oak Landing Road
Chestertown, MD 21620
410-778-5007
www.mearsgreatoaklanding.com

County: Kent County
Open: Seasonal
Latitude: N 39° 15' 48"   Longitude: W 76° 12' 12"
Body of Water: Fairlee Creek off the Chesapeake Bay
Dockage: Yes
Picture Code: GOL at www.crabdecksandtikibars.com/pix

Indoor Restaurant
Atmosphere Meter

casual | | | | | | | | | | | formal

Outdoor Bars
Atmosphere Meter

casual | | | | | | | | | | | formal

It seems you can't swing a dead cat in Kent County without hitting a peaceful B&B or historic inn. They're lovely destinations, but if you want an Eastern Shore retreat with activities to please the entire family, head over to Great Oak Landing.

This 70-acre bustling marina has 350 slips and 28 waterfront rooms in its rustic lodge. Parents can play a round on the six-hole golf course or master their serve on the tennis courts, and then unwind with a cool beverage from the thatched-roof bar adjacent to the pool and hot tub.

Kids can wear themselves out on the playground, moon bounce, water slide, or Wii games in the rec room. Weekend movie nights, picnics, and campfires bring everyone back together at the end of the day.

Dining is casual and regional. Mangrove's Bar & Grill serves traditional Eastern Shore seafood, sandwiches, and light fare appetizers in a relaxed environment. Green vinyl swivel stools compliment the bar's retro lounge feel.

Jellyfish Joel's offers tiki on the beach, where you can nibble on snacks or sandwiches under tall green palm trees and bright red umbrellas. Friday night luau parties are famous for mouth-watering Hawaiian barbeque.

Gracious bartenders offer to quench your thirst with cold beer or frozen drinks like Rum Runners or Pain n'de Ass.

When you hear the band playing and catch a picture-perfect sunset over the water, life on the Bay will seem a lot sweeter.

Shanty Beach Bar

21085 Tolchester Beach Road
Chestertown, MD 21620
410-778-1400
www.tolchestermarina.com/restaurants

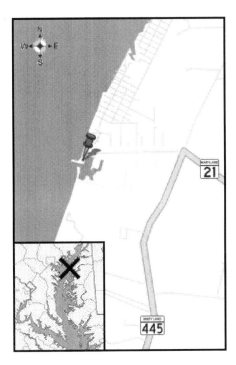

County: Kent County

Open: Seasonal

Latitude: N 39° 12' 49"

Longitude: W 76° 14' 38"

Body of Water: directly on the Chesapeake Bay

Dockage: Yes

Picture Code: SBB at www.crabdecksandtikibars.com/pix

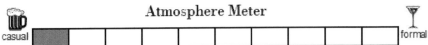

Atmosphere Meter

casual · formal

A 20-mile boat ride north of the Bay Bridge can transport you from a stressful, pressed-shirt and high-heel world to the laid-back, T-shirt and flip-flop life at Shanty Beach Bar.

Located right on the water's edge at Tolchester Marina, this popular watering hole is all about fun in the sun. The building might be small, simple, and rustic, but it's surrounded by big wooden decks, wide umbrellas, and plush tropical plants.

You can lie back on a comfy lounge chair at the waterfront pool with a frosty drink in your hand and refuse to move until you feel like it.

Or you can join in the revelry, because it seems like something's always happening at the Shanty Beach Bar. Pool parties, pirate days, band nights, and an antique car show in August contribute to the festive atmosphere.

Best of all is the beach. You can lay out a blanket in the sand and watch the sun set over the Chesapeake waters. And then raise a glass to toast all the folks who break their backs trying to protect sandy beaches like this one from disappearing.

Rising sea levels and relentless storms erode about 580 acres of Maryland each year. Entire islands, such as James, Holland, and Barren Island, have been abandoned by residents and are slowly sinking into the Bay.

Okay, enough said. No need to ruin that kick-back state-of-mind. But it never hurts to remember who's behind the scenes trying to keep the beach party going.

Channel Restaurant

21085 Tolchester Beach Road
Chestertown, MD 21620
410-778-1400
www.tolchestermarina.com/restaurants

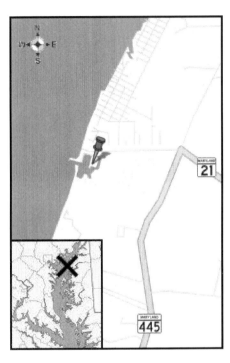

County: Kent County

Open: Seasonal

Latitude: N 39° 12' 47"

Longitude: W 76° 14' 29"

Body of Water: directly on the Chesapeake Bay

Dockage: Yes

Picture Code: CR2 at www.crabdecksandtikibars.com/pix

Atmosphere Meter

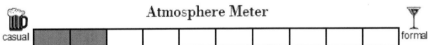

casual / formal

Channel Restaurant is nestled among the boats at Tolchester Marina on the Bay. It's a low-key kind of place that might be short on menu items but long on Eastern Shore hospitality.

Dishes center around seafood brought off the boats that day — crab cakes, shrimp, rockfish — pulled together with a wisp of a French touch. It's an ideal spot for grabbing a quick bite after a long day on the water.

The walls are covered with historic photos of an old-fashioned amusement park that once stood on this spot. If you ask why none of it remains, some locals will tell the story; others just shake their heads in disappointment.

Here's the scoop: Tolchester Beach and its sister resort 14 miles north in Betterton were born during the steamboat glory days from the 1880s to 1920s.

Tolchester Beach was a popular summer destination for heat-weary Baltimore residents who crossed the Bay on steamboats like the *Louise* and *Bay Belle*.

Inspired by Coney Island, the amusement park opened in 1877 with a picnic area, beach, and a twin-towered pavilion with ice cream and dancing. Next came the race track, paddle boats, hotel, mini-train, Ferris wheel, and roller coaster.

On weekends during its peak, up to 20,000 visitors flocked to the park. Then trouble started brewing. In the 1920s, paved roads allowed trucks to transport produce and freight from the region more cost-effectively. During the Depression, steamboats' popularity faded, and by the end of World War II, only a few remained.

The final nail in the coffin for steamboats and Tolchester Beach was the Bay Bridge's opening in 1952, which gave people easy access to Atlantic Ocean resorts.

Over the years, the amusement park buildings fell into ruin, were torn down, and eventually replaced by the marina you see here today.

Osprey Point Restaurant

20786 Rock Hall Avenue
Rock Hall, MD 21661
410-639-2194
www.ospreypoint.com

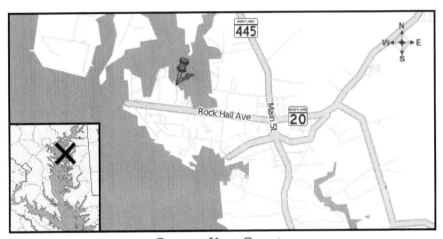

County: Kent County
Open: Year Round
Latitude: N 39° 8' 35"   Longitude: W 76° 15' 8"
Body of Water: The Haven off Swan Creek off the Chesapeake Bay
Dockage: Yes
Picture Code: OPR at www.crabdecksandtikibars.com/pix

Atmosphere Meter

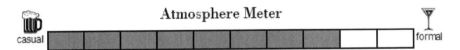

casual   formal

Some folks like to rough it in the great outdoors, doing that tent, mosquito, and tree root-in-your-back thing.

But others prefer to have their dose of nature in civilized locations like Osprey Point, where modern conveniences enhance the rural experience.

The long tree-lined driveway harkens back to a time when elegant country homes were the centerpiece of farms and tobacco plantations along the Bay. Inside the lovely white and blue inn, you're pampered in charming rooms with antiques, four-poster beds, and marble bath tubs.

The 30-acre wooded grounds are meticulously groomed, creating a peaceful retreat among the old pine trees and sea grass. A gazebo near the marina dares you to come out and watch the sun set over the water.

You can have a picnic, hike nature trails, swim in the pool, toss horseshoes, or go fishing. Whatever you want to do — as long as you build up an appetite for the gourmet food coming out of Osprey Point's kitchen.

The atmosphere oozes casual elegance welcoming you to have hors d'oeuvres at the bar or get settled in for a full meal in the dining room.

The chef creates fresh seasonal menus that give an upscale touch to regional seafood. Crab cakes are sprinkled with lime beurre blanc sauce, scallops arrive with ginger-carrot puree, and trout is grilled with malt vinegar brown butter.

Meat lovers can sink their teeth into slices of pecan-crusted leg of lamb or beef tenderloin with roasted garlic and goat cheese soufflé.

In short, it's all about graceful living along the Chesapeake.

Swan Point Inn

20658 Wilkins Avenue
Rock Hall, MD 21661
410-639-2500
www.swanpointinn.net

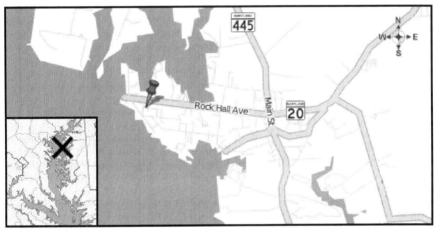

County: Kent County
Open: Seasonal
Latitude: N 39° 8' 23"   Longitude: W 76° 15' 25"
Body of Water: Swan Creek off the Chesapeake Bay
Dockage: No
Picture Code: SPI at www.crabdecksandtikibars.com/pix

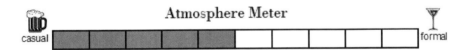

Atmosphere Meter

casual | | | | | | | | | | formal

Back in 1929, Swan Point was a waterman's home. Later it became the Wheelhouse, a local watering hole famous for cold beer, good food, and lively music.

A few years ago, new owners transformed the building into an inn with three comfortable rooms, a cozy bar, and two separate spaces for dining.

The cocktail lounge's walls are painted red and white with black accents, and that color theme is echoed on the tile floor and bar stools. Archways lead out to a pizza parlor where regulation red-and-white cloths cover the tables.

The main dining room creates a more sophisticated tone with white linens, ruby red napkins, and black chairs. Photographs of the Bay hang on the walls. Tall trees and red umbrellas cast shade on diners out on the wooden deck.

The menu covers all the Chesapeake basics like fried shrimp, crab cakes, New York strip steaks, chicken marsala or parmesan, caesar or spinach salads, and creamy crab or French onion soups.

But then it has a little fun with local fare by broiling shrimp that's laced with horseradish and wrapped in bacon, or topping oysters with crab meat and Béarnaise sauce.

The pizza parlor lets you cover the dough with anything you like, including crab meat, garlic, and artichoke.

When you're finished eating, take a walk around the marina a short block away and watch the stars come out over the Bay.

If you've had a lucky day on the water, bring your catch to Swan Point and they'll cook your fish and serve it with salad and sides for only $10.

Harbor Shack
Waterfront Bar & Grill

20895 Bayside Avenue
Rock Hall, MD 21661
410-639-9996
www.harborshack.net

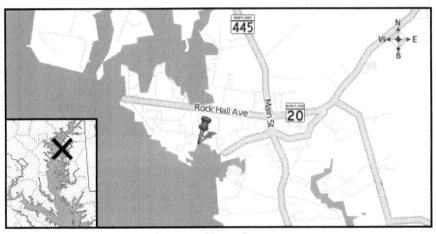

County: Kent County
Open: Year Round
Latitude: N 39° 8' 4"   Longitude: W 76° 14' 55"
Body of Water: Rock Hall Harbor off the Chesapeake Bay
Dockage: Yes
Picture Code: HSWBG at www.crabdecksandtikibars.com/pix

Atmosphere Meter

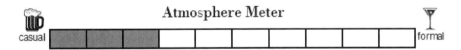

casual ▮▮▮ formal

In the dead of winter, Harbor Shack is an oasis of hopeful
color amidst the milky gray skies and dry-docked boats
wrapped like mummies in white plastic weather protection.

Walls painted the yellow and orange of a tequila sunrise promise that summer will return soon. Strings of colorful beer signs will flap in the wind, and palm trees will get planted in the sand.

And when the weather turns warm again, Harbor Shack becomes the Grand Central Station of Rock Hall — the busy neighborhood hangout where everybody is welcome to join in the revelry.

Charter boats with names like "Fish Fear Us" and "Rockaholic Fishing" buzz in and out of the marina. And people on the waterfront deck crack steamed crabs to the rhythm of a rock-and-roll band.

When new owners took the helm of this 200-seat waterfront bar in June 2006, they established a casual, upbeat atmosphere that's reflected in both the decor and menu.

According to the lively menu, "Warm Up Things" kick off meals with steamed clams, coconut shrimp, and crab dip. "Green Leafy Things" ensure you get enough fiber in your diet. "Local Dinner Things" fill your belly with crab cakes, stuffed rockfish, cowboy-crusted rib eye, and St. Louis ribs. "Mexican Things" bring South of the Border fajitas and nachos to the Bay. Then you can wash all this down with "Wet Things."

Harbor Shack is simply a fun place to unwind and have a good time.

Waterman's Crab House

21055 Sharp Street
Rock Hall, MD 21661
410-639-2261
www.watermanscrabhouse.com

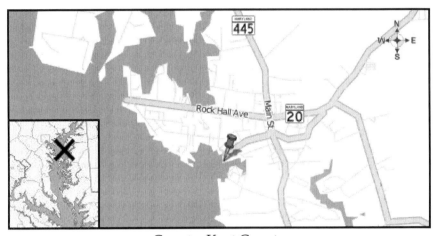

County: Kent County
Open: Seasonal
Latitude: N 39° 7' 59"   Longitude: W 76° 14' 36"
Body of Water: Rock Hall Harbor off the Chesapeake Bay
Dockage: Yes
Picture Code: WCH at www.crabdecksandtikibars.com/pix

Atmosphere Meter

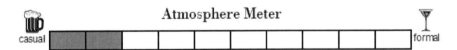

casual | | | | | | | | | | formal

   The dynamic duo of crabs and beer reigns supreme at Waterman's classic seafood house. For about 40 years, this Rock Hall landmark has successfully used the briny smell of steaming crabs to lure in diners from all walks of life.

   Leather-clad bikers, tourists with babies, locals in work shirts, and boaters in Ravens caps sit elbow-to-elbow at long picnic tables covered with mountains of hot red crabs and discarded shells.

The waterfront view from the massive wooden deck is incredible. When sensational sunsets fade into night, you can actually see the distant lights of Baltimore on the horizon across the water.

Children toss crackers left over from a bowl of vegetable she-crab soup over the railing into the beaks of insistent seagulls, while a reggae band gets everybody swaying.

Crab cakes are made in the Eastern Shore tradition, with just a hint of mustard, and you find fresh oysters at the raw bar, fried, or in a creamy stew.

The Rock Hall Combo piles locally caught crab cakes, flounder, shrimp, and scallops on a single platter with coleslaw and hush puppies.

And even though the menu offers burgers, prime rib, chicken, and BBQ ribs, you'll have a hard time taking your eyes off the crabs that your neighbor is picking next to you.

Crab Decks & Tiki Bars of the Chesapeake Bay

Rolph's Wharf Sandbar

1008 Rolphs Wharf Road
Chestertown, MD 21620
800-894-6347 or 410-778-6389
www.rolphswharf.com

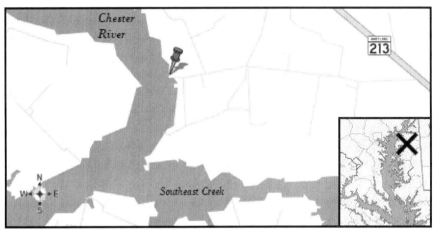

County: Queen Anne's County
Open: Seasonal
Latitude: N 39° 10' 27"   Longitude: W 76° 2' 13"
Body of Water: Chester River
Dockage: Yes
Picture Code: TRWS at www.crabdecksandtikibars.com/pix

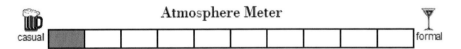

What do you do with an old boat that won't float because of a big hole in its bottom? Rather than chop it up for kindling, the folks at Rolph's Wharf turned it into a unique waterfront bar.

In its new life as the Sandbar, the boat rests on the shore a few yards away from the Chester River where it cruised the waters in its glory days. Cooking appliances, coolers, and blenders are now in the hull. Tall white bar stools around the outside allow patrons to rest their elbows on the gunwales of the boat, while a bartender inside hands out cold beer.

It's the embodiment of Eastern Shore resourcefulness and humor that makes everyone feel at home here. A pavilion stands overhead as protection from the rain, and soft white sand spread out on the beach creates a fabulous fun retreat.

It's not so much about food at the Sandbar: steamed shrimp, crab cakes, hot dogs, sandwiches, and spicy wings are served on paper plates.

Children dig in the sand, while parents relax on beach chairs in the sun. People lounge around the swimming pool, watching boats bustle in and out of the marina.

If an afternoon visit isn't enough, you can spend the night at the River Inn, which is part of the same marina. This beautiful circa 1830 Victorian farm house is flanked by ancient holly and pine trees and has a long front porch with a swing bench that's perfect for lazy days.

The widow's walk on top stirs up images of lonely women pacing the planks, waiting for their husbands to return from the sea.

The inn's rooms are quite comfortable, and they lack that "no touch" museum feel at some B&Bs that make you worry that you might break a crystal vase or porcelain doll that's been handed down for generations.

Best of all, the warm hospitality makes you want to return to Rolph's Wharf any chance you get.

Fish Whistle

98 Cannon Street
Chestertown, MD 21620
410-778-3566
www.fishandwhistle.com

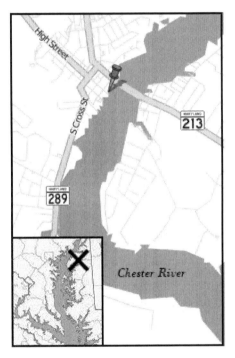

County: Kent County

Open: Year Round

Latitude: N 39° 12' 20"

Longitude: W 76° 3' 50"

Body of Water: Chester River

Dockage: Yes

Picture Code: FW at
www.crabdecksandtikibars.com/
pix

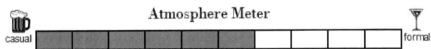

Atmosphere Meter

casual   formal

As you cruise around the Eastern Shore, be sure to stop at Fish Whistle. You'll be glad you did.

The restaurant is located at the marina within a stone's throw of the Chester River Bridge. Its warm salmon and pale green walls are tastefully decorated with carved wooden boats, fish, and other artifacts of the Bay.

The cuisine is upscale nouvelle and offers creative regional specialties such as oyster pot pie, catfish fingers with spicy remoulade, jumbo lump crab cakes, and cherry-smoked pork spareribs.

You can opt for more casual fare by ordering Cuban sandwiches, fish tacos, or nightly specials such as Monday's discounted burgers and wings, or Thursday's all-you-can-eat oysters.

When the kitchen closes on weekends, a DJ spins tunes in the bar and music flows out onto the waterfront deck.

After dinner, you should stroll around historic Chestertown. Founded in 1705, the town flourished during the shipping boom in the 18th Century, which created a wealthy merchant class that built elegant mansions along the river.

You can start at the waterfront on High Street, pass the gorgeous Imperial Hotel, and walk through the historic district until you reach Fountain Park and the quaint shops surrounding the town square. On top of the hill stands Washington College, established in 1782 with support from our nation's first president.

When the day is done, many urbanites leave Chestertown vowing to get out of their big-city homes more often and explore the Chesapeake's charming little towns.

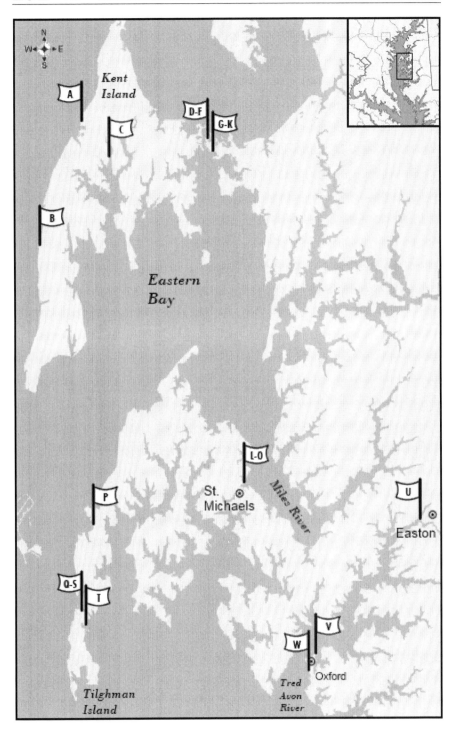

Middle Eastern Shore

Hemingway's Restaurant

357 Pier One Road
Stevensville, MD 21666
410-604-0999
www.hemingwaysbaybridge.com

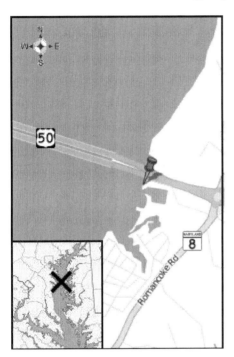

County: Queen Anne's County

Open: Year Round

Latitude: N 38° 58' 50"

Longitude: W 76° 20' 4"

Body of Water: directly on the Chesapeake Bay

Dockage: Yes

Picture Code: HR at www.crabdecksandtikibars.com/pix

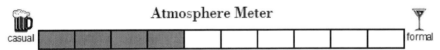

Atmosphere Meter

casual ———————————— formal

When the old Hemingway's fell under the wrecking ball in late 2010, it felt like something was missing along the Bay. For decades, it was the first thing you'd see as you headed east across the Bay Bridge — a beloved welcome sign that proved you landed safely on the Eastern Shore.

In early April 2011, after the owners of the Bay Bridge Marina pumped nearly $4 million into renovations, a new Hemingway's has risen. The entire marina is getting a make-over with another $8 million earmarked for the docks, pool, and other amenities, poising the property for future development.

The big question is how does the new Hemingway's stack up against the old icon? Well, it might take most of the 2011 summer to complete all the construction and iron out the kinks, but overall the new place is quite nice.

The huge red neon sign leaves no doubt that they're ready for business, and the two-tiered dining area, decks, and outdoor bar promise to make room for plenty of guests. Interior walls are painted white and a soft beige and decorated with black-framed vintage photos of local watermen, as well as nautical items such as fish nets, ship ropes, lanterns, and fish. An antique deep-sea diving suit stands at attention near the bar, and a waiting area is made cozy with comfortable furniture and a fire place.

The menu focuses on getting the basics right, but the staff promises that food selections will evolve after everybody gets his groove going. Starters include soups, salads, and a raw bar with fresh local oysters, mussels, and shrimp. Burgers and sandwiches come with fries and coleslaw.

Specialty entrees range from plump crab cakes and cedar-roasted Scottish salmon to root beer braised short ribs and slow-roasted prime rib. All in all, it's a good start, and the staff is friendly and eager to please.

So, don't be shy about stopping by to introduce yourself to your new neighbors at Hemingway's.

Kentmorr Restaurant

910 Kentmorr Road
Stevensville, MD 21666
410-643-2263
www.kentmorr.com

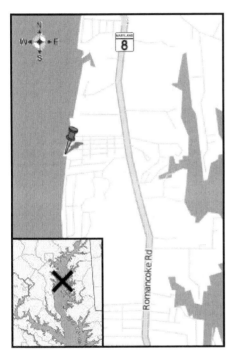

County: Queen Anne's County

Open: Year Round

Latitude: N 38° 54' 54"

Longitude: W 76° 21' 51"

Body of Water: directly on the Chesapeake Bay

Dockage: Yes

Picture Code: KR at www.crabdecksandtikibars.com/pix

Atmosphere Meter

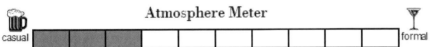

Whether you come by car, boat, or plane, Kentmorr Restaurant is well worth a visit. (Seriously, you really can fly into Kentmorr Airpark and take a short stroll to the restaurant.)

So, what makes this place special? You can stretch out on its beach while kids play in the sand and discover treasures of the Bay hidden in its gentle waves.

Or you can watch charter captains load their boats with excited passengers hoping for a lucky day and a bountiful catch. They even post a board with charter information and bragging rights for record catches of the season. It's a bustling little sport-fishing hub that's made folks happy since 1954.

The restaurant sits out on the water's edge with wooden picnic tables lined up along the dock. The dining area is open and airy, with enough space between tables to ensure you won't get hit by flying shrapnel when other diners crack open their crabs.

The menu showcases classic Chesapeake fare including rockfish, shrimp, oysters, and littleneck clams. The kitchen executes those standard dishes masterfully, yet has a little fun with crabs along the way.

Crab cake sliders make a perfect mid-day snack, while "Crabmole" with fresh avocado takes traditional guacamole to new heights. Half-and-Half dares to mix cream of crab soup with its red vegetable counterpart, and Softshell BLT tops crabs with applewood smoked bacon and fresh-picked tomatoes. For a few bucks more, you can add a crab cake to steak, chicken, or rib entrees.

And if you time your trip just right, you can cash in on one of the Eastern Shore's more precious commodities — a glorious sunset over the water reflecting off the Bay Bridge in the distance.

Kent Manor Inn
& Restaurant

500 Kent Manor Drive
Stevensville, MD 21666
410-643-7716
www.kentmanor.com/finedining.html

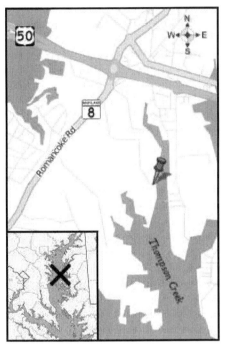

County: Queen Anne's County

Open: Year Round

Latitude: N 38° 57' 51"

Longitude: W 76° 18' 56"

Body of Water: Thompson Creek off Cox Creek off Eastern Bay

Dockage: Yes

Picture Code: KMIR at www.crabdecksandtikibars.com/pix

Atmosphere Meter

casual — formal

Fine dining accented with Old World elegance and natural beauty await you at Kent Manor Inn & Restaurant.

The beautiful Victorian building (circa 1820) and gorgeous grounds set the stage for an upscale culinary experience.

Italian marble fireplaces and classic English decor create a serene, romantic atmosphere in the dining rooms. An outdoor deck overlooks the charming garden house and the waters of Thompson Creek.

American nouvelle cuisine is masterfully fused with Eastern Shore influences, offering presentations so lovely that the most discriminating chefs would nod their heads in approval.

The menu changes often to capture the seasons' harvests and fresh ingredients. As you walk in the door for Sunday brunch, the aroma of applewood smoked bacon and just-baked pastries might make your stomach rumble in a rather unladylike fashion.

After dining, take time to stroll around the estate. The land was granted to Thomas Wetherall in 1651, only 17 years after Lord Calvert set foot in Maryland.

In 1843, Alexander Thompson inherited the property and decided to build an addition to the house right before the Civil War broke out. Local historians describe old A.T. as quite the character — rich, flamboyant, cigar-smoking, and fond of women.

He married three times but had no children, and was famous for his social graces and love of horseback riding. Some say Thompson's ghost still gallops around the grounds on his white steed and roams the halls of the inn, mysteriously turning on lights or opening locked doors. When you visit this lovely estate, perhaps you'll get a chance to meet him.

Annie's Paramount Steak & Seafood House

500 Kent Narrows Way North
Grasonville, MD 21638
410-827-7103
www.annies.biz

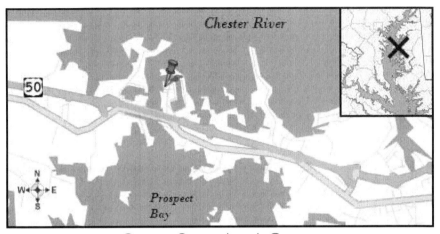

County: Queen Anne's County
Open: Year Round
Latitude: N 38° 58' 27"   Longitude: W 76° 14' 41"
Body of Water: Kent Island Narrows off the Chester River
Dockage: Yes
Picture Code: APSSH at www.crabdecksandtikibars.com/pix

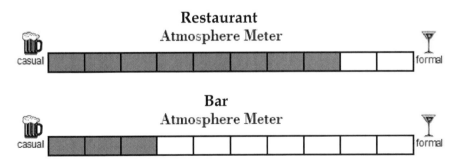

Annie's is the Chesapeake's way of saying, "Look how we do surf and turf." It's located smack dab in the middle of Mears Point Marina's parking lot, so you won't find outdoor deck seating — yet. But plans are underway to move a few hundred yards down the road, increase its footprint, and add a second floor.

In the meantime, tall windows open out to a gorgeous view of Kent Narrows and the bridge. The lounge sports a casual feel with a pool table, TVs lined up along the walls, and time-worn wood floors.

Carpeted, and more upscale, dining rooms glow with hushed pink lighting. Here you'll find feminine touches like towering floral arrangements near the black grand piano and bud vases with petite clusters of flowers on tables covered with pink and white linens.

The restaurant takes pride in its prime cuts of beef, dry aged and hand-cut on the premises, complemented by an extensive wine menu. Colorado lamb chops, prime rib, and marinated tenderloin tips, a.k.a. "Bull in the Pan," are guaranteed to make your mouth water in anticipation.

"Toast of the Town" crab cakes, jumbo breaded oysters, and stuffed shrimp imperial are the house pride and joy on the seafood side.

Annie's cream of crab soup is so good that it's now sold at select supermarkets in Annapolis and other Bay locations.

Red Eye's Dock Bar

428 Kent Narrows Way North
Grasonville, MD 21638
410-827-EYES
www.redeyedockbar.com

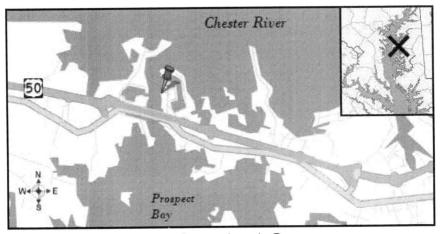

County: Queen Anne's County
Open: Year Round
Latitude: N 38° 58' 24"   Longitude: W 76° 14' 44"
Body of Water: Kent Island Narrows off the Chester River
Dockage: Yes
Picture Code: REDB at www.crabdecksandtikibars.com/pix

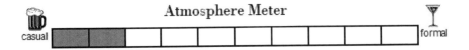

If you look all the way up at the top of the building, you'll notice a large eyeball painted on the wall, and you might wonder why that eye is so red.

Maybe it's tired? For decades, The Red Eye has been the last stop for a final view of the Bay and a sunset cocktail before heading home to Washington or Baltimore.

A welcoming port for a little hair of the dog after a busy beach weekend.

Okay, so maybe the eye turned red because it doesn't dare to blink for fear of missing the merriment happening down below. Neon palm trees and colorful tiki masks carved on pylons stand guard along the water's edge, and boaters pull up ready to rumble. Rock-and-roll bands crank tunes from the stage.

Perhaps those famous Sunday bikini contests made that eye blood-shot? Probably not. At best it might raise its eyebrow with amusement.

The redness could be from those cold easterly winds that blow across the Bay during the off-season, when locals camp out in the heated Upstairs Dock Bar to watch NFL playoffs or March Madness on 16 HD TVs.

We may never solve the mystery of what turned that eyeball red, but it's worth the trip to investigate — even if you wake up the next morning with eyes of a similar hue.

Harris Crab House

43 Kent Narrow Way North
Grasonville, MD 21638
410-827-9500
www.harriscrabhouse.com

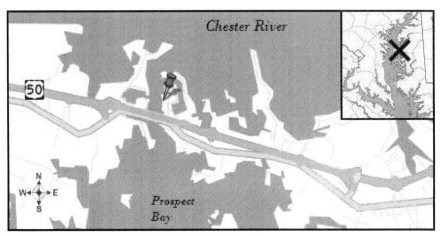

County: Queen Anne's County
Open: Year Round
Latitude: N 38° 58' 23" Longitude: W 76° 14' 43"
Body of Water: Kent Island Narrows off the Chester River
Dockage: Yes
Picture Code: HCH1 at www.crabdecksandtikibars.com/pix

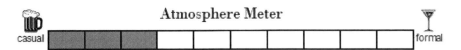

When asked Harris' secret for making perfect fried oysters, the waitress leaned in close and whispered, "Shake off the excess flour, make sure your grease is good and hot, and pull 'em out fast right when they turn a crispy golden brown."

Before tending to the rest of her tables, she winked and added, "And don't you dare settle for anything less than fresh Bay oysters! The rest ... hummpf ... well, why bother?"

She's right about the oysters — and everything else you pop into your mouth at Harris Crab House. Only the best of the Chesapeake lands on your table.

As proof, you can sit on the outside decks and watch local watermen unload just-caught crabs and oysters, and haul them into the kitchen.

Soft shell po boys come in a warm toasted baguette. Vegetable and cream of crab soups are legendary for robust flavors. And steamed seafood — local crabs, shrimp, mussels, and clams — win awards for freshness and the special house seasonings.

Harris' long-term commitment to local seafood is underscored as you look around the restaurant. The walls are covered with vintage oyster cans and posters of dancing bivalves and crabs. Locals keep this cozy crab house bustling day and night, all year round.

Walking along the dock, watching the sun set over Kent Narrows Bridge, and sipping a nightcap at the Red Eye next door is the finishing touch to a memorable evening on the Bay.

The Big Owl Tiki Bar

3000 Kent Narrows Way South
Grasonville, MD 21638
410-827-6523
www.thebigowl.com

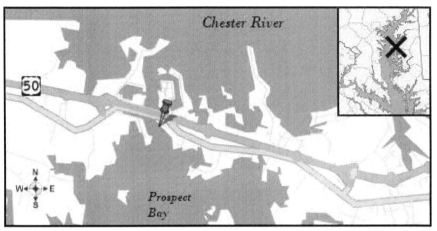

County: Queen Anne's County
Open: Seasonal
Latitude: N 38° 58' 8"   Longitude: W 76° 14' 44"
Body of Water: Kent Island Narrows off Prospect Bay
Dockage: Yes
Picture Code: BOTB at www.crabdecksandtikibars.com/pix

Atmosphere Meter

casual |████| | | | | | | | | | formal

When you hear the sounds of raucous laughter, clinking glasses, and Jimmy Buffet tunes as you walk out the pier to The Big Owl Tiki Bar, you know right away that they take the business of having fun very seriously.

Perched on the water at Kent Narrows, the building and pylons are painted neon Key West orange and turquoise, with hand-carved tiki masks grinning from their posts on the walls and bar.

Bright blue and yellow umbrellas offer relief from the sun on the long wooden deck. You can capture memories of your visit by taking a photo with your arm around a giant cut-out owl wearing jet-black Ray Ban shades, a Hawaiian shirt, and flip-flops.

The menu is simple: Caribbean-influenced pub food of crab balls, steamed shrimp, chicken or rockfish nuggets, burgers, and sandwiches. And the wide selection of cold beer takes the edge off the summer heat.

At Big Owl, it's easy to sit back, catch an amazing sunset, and let the reggae music lull you into a happy relaxed state.

On your way out when you first step on land again, be sure to check out two cemetery stone markers. They serve as memorials to Hazel and Mamma Cass, a pair of visionary women who were instrumental in fostering business development on the southern part of Kent Narrows.

The Narrows Restaurant

3023 Kent Narrows Way South
Grasonville, MD 21638
410-827-8113
www.thenarrowsrestaurant.com

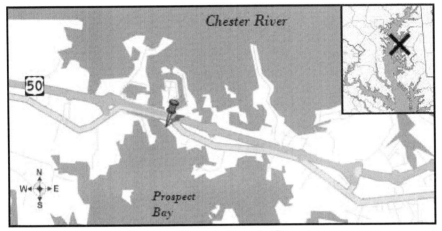

County: Queen Anne's County
Open: Year Round
Latitude: N 38° 58' 7"   Longitude: W 76° 14' 42"
Body of Water: Kent Island Narrows off Prospect Bay
Dockage: Yes
Picture Code: TNR at www.crabdecksandtikibars.com/pix

Atmosphere Meter

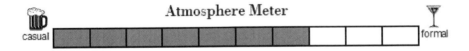

casual — formal

If a restaurant is built upon the foundation of an old oyster-shucking house, there's almost an obligation to serve top-quality local seafood. And that's been happening since 1983 at The Narrows.

For years, its chefs have taken home prizes for the best crab cake, crab soup, and romantic restaurant.

The menu shows a thoughtful marriage of traditional Bay cuisine with innovative cooking. You'll have a hard time choosing among mouth-watering treats like crab tart with feta, spinach and tomato, golden brown fried oysters, crab imperial topped with applewood smoked bacon, tempura lobster tail with seaweed and wasabi, and pecan-crusted catfish.

Meat dishes — slow-roasted BBQ short ribs, grilled chicken pesto sandwich, filet mignon over garlic mashed potatoes, and rosemary-crusted rack of lamb — make sure everyone leaves happy.

A picturesque view of the Chesapeake's sail and power boats, sparkling waters, and migratory geese and swans adds the final touch to a lovely dining experience.

If you're in a rush and can't sit down for a meal, The Narrows will ship crab cakes and soups overnight right to your door.

Fisherman's Inn & Crab Deck

3116 Main Street
Grasonville, MD 21638
410-827-8807 Inn, 410-827-6666 Crab Deck,
410-827-7323 Seafood Market
www.crabdeck.com

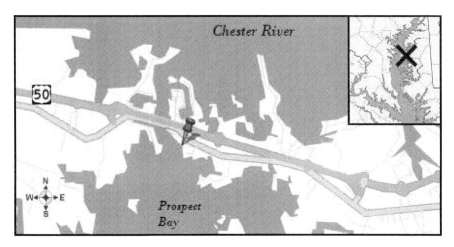

County: Queen Anne's County
Open: Inn open year round;
crab deck, tiki bar and seafood market open April-October
Latitude: N 38° 58' 3"   Longitude: W 76° 14' 37"
Body of Water: Kent Island Narrows off Prospect Bay
Dockage: Yes
Picture Code: FICD at www.crabdecksandtikibars.com/pix

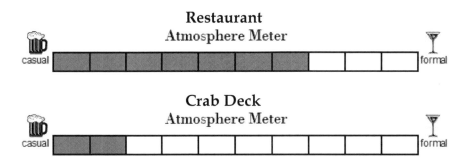

If you're looking for a single spot to fulfill all your Chesapeake dreams, then head for Fisherman's Inn.

Since 1930, this Kent Narrows landmark has survived everything from tough economic times to Hurricane Isabel. And somehow it keeps growing and getting better.

The Inn's main restaurant shows its nautical roots with a huge aquarium at the entrance, a collection of more than 300 antique oyster plates decorating the walls, and a bar shaped like a boat. The menu presents an impressive array of local seafood, pasta, beef, and sandwiches.

The long wooden Crab Deck offers a more casual waterfront experience, where cooks gladly steam, grill, or fry crabs, shrimp, rockfish, oysters, clams, and other daily catch that local fishermen bring to their door.

Rolls of paper towels, brown paper on the tables, and the aroma of Old Bay in the air leave no doubt that this place is the real deal.

Waiters at Cappy's Tiki Bar quickly place a cool beverage in your hand while you watch a live band or inspect the boats passing by the dock.

And that's not all! If you want to charter a fishing or sight-seeing boat, Fisherman's Inn hooks you up with a seasoned captain. And if you want to get married at the water's edge, the banquet hall can accommodate all your family and friends.

In a nutshell, Fisherman's Inn is the one-stop shop for Bay lovers.

Bridges Restaurant

321 Wells Cove Road
Grasonville, MD 21638
410-827-0282
www.bridgesrestaurant.net

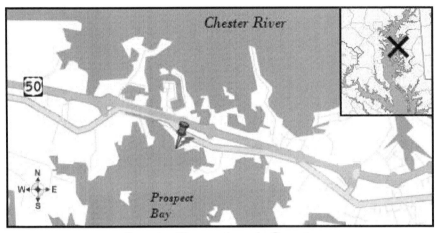

County: Queen Anne's County
Open: Year Round
Latitude: N 38° 57' 57"   Longitude: W 76° 14' 34"
Body of Water: Kent Island Narrows off Prospect Bay
Dockage: Yes
Picture Code: BR at www.crabdecksandtikibars.com/pix

Atmosphere Meter

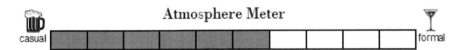

This is not your traditional crab deck. Bridges could be described as a contemporary nautical cafe, with an upscale flare — the kind of place where you might take a date, rather than find one.

But you can't beat the location, right on the water's edge with spacious decks offering a heavenly view of Prospect Bay.

Its yellow-and-white striped awnings, red roof, and golden mustard walls seem to glow at sunset.

Inside, the blond wood and black chairs set the tone for stylish yet casual dining with a French cafe twist. The massive chandelier made of wine bottles foreshadows an extensive wine list that tempts you to sample anything from a sauvignon blanc to a shiraz. Specialty drinks feature mojitos and martinis.

The menu presents an innovative fusion of local seafood spruced up with Mediterranean and Caribbean influences. Chesapeake crab cakes, rockfish, and steaks peacefully coexist with crab pesto pizza, jerk chicken, roasted pork Cuban sandwiches, Mediterranean seafood stew, chicken and shrimp picatta, and veal osso bucco.

The Jetty Restaurant & Dock Bar

201 Wells Cove Road
Grasonville, MD 21638
410-827-4959
www.jettydockbar.com

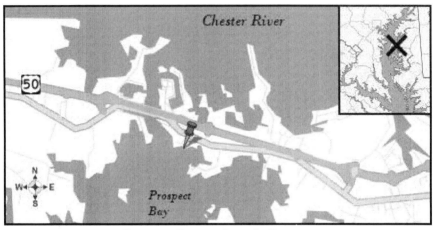

County: Queen Anne's County
Open: Year Round
Latitude: N 38° 57' 57"   Longitude: W 76° 14' 29"
Body of Water: Kent Island Narrows off Prospect Bay
Dockage: Yes
Picture Code: TJRDB at www.crabdecksandtikibars.com/pix

Atmosphere Meter

casual ▮▮▯▯▯▯▯▯▯▯ formal

A cacophony of color — electric blue, green, yellow, and a touch of magenta — paint a fun-inspiring tropical image at The Jetty.

Towering palm trees, thick green foliage and rustling sea grass make you feel like you've landed on a little slice of paradise. Vintage Harleys parked out front imply that good times have just rolled in.

There's an open, breezy feel to this place, almost as if you're required to check your worries at the door before entering. Children dig in the sandy beach area, while mothers steal a moment to relax over a crisp Chardonnay and a crimson sunset.

Friends linger at the tables, washing down a mountain of hot steamed crabs with icy beer. The menu infuses Bay ingredients with Caribbean flavors, creating food that is simple, fresh, and delicious.

Local seafood standards of crabs, shrimp, and daily catch are served with creamy coleslaw and salty fries. Hearty sandwiches, jerk chicken, sizzling steaks, and crisp salads round out your dining options.

On warm summer evenings, the energy level and crowd size picks up considerably, so parking can be a challenge. But never fear, The Jetty Bus thoughtfully shuttles people to and from nearby hotels and parking lots.

Bob Pascal's
Harbour Lights Restaurant

101 North Harbor Road
St. Michaels, MD 21663
410-745-9001 or 800-955-9001
www.harbourinn.com

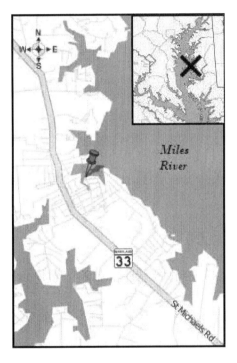

County: Talbot County

Open: Year Round

Latitude: N 38° 47' 6"

Longitude: W 76° 13' 10"

Body of Water: St. Michaels
Harbor off the Miles River

Dockage: Yes

Picture Code: BPHLR at
www.crabdecksandtikibars.com/
pix

Atmosphere Meter

casual formal

When you pull up your boat to Harbour Inn, prepare to get pampered with casual elegance. It's part of a full-service luxury resort that's probably more appealing to Mr. Howell than Gilligan. The waterfront view of the Miles River and St. Michaels is gorgeous.

The restaurant features Chesapeake seafood specialties blended with Mediterranean flavors. On crisp white tablecloths rest plates of jumbo lump crab cakes, saffron seared red snapper, pan-seared local rockfish, wild king salmon, and oysters on the half shell.

Meat lovers lick their chops over grilled New York strip steaks and braised veal shank. Bread, pasta, and desserts, made in-house, are a carb-lovers dream.

If you're in the mood for more casual fare, take a seat at the waterfront deck and tavern, where you can sample gourmet bar bites such as corn and crab fritters with red chili and lime dressing, lobster and shrimp ravioli, classic creamy crab dip, grilled lamb sliders, or pizza of the day.

If you're worn out from a day on the Bay, you can stay overnight in luxury at one of the inn's 38 suite rooms or eight single guest rooms. Heated massage tables and hot towels in the spa await your aching muscles.

Best of all, the outdoor pool invites you to grab a cool martini, gaze at the water, and wash away all stress from your work week.

St. Michaels
Crab & Steakhouse

305 Mulberry Street
St. Michaels, MD 21663
410-745-3737
www.stmichaelscrabhouse.com

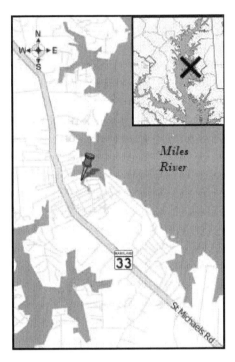

County: Talbot County

Open: Year Round

Latitude: N 38° 47' 6"

Longitude: W 76° 13' 14"

Body of Water: St. Michaels
Harbor off the Miles River

Dockage: Yes

Picture Code: SMCS at
www.crabdecksandtikibars.com/
pix

Atmosphere Meter

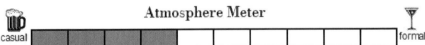

casual

formal

Did you know that when you walk up to St. Michael's
Crab & Steakhouse, the patio bricks under your feet were
kilned in the 1800s?

And did you know that the building was home to one of the area's earliest oyster shucking sheds? The thick wooden ceiling joists holding up the tavern serve as proof to its authenticity.

History is all around you here, but so is really good food, and it's all prepared to order. The extensive menu takes you on a culinary tour of regional treasures — succulent crab cakes, oysters on the half shell, steamed mussels and clams, Chesapeake chicken, and more.

Crowd pleasers include Crab Benedict (crab imperial with tomato and bacon on an English muffin), char-broiled New York strip steaks, and the seafood platter with a crab cake, founder, shrimp, and scallops.

The outside deck is often packed with local watermen who proudly tell about how their town once fooled the British.

In 1813, British ships planned to attack St. Michaels. Forewarned, the quick-thinking residents hoisted lanterns to the masts of ships and tops of trees, causing the cannons to overshoot the town.

Only one house was hit when a cannonball cut through the roof and rolled down the staircase as the mother carried her infant daughter downstairs. The town was saved.

Want to learn more? Walk over to the Chesapeake Bay Maritime Museum that celebrates the region's culture, seafood, and history. Its collection of Chesapeake watercraft, crabbing skiffs, workboats, and log canoes is sure to amaze you.

Town Dock Restaurant

125 Mulberry Street
St. Michaels, MD 21663
410-745-5577
www.towndockrestaurant.com

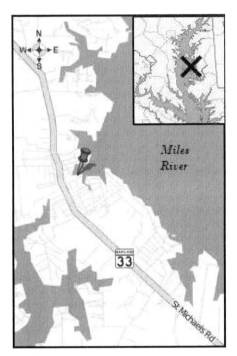

County: Talbot County

Open: Year Round

Latitude: N 38° 47' 6"

Longitude: W 76° 13' 16"

Body of Water: St. Michaels Harbor off the Miles River

Dockage: Yes

Picture Code: TDR at www.crabdecksandtikibars.com/pix

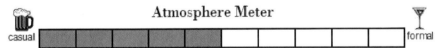

Atmosphere Meter

casual | | | | | | | | | | formal

Town Dock closed for a while to repair damage from a fire in 2010. But thank heavens, it reopened in April 2011 to complete the trinity of traditional Bay dining on the harbor, along with The Crab Claw and St. Michaels Crab & Steakhouse.

The two-tiered building, gazebo, and deck afford every table an unobstructed and gorgeous view of the water. Tables inside are covered with white linens, but the atmosphere is still comfortable and welcoming.

If you're looking for a more laid-back feel, Foxy's Marina Bar provides a casual spot to enjoy crisp cocktails and watch the people parade on a warm summer evening.

Its ideal location — right in the heart of St. Michaels harbor — is frequented by locals and tourists alike. Town Dock's specialty is seafood, but it also delivers delicious land-based alternatives.

Folks rave about the crab cakes and oysters, but other treasures from the sea await on and off the menu. Penne Puttanesca tosses jumbo shrimp in a rich tomato sauce with anchovies, fresh basil, and Kalamata olives, and seared sea scallops are gently placed on top of matchstick-cut vegetables with a lemon butter sauce.

Plus, the Fresh Seafood Chalk Board recommends fish that were unloaded at the docks that morning.

New Zealand rack of lamb, marinated pork tenderloin with home made chutney, and chicken scallopini with crimini mushrooms and sweet peas are star attractions for meat-eaters.

And you won't leave a crumb on the plate if you order the bleu cheese torte with artichoke hearts, red onion, and crisp bacon.

If you're looking for a venue to accommodate a larger crowd or special event, Town Dock has two waterfront banquet rooms with seating for up to 60 guests.

The Crab Claw Restaurant

304 Burns Street
St. Michaels, MD 21663
410-745-2900
www.thecrabclaw.com

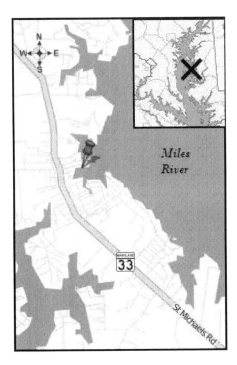

County: Talbot County

Open: March thru November

Latitude: N 38° 47' 13"

Longitude: W 76° 13' 14"

Body of Water: St. Michaels
Harbor off the Miles River

Dockage: Yes

Picture Code: TCCR at
www.crabdecksandtikibars.com/
pix

Atmosphere Meter

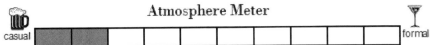

casual ... formal

Crabs, clams, oysters, and shrimp. Steamed, fried, broiled, or raw. You name it, they've got it, because The Crab Claw is all about fresh Chesapeake seafood.

How fresh? "If he don't kick, we don't cook!" promises the kitchen staff. And they've upheld this high standard for decades.

The restaurant evolved from a clam shucking and crab harvesting business in the 1950s to a seafood eatery in 1965. You can feel the sense of tradition as you climb the stairs inside the rustic two-story wood and clapboard building to get a seagull's view of the harbor.

Down below on the expansive outdoor decks, waitresses scurry among the crowded picnic tables delivering frosty beers to thirsty crab-picking customers.

You can get the meal started with clams casino, crab balls, or spicy chicken wings, then move on to creamy oyster stew, crab soup, or a salad.

The raw bar list reads like a Who's Who of Chesapeake favorites: fresh clams, fried shrimp, steamed mussels, and raw oysters. Entrees range from seafood samplers to soft shells, and Maryland fried chicken is the pride of Eastern Shore kitchens.

When you finish your last bite and still want to experience more of the Bay, go next door and get on board the *St. Michaels Patriot.* For 90 minutes, you can cruise the waters, taking in views of the unique wildlife that lives along the Miles River and the historic mansions that date back to Colonial and Victorian eras.

Lowes Wharf
Bayside Grill & Tiki Bar

21651 Lowes Wharf Road
Sherwood, MD 21665
Toll Free 888-484-9267; local 410-745-6684
www.loweswharf.com/yacht.htm

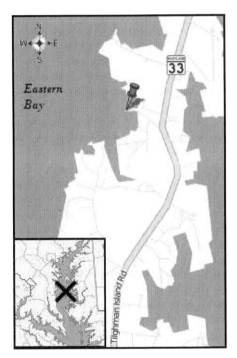

County: Talbot County

Open: Year Round

Latitude: N 38° 45' 57"

Longitude: W 76° 19' 42"

Body of Water: Ferry Cove off
the Chesapeake Bay

Dockage: Yes

Picture Code: LWBG at
www.crabdecksandtikibars.com/
pix

Atmosphere Meter

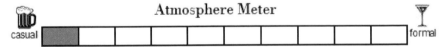

casual   formal

One of the best-kept secrets on the Eastern Shore is Lowe's
Marina Grill & Tiki Bar. You won't find much about it online
or in guide books. So as you travel south on Route 33 from
St. Michael's to Tilghman Island, keep your eyes peeled near
the town of Sherwood.

Upon arrival, you won't believe what you see — a two-story inn, cozy restaurant, and sunny beach with colors that make you feel like you're in Key West.

Bathing suit-clad guests kick back in bright red, blue, and yellow Adirondack chairs and picnic tables with cool beverages clenched in their hands. The wind gently tugs at red and blue umbrellas as they try to cast a little protective shade.

A two-foot tall retaining wall encircles the beach area — tall enough to prevent waves from washing away the sand, short enough to reveal a spectacular view of the Bay, and just the right height for children to jump off into the water.

The entire place is flanked by two scenic coves that offer hours of entertainment to daring children who explore their shores at low tides. Volleyball, horseshoes, jet skis, fishing boats, and kayaks round out the possibilities of day-time activities.

As the sun sets, you might get hit with the sinking feeling that it's time to go home. Keep in mind, the inn's 20+ rooms could solve your problem and delay the return to civilization for a day. Rooms are comfortable and clean, but you might not spend much time in them. The lure of a warm summer breeze, tasty seafood treats in the restaurant, and the temptation to throw darts or play billiards in the bar could draw you back into the heart of Lowe's Wharf Grill.

During a recent visit, the bartender confessed, "The best thing about my job is when I get hot, I jump into the water, cool off, and then come back to serving drinks dripping wet." She sent a clear message that after 15 years in the business, Lowe's owners know how to help you relax and enjoy life.

Bay Hundred
Restaurant & Tiki Bar

6176 Tilghman Island Road
Tilghman, MD 21671
410-886-2126
www.bayhundredrestaurant.net

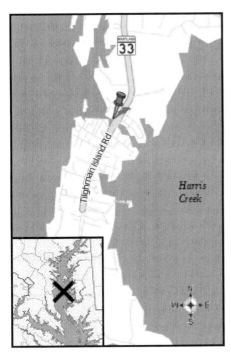

County: Talbot County

Open: Year Round

Latitude: N 38° 43' 12"

Longitude: W 76° 19' 57"

Body of Water: Knapps
Narrows between Harris Creek
and the Chesapeake Bay

Dockage: Yes

Picture Code: BHR at
www.crabdecksandtikibars.com/
pix

Atmosphere Meter

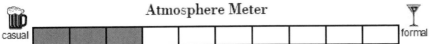

casual   formal

Have you ever seen a hairy umbrella? Well, you'll get that
and a whole lot more at Bay Hundred Restaurant.

The outside crab deck provides a front-row seat to watch
fishermen hauling up their daily catch and boats chugging

through Knapps Narrows. And yes, umbrellas that shade diners from the relentless August sun really are covered with a furry fabric that rustles in the breeze and simply makes you smile.

The bar area's decor could be considered "subtle tiki," with bead curtains, rattan barstools, and grass-matted walls. But four dart boards suggest that subtle decor gives way to raucous play when 301 or cricket matches kick into high gear.

The air-conditioned dining room offers a respite from the heat but still lets you enjoy the view while picking a dozen steamed crabs or nibbling on appetizers like conch fritters or coconut shrimp.

Also in the cook's repertoire are rockfish imperial, ahi tuna sliders with wasabi mayo, and a savory 14 ounce rib-eye steak.

When you're done with your meal, you can check out *The Lady Patty,* one of the few remaining skipjacks left on the Bay available for charter.

In case you're wondering, "Bay Hundred" refers to the strip of land between Oak Creek and the tip of Tilghman Island. Talbot County was divided into "hundreds" for administrative purposes by the mid-1670s.

The term "Hundred" comes from medieval England when shires were parceled into segments that could produce 100 fighting men.

The Bridge Restaurant

6136 Tilghman Island Road
Tilghman, MD 21671
410-886-2330

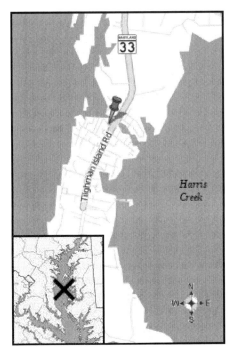

County: Talbot County

Open: Year Round

Latitude: N 38° 43' 9"

Longitude: W 76° 19' 59"

Body of Water: Knapps Narrows between Harris Creek and the Chesapeake Bay

Dockage: Yes

Picture Code: TBR at www.crabdecksandtikibars.com/ pix

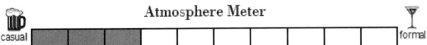

Atmosphere Meter

casual   formal

You have two choices at The Bridge Restaurant. You can grab a table on the second floor to get a bird's eye view of the busy boat traffic making its way under the Tilghman Island Bridge. Or you can venture down to the water's edge, take a seat at a picnic table on the deck, and enjoy the watermen's perspective.

Either way, you can't go wrong. This bustling place upholds the best of traditional Bay dining and merriment.

Crabs, shrimp, and other local seafood share menu space with flavorful chicken and tender beef. Dining room seating offers a quaint panoramic view enhanced by a couple of rusty old boats docked along the shore.

Newer, better maintained watercraft passing by remind you that life on Tilghman Island never stands still. When you look to the right of the restaurant, you might wonder what's so special about this drawbridge.

Since the 1840s, various types of bridges have spanned Knapps Narrows. Built in 1998, the current one is called a bascule bridge, and is Maryland's only overhead counterweight bridge (others have counterweights underneath).

It's also the nation's busiest bridge. In 2009, it opened up 10,276 times to let nautical traffic drift through. So chances are pretty good that you'll get to witness a little local history as the bridge raises its moveable span.

The Tilghman Island Inn

21384 Coopertown Road
Tilghman, MD 21671
Toll Free 800-866-2141, local 410-886-2141
www.tilghmanislandinn.com

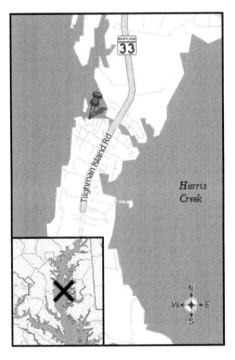

County: Talbot County

Open: Year Round

Latitude: N 38° 43' 12"

Longitude: W 76° 20' 14"

Body of Water: Knapps
Narrows between Harris Creek
and the Choptank River

Dockage: Yes

Picture Code: TTII at
www.crabdecksandtikibars.com/
pix

 Atmosphere Meter

casual | | | | | | | | | | formal

Tilghman Island Inn has created the perfect marriage of elegant contemporary and traditional style.

It hosts one of the most beautiful dining areas on the Bay, as oriental-rug runners lead the way to tables set with white linens on gorgeous wooden floors.

You'll want to stop and look at the artwork accentuating the warm blue and salmon walls. But save some time to soak in the wall of block glass as the afternoon sun creates a kaleidoscope of light and color.

The outside deck bar, walls speckled with gray oyster shells, presents two essential Bay views: Look to your left to see an expanse of open water; to your right you gaze at grassy marshlands that provide a sanctuary for fledgling crabs, shrimp, and other aquatic life.

Sunsets are amazing at the Tilghman Island Inn, and its fine cuisine is an innovative treat. The chef changes menu items to match the seasons. A recent Tasting Menu let you choose between lamb chops with potato-turnip gratin or rockfish with lobster and crawfish risotto.

Treasures on the a la carte menu include black-eyed pea cakes, Choptank oysters in a champagne cream sauce, and grilled pork tenderloin with polenta.

You can complement the flavors of local seafood dishes with one of the most extensive wine collections in the area.

If you want to linger longer than one meal, make a reservation to stay at its lovely inn, complete with spa, tennis courts, swimming pool, and other relaxing amenities.

Harrison's Chesapeake House

21551 Chesapeake House Drive
Tilghman, MD 21671
410-886-2121 or 410-886-2109
www.chesapeakehouse.com

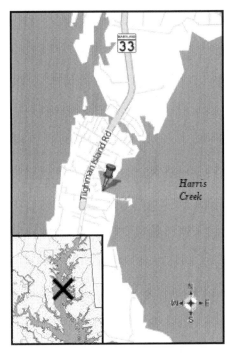

County: Talbot County

Open: Year Round

Latitude: N 38° 42' 39"

Longitude: W 76° 20' 8"

Body of Water: Dogwood
Harbor off the Choptank River

Dockage: Yes

Picture Code: HCH2 at
www.crabdecksandtikibars.com/
pix

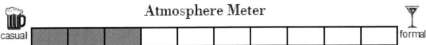

Atmosphere Meter

casual ▢▢▢▢▢▢▢▢▢▢ formal

"If you like chrome and glass high-rise hotels, hot tubs, and sushi bars, we're not the place for you. On the other hand, if your taste tilts toward waterfront decks with picnic tables that groan under the weight of huge platters of hot steamed crabs and sweating pitchers of icy beer and brewed tea, we're for you." That's how Harrison's owners describe their Chesapeake gem.

The restaurant and inn have an old-fashioned charm that makes you want to kick back and get comfortable when you come to visit.

Ten years after the Civil War ended, Captain Levin Harrison opened his doors to entertain guests with Chesapeake sports fishing, duck hunting, and gracious local dining. And the tradition continues with charter fishing and hunting packages offered year-round.

As you stroll around the facilities, you will find a swimming pool, white picnic tables and rocking chairs, and a sand-and-brick patio overlooking a fabulous view of the Bay.

The rustic Captain Buddy's Deck Bar rests precariously on pylons above the water. Its brightly colored over-sized crab decorations and beer signs invite you to come inside for a game of pool or a cold beer. *The Tilghman Lady*, a dilapidated old wooden boat next door, does its best to stay afloat.

Family-style dinners, with show-stoppers like local steamed crabs, oysters, and rockfish, are fresh, hearty, and homemade. Warm biscuits, buttered corn-on-the-cob, and crunchy coleslaw make you feel like you're at a picnic in the country.

Tip for arriving safely at Harrison's: Make sure you write down the final directions on a piece of paper or bring along a map. Cell phone coverage gets spotty, and you wouldn't want to miss this treasure because you relied solely on your GPS system.

Irish Crab Waterside Pub

975 Port Street
Easton, MD 21601
410-822-1201

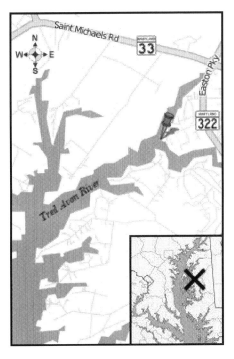

County: Talbot County

Open: Year Round

Latitude: N 38° 46' 5"

Longitude: W 76° 5' 41"

Body of Water: Tred Avon River

Dockage: Yes

Picture Code: ICWP at www.crabdecksandtikibars.com/pix

Atmosphere Meter

casual   formal

When visitors come to historic Easton, MD, they're rewarded with gourmet restaurants, Colonial and Victorian architecture, fine antique shops, award-winning gardens, and seven golf courses.

But most people don't know that just southwest of town is a hidden jewel with a much more casual flare called the Irish Crab Waterside Pub.

Located at Easton Point Marina on the tip of the Tred Avon River, this delightful place gives a whole new meaning to the word "rustic."

Several signs welcome you: one is missing letters critical to the pub's name (like the "I" in Irish), and on another, a smiling crab waves a shamrock in its crimson claw.

Mismatched bar stools and plastic chairs offer seating at the bar, where old Christmas lights strung around the edges add a little cheer. Three tables covered with green-and-white checkered oilcloths tempt you to take a seat on the small deck and enjoy the stunning view of the river.

A local patron affectionately referred to Irish Crab as their "redneck yacht club," where everybody can drink cold beer, eat good food, and relax. And that's the truth

. Irish Crab intentionally keeps its menu simple and fresh — crab cakes, rockfish, mussels, burgers, soup, and Black & Tan onion rings (a salute to its heritage).

If that's not enough to get your juices flowing, you can also become a pirate when you're here. Right next door docks a replica of an 18th century wooden pirate ship, its helm decorated in bright orange, red, and yellow designs.

Wanna-be swashbucklers can climb aboard the *Sea Gypsy III* to fulfill dreams of finding buried treasure or hitting the high seas to raid the king's bounty.

Schooners on the Creek Restaurant

314 Tilghman Street
Oxford, MD 21654
410-226-0160
www.schoonersonthecreek.com

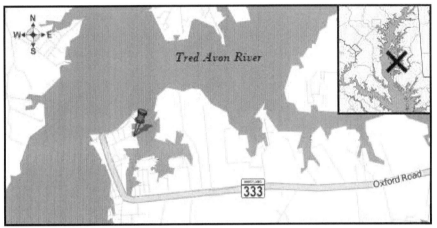

County: Talbot County
Open: Seasonal
Latitude: N 38° 41' 34"   Longitude: W 76° 10' 6"
Body of Water: Town Creek off the Tred Avon River
Dockage: Yes
Picture Code: SCR at www.crabdecksandtikibars.com/pix

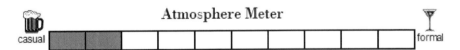

Whether you come by land or sea to Schooners in Oxford, MD, you'll know you found a real Chesapeake jewel.

The building was an oyster-shucking plant in the early 1900s. Today, a large plastic shark greets landlubbers entering from the parking lot, and a big red sign invites you to sip a Schooner's Squeeze after you dock your boat.

Featuring classic Eastern Shore cuisine, this waterfront crab house with a bar and large outdoor deck offers plump steamed crabs and fresh seafood caught daily by fishermen cruising the Tred Avon River and the Bay.

Steamed shrimp, fried oysters, and local clams are big hits on the menu. The atmosphere is laid-back, and the view can't be beat.

If you're lucky, you might hear locals tell tales of their historic little town. Oxford, established in 1683, became an important trading center on the Chesapeake.

British ships unloaded goods imported from Europe to exchange for tobacco grown on local plantations. Rosters of 17th Century residents read like a Who's Who of American history.

Most noteworthy was Robert Morris Jr., a signer of the Declaration of Independence and financier of the American Revolution.

After the Civil War and completion of the local railroad in 1871, Oxford grew into a central hub for canning and shipping local seafood.

Even today, a stone's throw away from your cold beer and hot crabs is the historic Oxford Boatyard, founded in 1866, which still provides a gamut of services for boaters.

The Masthead
at Pier Street Marina

104 West Pier Street
Oxford, MD 21654
410-226-5171
www.themastheadatpierstreetmarina.com

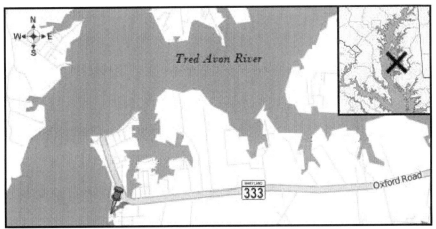

County: Talbot County
Open: Seasonal, open April through October
Latitude: N 38° 40' 58"   Longitude: W 76° 10' 24"
Body of Water: Tred Avon River
Dockage: Yes
Picture Code: TMPSM at www.crabdecksandtikibars.com/pix

Atmosphere Meter

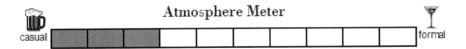

casual ⸻ formal

If you want to enjoy sensational sunsets and seafood in a quaint historic town, head for The Masthead at Pier Street Marina in Oxford, MD.

The location is perfect. Jutting out where the Tred Avon River pours into the Bay, this place encourages you to grab a cold beverage at its outdoor gazebo bar and take in the heavenly waterfront views from its massive wooden deck.

The menu performs a delightful two-step of mixing traditional Bay cuisine with Caribbean fun. You can bounce from blue crabs to conch fritters, or from cherrystone clams to mahi mahi with mango salsa.

Either way, you won't be disappointed. The Slammin' Soft Crab Sandwich and Totally Tuna Tacos are light fare treats. Sunset dinners are made memorable with tender crab cakes, rockfish stuffed with crab imperial, and seafood scampi that pours shrimp, lobster, and scallops over a bed of delicate penne pasta.

The owners completely renovated the restaurant in 2004 to repair damages from Hurricane Isabel and created seating for 250 guests on the deck and 85 indoors. (They also own Latitude 38 in Oxford for year-round dining.)

Although it's tempting to linger longer in this idyllic spot, save some time to cruise into downtown Oxford for its colonial architecture and charm.

The best part: riding the ferry that runs between Oxford and Bellevue. Started in 1683, it's the oldest privately owned ferry in the United States.

The 20-minute round-trip ride gives you a duck's eye view of the water and harkens back to a time when life was less hectic and hurried.

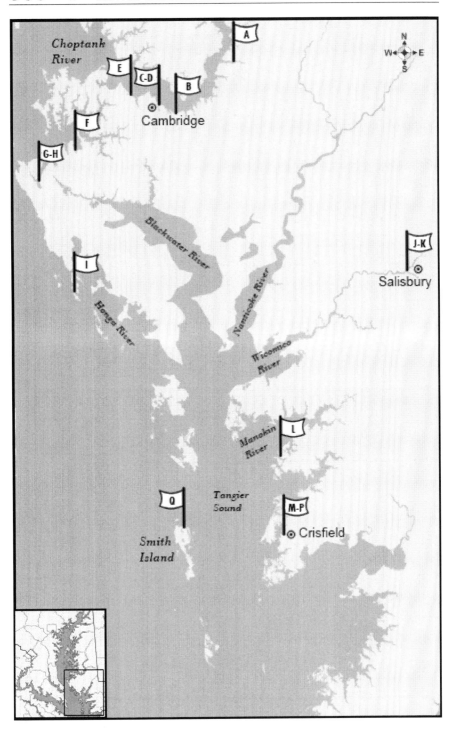

Lower Eastern Shore

Suicide Bridge Restaurant

6304 Suicide Bridge Road
Hurlock, MD 21643
410-943-4689
www.suicide-bridge-restaurant.com

County: Dorchester County
Open: Year Round
Latitude: N 38° 37' 59" Longitude: W 75° 56' 49"
Body of Water: Cabin Creek off the Choptank River
Dockage: Yes
Picture Code: SBR at www.crabdecksandtikibars.com/pix

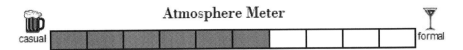

There's something about a name like Suicide Bridge that makes you want to ask questions. Has anyone really ...? When? How?

Depending on the size of the crowd, the bartender in the Light House Lounge will either patiently answer or hand you a piece of paper with enough local lore to satisfy your inquiring mind.

The original wooden bridge was erected in 1888; another took its place in 1910. The current 21-foot high structure, still wooden but now covered with asphalt, was dedicated in 1968. Almost a dozen people chose this location as the place to meet their maker.

Several shot themselves, then toppled into the river below. After one man jumped off the bridge and hit his head on a piling, locals suspected foul play and performed the autopsy on his body at a nearby picnic table.

But there's more to this place than stories of unfortunate demise. The restaurant's two-story clapboard building offers a lovely waterfront view in a charming setting. Walls of knotty pine and stone are decorated with super-sized metallic crabs and local wildlife.

Bustling crowds sit at wooden tables while scanning menus that offer an extensive selection of fresh seafood, aged steak, chicken, and pasta. Backfin crab cakes, shrimp and scallops a la Suicide (cream sauce over pasta), and coldwater lobster tails are dinner favorites.

Landlubbers prefer to cut into a juicy prime rib, tender lamb chops, or sautéed liver and onions. Sandwiches and baskets are available for smaller appetites.

If you want a closer look at the water, you can cruise the Choptank River on board two reproductions of 80-foot turn-of-the-century paddlewheel riverboats, named *The Dorothy & Megan* and *The Choptank River Queen*. Restaurant staff will prepare meals for you to take along.

Blue Point Provision Company & Water's Edge Grill

100 Heron Boulevard
Cambridge, MD 21613
410-901-6410
www.chesapeakebay.hyatt.com/hyatt/
hotels/entertainment/restaurants

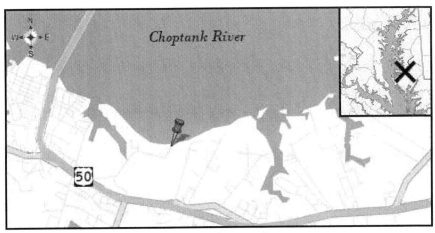

County: Dorchester County
Open: Year Round
Latitude: N 38° 33' 41"   Longitude: W 76° 2' 32"
Body of Water: Choptank River
Dockage: Yes
Picture Code: BPPC at www.crabdecksandtikibars.com/pix

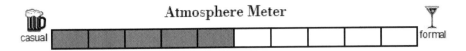

When in pursuit of the authentic Bay experience, a Hyatt Regency resort doesn't usually top the priority list. So Blue Point Provision Company comes with a disclaimer: If you're a Bay purist, with visions of crusty boat captains and rusty crab pots, then consider another crab deck. You've got plenty of others to choose from.

But if you're willing to keep an open mind and look beyond the manicured golf course, spacious swimming pool, and big-hotel backdrop, then you might be in for a pleasant experience.

Blue Point made it into this list for several reasons. First of all, it's got an incredible panoramic view of the Choptank at River Marsh Marina, and it's tucked away in a far corner of the resort.

The grounds' 400 acres of gorgeous marshland should give you plenty of room to avoid the resorty stuff, if you choose.

Second, it has a good attitude and shows an appreciation for Bay traditions and heritage. Oyster tongs and a crab dredge hang prominently on the entry wall, and somebody with a sense of humor uses an oversized fishing lure for a mailbox.

And even though the restaurant's floors are a bit too shiny and the decor feels a tad contrived, the menu carries a wide selection of fresh Chesapeake seafood that's delivered daily by local watermen.

So what the heck? When they're serving up good rockfish, blue point oysters, crab cakes, and other regional specialties, Blue Point is worth a try.

Portside Seafood Restaurant

201 Trenton Street
Cambridge, MD 21613
410-228-9007
www.portsideseafood.com

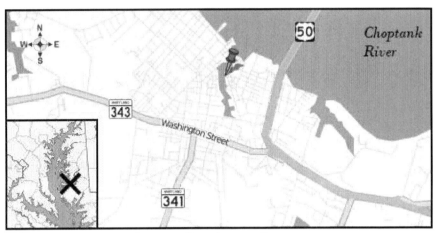

County: Dorchester County
Open: Year Round
Latitude: N 38° 34' 13"   Longitude: W 76° 4' 22"
Body of Water: Cambridge Creek off the Choptank River
Dockage: Yes
Picture Code: PSR1 at www.crabdecksandtikibars.com/pix

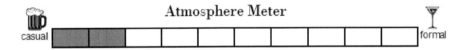

Atmosphere Meter
casual   formal

You get the best of both worlds at Portside Restaurant —
indoor and outdoor good times at the Eastern Shore.

When the weather's warm, bright blue and red umbrellas
mark the way to the outside upper deck. That's where you'll
find relaxed waterfront dining overlooking a bridge that spans
Cambridge Creek, just shy of the Choptank River.

The inside sports haven gives you a front-row seat to the autumnal football frenzy as zealous fans toast the Maryland Terps or Baltimore Ravens (Steelers fans beware!).

Whether you work up an appetite from the fresh air or an amazing touchdown pass, Portside's menu aims to please. Snacks include wings, crab dip, nachos, and potato skins.

Crab soup is award winning and creamy smooth. Soft-shell sandwiches and crab melts are perfect for lunch, along with garden-fresh salads.

Landlubbers can opt for Delmonico steaks, chicken Chesapeake, or pasta. Steamed shrimp, clams, and mussels prefer to get dipped in warm drawn butter. Crab cakes are the size of baseballs. And it's all available for a reasonable price.

Not sure what to order? Ask one of the locals. Since the 1950s when it was called Eastside, Cambridge residents have chosen this restaurant as a favorite watering hole, steeped in Chesapeake tradition.

Snappers Waterfront Café

112 Commerce Street
Cambridge, MD 21613
410-228-0112
www.snapperswaterfrontcafe.com

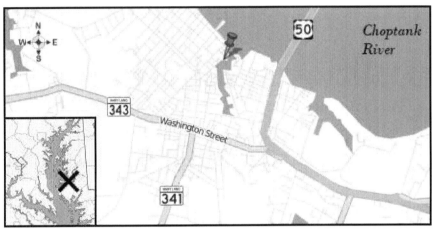

County: Dorchester County
Open: Year Round
Latitude: N 38° 34' 21"   Longitude: W 76° 4' 23"
Body of Water: Cambridge Creek off the Choptank River
Dockage: Yes
Picture Code: SWC at www.crabdecksandtikibars.com/pix

Atmosphere Meter

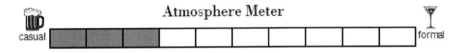

casual   formal

At first glance, Snappers looks like a garden-variety crab deck. But once you start cruising around this place, you discover it's got something to make everybody happy.

For a first blast of fun, belly up to the tiki bar. You can toss back an oyster shooter, wiggle your toes in the sand, test an icy margarita, kick back and watch the band, or even wear a sombrero if you like.

When you're ready to move on, head for the dining areas where you can go alfresco with a waterfront view or take a seat inside where subtle tiki touches garnish the walls. Either way, the atmosphere is quite pleasant, and the service is friendly.

The menu offers an extensive mix of local sea food, ribs, steak, Tex-Mex specialties, burgers, pasta, and salads. House specialties include jumbo jerk shrimp fajitas, Eastern Shore fried chicken, and filler-free crab cakes. Only the daring order fried pickles.

Then comes the best part — climb up the stairs to The Rave Cave. It's billed as "Real Sports Fan's Ultimate Hide-Away," and it delivers.

Wide-screen TVs, overstuffed leather sofas, La-Z-Boy recliners, and low-set coffee tables tempt you to kick up your feet, while waitresses deliver icy cold beer. You can almost feel the residue of cigar smoke from the days of when tobacco was permitted indoors.

It's a heavenly spot for sneaking away from visiting in-laws or sharing a good game with fellow Baltimore fans. After almost 20 years in the restaurant biz, Snappers knows how to do things right.

Clearview at Horn's Point Restaurant & Bar

5650 Country Club Road
Cambridge, MD 21613
410-221-0521
www.clearviewathornspoint.com

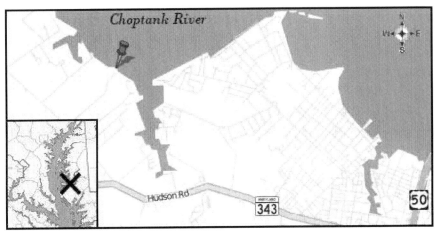

County: Dorchester County
Open: Year Round
Latitude: N 38° 35' 5"   Longitude: W 76° 7' 5"
Body of Water: Choptank River
Dockage: No
Picture Code: CHPRB at www.crabdecksandtikibars.com/pix

Atmosphere Meter

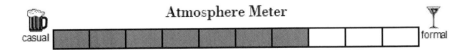

Eastern Shore casual elegance is a fine way to describe Clearview at Horn's Point. It's located on 130 acres of waterfront property that used to belong to a duPont estate. The 18-hole golf course was designed by renowned architect

Russell Roberts who blended the natural beauty of the Bay with the gentle contours of the greens.

Located just two miles outside of Cambridge, the beautiful grounds and facilities are a favorite venue for weddings and business retreats.

Formerly the Cambridge Country Club, Clearview treats guests to a fabulous view of the Choptank River from a large outdoor deck. White Adirondack chairs are placed on the grassy lawn, and couples hold hands while strolling on the long wooden pier that leads out to the water. Sunsets are dazzling.

Inside, the walls are painted a creamy beige, and modern square light fixtures cast an amber glow from the ceiling. Tall leather chairs encircle tables set with white linen tablecloths.

Two fireplaces set a soothing romantic tone. Between the dining rooms is a bar area, complete with a wooden bookcase and flat-screen TVs turned down low.

The sophisticated, yet warm, ambiance provides an ideal backdrop for a fine-dining experience that features fresh local ingredients. Mussels are steamed in white wine, crab dip welcomes tiny pieces of Smithfield ham, and Caesar salads are topped with crispy fried oysters. Beef tips over garlic mashed potatoes are lightly blanketed in a bordelaise sauce.

The menu changes to capture the season's harvest, so you never know what pleasant surprises await you at this lovely spot along the Bay.

Madison Bay
Restaurant & Raw Bar

4814 Madison Canning House Road
Madison, MD 21648
410-228-1108

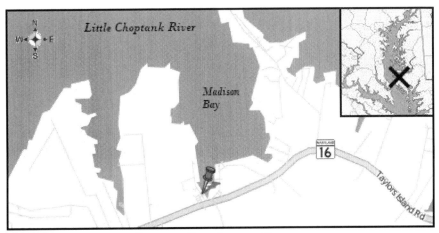

County: Dorchester County
Open: Year Round
Latitude: N 38° 30' 29"   Longitude: W 76° 13' 26"
Body of Water: Madison Bay off the Little Choptank River
Dockage: Yes
Picture Code: MBRRB at www.crabdecksandtikibars.com/pix

Atmosphere Meter

casual | | | | | | | | | | | formal

Madison Bay is only 11 miles southwest of Cambridge, but you feel like you've been transported into an entirely different world.

It's tucked between a campground and marina, so you see more boats and campers than cars and brick buildings. People enjoy the slowed-down pace of rural living, with excellent sports fishing, hiking trails, and crabs galore. The white one-story building is topped with a red roof, and a beer-slinging crab wearing sunglasses is painted on the sign.

The atmosphere is rustic casual. Locals strike up a game of pool located behind the rounded formica bar, while country music plays on the radio.

The outdoor deck's aluminum cover is lined with strings of colorful lights. People convene at wooden picnic tables to watch boats shuffle in and out of the marina.

The kitchen serves Eastern Shore home-style cooking. Appetizers include crab pizza, bacon-wrapped oysters, and steamed shrimp or clams. Filler is not allowed in the jumbo lump crab cakes. Tables are crowded with sandwiches, burgers, seafood platters, ribs, and fried chicken. Pickled beets, stewed tomatoes, and beer-battered onion rings garnish plates with blue crabs painted around the rim.

Originally, this area was called Tobacco Stick Bay. According to local lore, an Indian fleeing from white settlers used a tobacco stick to jump across the channel at the mouth of the cove, and ran into the woods to safety. The name stuck until around 1881 when it was changed to Madison Bay.

During the War of 1812, British ships entered Tobacco Stick's harbor to carry out their agenda of ransacking the Maryland countryside. They torched several vessels, including a ship owned by Captain Thomas Linthicum. But that wasn't enough to satisfy the Brits' thirst for destruction. They carted off Captain Linthicum and held him prisoner for months. Eventually they dumped him off in a remote corner of the Bay, half-clad and barefoot, leaving him to walk all the way back to his home in Dorchester County.

Palm Beach Willie's Fine Food & Spirits

638 Taylors Island Road
Taylors Island, MD 21669
410-221-5111
www.palmbeachwillies.com

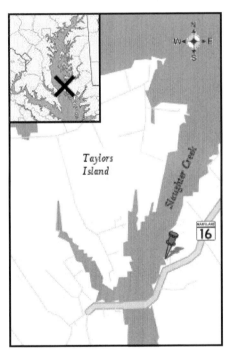

County: Dorchester County

Open: Year Round

Latitude: N 38° 28' 34"

Longitude: W 76° 17' 11"

Body of Water: Slaughter Creek off the Little Choptank River

Dockage: Yes

Picture Code: PBWFFS at www.crabdecksandtikibars.com/pix

Atmosphere Meter

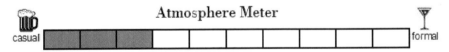

casual   formal

Along the Bay, it's common to hear places named after brave historic figures, family patriarchs, or even crusty ship captains. But Palm Beach Willie's stands alone for naming its restaurant after the owner's dog. Apparently the Labrador retriever, originally called plain-old "Willie," developed a strong preference for warm water rather than icy cold waves and became known as "Palm Beach Willie."

That's not the only unique feature of this delightful place on the banks of Slaughter Creek. The entire restaurant resides inside a floating houseboat, resting in the water. Sunset views are spectacular. An enclosed deck that's attached to the building has been newly renovated with tall windows opening up to catch the breeze off the water. Heaters are thoughtfully turned on during chilly days. Tropical plants are placed out front, and thatched umbrellas sway above round wooden picnic tables on the deck.

The island motif is carried inside with portraits of parrots staring down at tables covered in colorful tropical prints. Twine rope and lights shaped like flip-flops are wrapped around poles at the bar, with a few coconuts dangling near the ceiling.

The atmosphere is casual and friendly. If you're looking for fresh seafood, you've come to the right place. Traditional jumbo lump crab cakes and steamed shrimp are cooked just right, and creative dishes show the kitchen has a little fun with the classics. Willie's Seafood Stew is a savory steaming cauldron of the daily catch, homemade clam strips offer the perfect crunch, and Poncho's Club Sandwich is a multi-layer feast of crab cakes, grilled shrimp, bacon, ham, cheese, lettuce, and tomato. Burgers, fried chicken, prime rib, and egg salad with bacon can satisfy any appetite. Desserts are made in-house and scrumptious.

By car, Palm Beach Willie's is a pleasant 15-mile drive from Cambridge. But it's also a boater's dream location, because new management has given the marina a facelift and now offers updated facilities, a swimming pool, showers, and overnight transient slips.

The Island Grille

514 Taylors Island Road
Taylors Island, MD 21669
410-228-9094

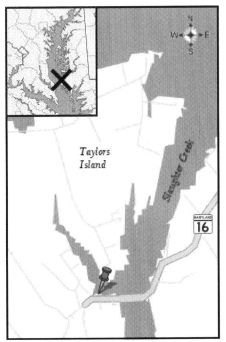

County: Dorchester County

Open: Year Round

Latitude: N 38° 28' 11"

Longitude: W 76° 17' 51"

Body of Water: Slaughter Creek off the Little Choptank River

Dockage: No

Picture Code: TIG at www.crabdecksandtikibars.com/pix

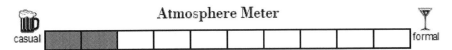

Atmosphere Meter

casual ▯▯▯▯▯▯▯▯▯▯ formal

If the Island Grille looks like a general store, that's because it was one. Around 1816, the people of Taylors Island erected the building to replace a previous store that burned down.

As time passed, it became the post office, gathering place, and market for folks living in this remote neck of the Bay. When Hurricane Isabel stormed through in 2003, she flooded

Taylors Island and the store. After extensive renovations, the building began its new life as the local cafe and watering hole.

Chapel Cove Marina office and tackle shop are next door, adding a charming small-town feel. Island Grille's exterior walls are painted pale green, and its sign out front shows a heron wearing a chef's hat and bow tie serving beverages along the water.

The inside still feels like a general store. On the walls and shelves are vintage knickknacks, maps, deer heads, ships, carved waterfowl, books, and old photos.

Tables covered with red oilcloths and a wooden bar in the back are dead give-away clues that it's been converted to a restaurant. The atmosphere is relaxed, accented with a lovely view of the water.

The kitchen dishes out casual fare — wings, beer-battered shrimp, burgers, sandwiches, salads, and of course, fresh seafood delivered daily by local watermen.

History buffs might be interested in seeing a relic from the War of 1812 a few yards from the restaurant. The Becky Phibbs Cannon was captured from the British war ship, *Dauntless,* in 1815 by Joseph Stewart and local militiamen near James Island. Freezing winter temperatures and ice along the shore allowed the men to get within firing range of the ship and make off with the cannon.

Its name is a combination of the ship's commander, Matthew Phibbs, and a black woman named Becky, who had been captured and forced to work as a cook on the British vessel.

Old Salty's Restaurant

2560 Hoopers Island Road
Fishing Creek, MD 21634
410-397-3752

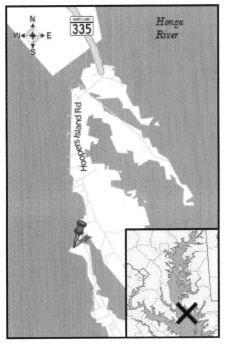

County: Dorchester County

Open: Year Round

Latitude: N 38° 19' 27"

Longitude: W 76° 13' 51"

Body of Water: between the Chesapeake Bay and Back Creek off the Honga River

Dockage: No

Picture Code: OSR at www.crabdecksandtikibars.com/pix

Atmosphere Meter

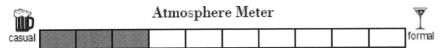

casual   formal

If you're looking for an authentic Bay adventure, put Old Salty's on the top of your must-see list. It's in a remote location about 45 minutes south of Cambridge on the Eastern Shore, but the rural landscape is so dramatically beautiful, you'll be sorry when the ride is over.

You drive past crab-picking plants, white-washed Methodist churches, workboats tied up to rickety docks, and miles of golden marshland interrupted by clusters of loblolly pines. You pass Blackwater National Wildlife Refuge, home to egrets, eagles, and a menagerie of waterfowl and wildlife. Eventually you arrive at Hoopers Island, which is a string of three islands connected by a narrow two-lane causeway that separates the Chesapeake Bay and the Honga River.

Old Salty's is located in the former school house of Fishing Creek (population 163). In this historic fishing village, watermen have harvested the Bay's sweetest crabs and oysters for generations. The atmosphere at Old Salty's is timeless and casual. Dining room chairs are upholstered in a nautical fabric, and duck decoys rest quietly on window ledges. On the wood panel walls, paintings of ship captains smoking long-stem pipes watch your back as you have a drink at the bar. Some wonder if one of the sailors is Old Salty himself.

The food is home-style and traditional. Juicy hand-cut steaks appear on the menu, but it's hard to resist the fresh local seafood when you've just driven past fishermen pulling it out of the water. House specialties include crab cakes, fried oysters, spicy steamed shrimp, sautéed peelers (soft-shells), and warm homemade rolls.

The service is friendly and laced with stories told by folks who are proud of their local heritage. On a recent visit, the bartender left his post to show off the former gymnasium that now is used for large parties and special events.

Captain John Smith first discovered the islands in the early 1600s. Local legend says European settlers bought the land from the Yaocomaco Indian tribe for five woolen blankets. The island was named after a friend of the Calverts, Henry Hooper, who purchased a large parcel of land in 1668. His descendants still live in the area to this day.

Brew River Restaurant

502 West Main Street
Salisbury, MD 21801
410-677-6757
www.brewriver.com

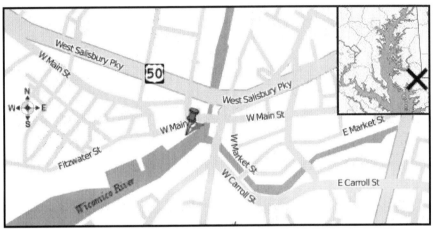

County: Wicomico County
Open: Year Round
Latitude: N 38° 21' 52" Longitude: W 75° 36' 21"
Body of Water: Wicomico River
Dockage: Yes
Picture Code: BRR at www.crabdecksandtikibars.com/pix

Atmosphere Meter

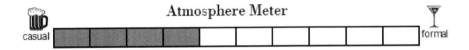

casual   formal

Can you believe there's a crab deck so far up the
Wicomico River that you could throw a rock from one bank to
the other? Well, it's true.

Brew River Restaurant carries the spirit of the Bay about
16 miles inland to a marina in downtown Salisbury, MD. It
opened in the spring of 2000 by a family that's worked in the

restaurant business on the Eastern Shore since 1974 and also owns Harpoon Hanna's on Fenwick Island, DE.

Brew River is casual and comfortable inside with knotty pine walls decorated with pictures of Chesapeake crabs, oyster boats, and watermen.

Wooden barrels and hand-painted fish hang from the ceiling, and antique stained glass windows serve as dividers between cozy wooden booths. A massive stone fireplace warms the air during the winter.

But in the summer, head outside to the expansive deck and dock bar where cold beer, frozen concoctions, and martini mixers are plentiful. Live music, tiki torches, and fire pits spice up the waterfront view.

When your stomach starts to rumple, you can order inside or outside from the full menu. Seafood leads the charge with crab dip, coconut shrimp, and a raw bar for appetizers. Crab cakes, seafood alfredo, and prime rib cater to hearty appetites, and sandwiches and salads offer lighter fare.

After dinner, you can end the evening by dancing at the waterfront nightclub or taking a moonlit stroll along the river.

Market Street Inn

130 West Market Street
Salisbury, MD 21801
410-742-4145
www.marketstreetinnsalisbury.com

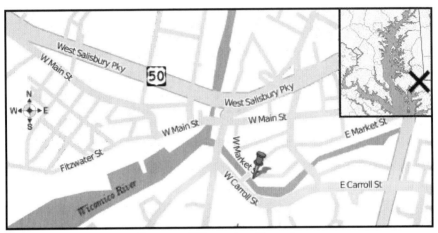

County: Wicomico County
Open: Year Round
Latitude: N 38° 21' 48"   Longitude: W 75° 36' 8"
Body of Water: Wicomico River
Dockage: No
Picture Code: MSI at www.crabdecksandtikibars.com/pix

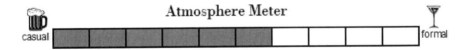

The building where Market Street Inn now resides has gone through almost as many lives as a cat. Built in 1941, it was originally a seafood market, and in the 1960s it became a sports bar owned by a couple of Baltimore Colts.

It got painted bright pink in the '70s while serving margaritas and burritos. In the '80s, owners covered up the pink paint, added a floating dock, and turned it into an open air sandwich shop. In 2001, the current owner transformed Market Street into an upscale casual dining establishment with gourmet food and an excellent wine selection.

But you'll see clues that it doesn't take itself too seriously. The giant red martini glass sculpture and a mailbox shaped like a big beer tap out front say somebody's having fun here. And the cheery blue umbrellas on the outdoor waterfront BARge are clear signs of merriment.

Depending on your beverage of choice, you can join clubs with fellow fans of good wine, beer, or martinis. The rustic pub's low ceiling is covered with a huge martini glass with mini offspring glasses all around it.

The walls of the dining area are painted in rich earth-tones with beautiful hand-painted murals of village scenes and landscapes. Black-and-tan wooden chairs are accented with gray tables and soft lighting.

For lunch, you can go light with jerk chicken Caesar or tropical salmon salad, or be more ambition with the black-and-bleu burger or pulled BBQ beef sandwich.

At dinner, the kitchen shines with perfectly prepared crab cakes, roasted rack of lamb, applewood smoked pork medallions, and Black Angus sirloin steak.

At Market Street Inn, it's all about fine food with a laid-back upbeat attitude.

Hide Away Grill

25763 Rumbley Road
Westover, MD 21871
410-651-1193
www.goosecreekmarinaandhideawaygrill.com

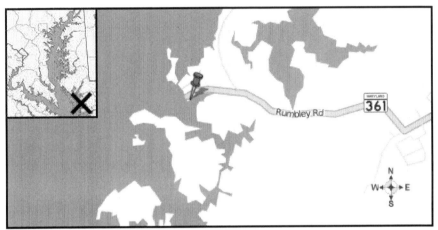

County: Wicomico County
Open: Seasonal
Latitude: N 38° 5' 33"   Longitude: W 75° 51' 40"
Body of Water: Goose Creek off Tangier Sound
Dockage: Yes
Picture Code: HAG at www.crabdecksandtikibars.com/pix

Atmosphere Meter

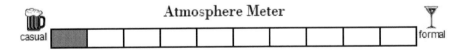

casual   formal

Tucked away in a remote part of Somerset County awaits one of the sweetest hidden jewels of the Bay, appropriately called Hide Away Grill.

To get there, boaters relish the uncrowded open waters of Tangier Sound, and drivers are treated to scenic country roads lined with tall loblolly pines and golden marshy grasslands that serve as incubators for infant crabs, fish, and shrimp.

The restaurant is located at Goose Creek Marina in the quaint fishing village of Rumbley, where life revolves around water, boats, and crabs. A campground is nearby if you want to linger a while.

Hide Away is "rustic tiki" at its best. The tiny building is painted tropical turquoise and rosy pink, and its sign is made of letters nailed to a gnarly piece of driftwood.

Sand covers the ground outside near the boats, and a "palm tree" consisting of blue and green wine bottles stuck on an old tree trunk adds a colorful island touch.

The view is unobstructed and gorgeous. Neighbors toss horseshoes, while children splash in the gentle Chesapeake waves.

Inside, the walls are painted with palm trees and a pastel Caribbean sunset. Six chrome-and-black vinyl bar stools line up along the thatched roof and bamboo bar. The indoor dining room holds about a dozen tables, but crowds of diners overflow onto the picnic tables outside.

The bathrooms, labeled Sooks and Jimmys, forewarn that crabs are prominent players around here. Food is simple, fresh, and caught locally. Steamed crabs doused in Old Bay seasoning, fried rockfish with creamy coleslaw, and juicy burgers accompanied by fries with melted cheddar and bacon provide delightful summer treats.

Add a cold beer and you've found a little piece of Chesapeake heaven.

Olde Crisfield
Crab, Steakhouse & Tiki Bar

204 South 10th Street
Crisfield, MD 21817
410-968-2722
oldecrisfield.angelfire.com

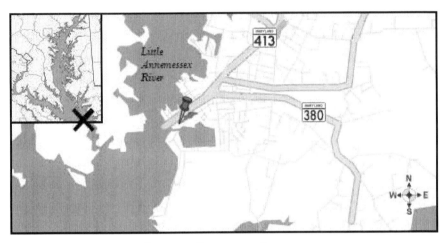

County: Somerset County
Open: Seasonal
Latitude: N 37° 58' 42"   Longitude: W 75° 51' 41"
Body of Water: between Somers Cove and
the Little Annemessex River off Tangier Sound
Dockage: No
Picture Code: OCCSTB at www.crabdecksandtikibars.com/pix

Atmosphere Meter

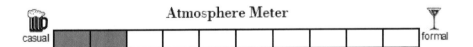

casual   formal

You can't miss it when you roll into town. Olde Crisfield's
neon yellow, orange, and green walls with a gigantic orange
crab on the roof create an electric burst of color amidst a

---

backdrop of blue sky and water. Renovated by new owners in 2009, the large two-story building offers enough seating to accommodate about 300 guests who are treated to an incredible view of the historic harbor.

Tall palm trees sway above the tiki bar, and crab bushels are turned upside-down to serve as lampshades. Wooden tiki masks grin from poles under bright yellow awnings.

When you walk inside, you enter a world of "total tiki." Bamboo walls accented with banana yellow are decorated with crabs and plush island scenes. Chairs and barstools display every color of the rainbow, while tabletops are hand-painted with tropical fish and parrots.

The kitchen offers something for everyone — sandwiches, burgers, and steaks — but you need to taste the local seafood that's been considered a delicacy around the globe for centuries. The Oyster Bar showcases the catch of the day, including steamed shrimp, clams, mussels, and oysters. Hot steamed crabs and crab cakes are among the best on the Bay. You can wash them down with a cold beer or a signature drink, such as Category 3: Dark and Stormy, Electric Lemonade, Last of the Mojitos, or Drunken Golfer. From the deck you can watch a dazzling array of boats bustling around the harbor, including the huge cruise ships that ferry passengers to Tangier Island. If you have the time, it's worth a trip out to the island.

First spotted by John Smith in 1608 as he explored the Chesapeake, Tangier Island is now home to around 500 residents. Linguists come to hear the unique American English dialect that's been preserved through residents' isolation from the mainland. Tourists flock to the island to see the beautiful fishing villages where watermen have harvested top-quality crabs and oysters for generations.

The Watermen's Inn

901 West Main Street
Crisfield, MD 21817
410-986-2119
www.crisfield.com/watermens

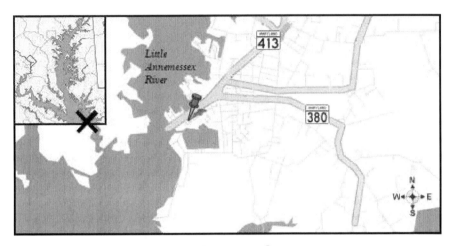

County: Somerset County
Open: Year Round
Latitude: N 37° 58' 44"   Longitude: W 75° 51' 37"
Body of Water: between Somers Cove and
the Little Annemessex River off Tangier Sound
Dockage: No
Picture Code: TWI at www.crabdecksandtikibars.com/pix

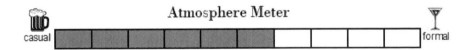

Fine casual dining mixed with a pinch of local folklore await you at Watermen's Inn. The old building is painted burnt orange, and above the covered front porch rests a lovely mural of a sailboat coasting toward the sunset.

The interior walls have a soft warm glow of amber and beige, and large windows create an open airy feel. Pictures of Chesapeake boats and wildlife hang on the walls, and etched glass depictions of herons separate the cozy dining area from the kitchen. Tables are set with bud vases holding fresh-cut flowers and glass tops covering crisp white linens.

Since 1988, the owners have created a gourmet experience that makes the most out of local and seasonal ingredients. Menu highlights include shrimp, scallops, and crab bathed in a cream sauce and topped with puff pastry, hand-cut rib-eye steaks with red onion and black olive marmalade, and Oyster Rockefeller, farmed by a local waterman named Ernie. Homemade desserts, prominently displayed on an antique desk, tempt you to indulge your sweet tooth.

The tap room has an old-fashion saloon feel, which is underscored by vintage photos of Crisfield hanging on the walls. Long known for its treasure trove of local seafood, the town hit an economic boom during the mid-1800s, thanks to the railroad's arrival and the invention of refrigeration for transporting perishable items. Seafood processing plants and other marine-related businesses sprang up all around the area. According to the bartender, workers from nearby plants liked to hang out at the honky-tonk bar where Watermen's now resides. During breaks, they'd dash over, put down a couple drinks, and chat with their buddies. Coaxing them back to work was no easy task, so plant managers would sound steam whistles to mark the end of the break, but the workers didn't always listen.

To fix the problem, each plant developed its own special whistle, and when their workers heard it blow, they had no excuse but to return to their jobs. So, at Watermen's Inn, you get gourmet food at a reasonable cost and local stories that are priceless.

Blue Crab Garden Café

801 West Main Street
Crisfield, MD 21817
410-968-0444

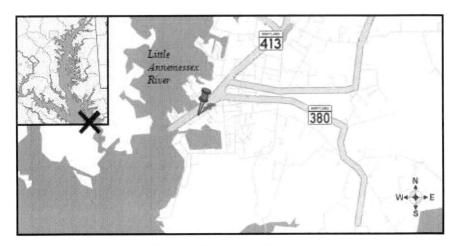

County: Somerset County
Open: Year Round
Latitude: N 37° 58' 47" Longitude: W 75° 51' 33"
Body of Water: between Somers Cove and
the Little Annemessex River off Tangier Sound
Dockage: No
Picture Code: BCGC at www.crabdecksandtikibars.com/pix

Atmosphere Meter

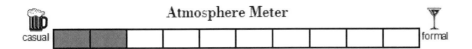

casual   formal

Every small town needs a corner café where folks can
gather and share news over a cup of coffee in the morning or
a cold beer later in the day.

In Crisfield, that place is the Blue Crab. Conveniently located on main street near the town pier and main attractions, this little hot spot is big on hospitality.

The owners welcome visitors with a casual warmth that makes you feel like you're part of the community. Locals squeeze together at wooden picnic tables on the deck to share hot steamed crabs that were just unloaded at the docks.

The menu is simple and fresh, served on plates shaped like sunfish. Starters like BBQ shrimp on skewers, creamy crab dip, and Tangier clam chowder lead into salads and sandwiches for the main course. Soft-shell crabs are tucked between slices of white bread, and chicken salad is accented with a pinch of dill.

Root beer floats or strawberry shortcakes give an old-fashioned ending to your meal. A small dance floor in the back picks up the energy level in the evenings.

If you need more than one day to experience Crisfield, the Blue Crab's owners can accommodate guests at Marquis Manor, a lovely Victorian home they've spent years painstakingly renovating.

They even put together weekend packages that encourage you to tour local points of interest, take a crab shanty tour with a waterman, or unwind with a spa treatment and wine tasting.

And they know where to hook you up with the famous 10-layer Smith Island Cake to help you savor fond memories of your trip to their charming part of the Bay.

The Cove Restaurant

718 Broadway
Crisfield, MD 21817
410-968-9532

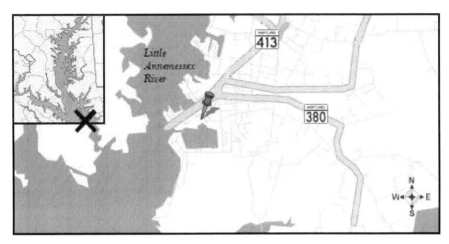

County: Somerset County
Open: Year Round
Latitude: N 37° 58' 45"   Longitude: W 75° 51' 30"
Body of Water: between Somers Cove and
the Little Annemessex River off Tangier Sound
Dockage: No
Picture Code: TCR at www.crabdecksandtikibars.com/pix

Atmosphere Meter

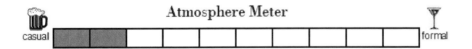

casual — formal

When you gaze up at the weather-worn, vintage sign above The Cove, you get a sense that this restaurant has been around for decades, upholding traditions of a classic Bay seafood house.

The ground floor walls are cinder block painted white, and the second story is clapboard with a wooden deck facing the water. The large inside dining area sports a maritime theme featuring decorative plates and pictures of lighthouses and statuettes of boat captains. A brick fireplace emits warmth to the wooden tables and tall-back booths.

The home-style cooking is hearty, and dishes are served in hefty portions. Crab cakes are the size of a fat man's fist, and slabs of rockfish are fried to a golden crisp. Steamed shrimp and Maryland fried chicken are adorned with creamy coleslaw, beets, or biscuits.

In the background, the crab-emblazoned Crisfield water tower stands watch over the town that has played a key role in Chesapeake history for centuries.

The city of Crisfield was previously called Somers Cove to honor Benjamin Somers, who settled the area in 1663. That name might have stuck, if it hadn't been for John Woodland Crisfield, a local lawyer and Congressman.

Mr. Crisfield was instrumental in bringing the railroad to this neck of the Bay, sparking a boom time for the crab, oyster, and seafood industry.

One day in the mid-1860s, Mr. Crisfield was inspecting the docks near the steamboat landing. While walking across a section of rotten boards, he crashed through the planks and toppled into the frigid water. After fishing him out, local officials named their town after him in a gesture of apology and appreciation to this formidable benefactor.

To learn more about Crisfield — both the man and the town — check out the J. Millard Tawes Historical Museum, just down the street from The Cove.

Bayside Inn Restaurant

4065 Smith Island Road
Smith Island, MD 21824
410-425-2771

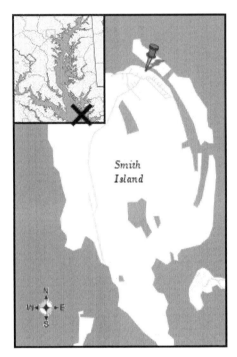

County: Somerset County

Open: Seasonal

Latitude: N 37° 59' 45"

Longitude: W 76° 1' 57"

Body of Water: Big Thorofare
Channel off Tangier Sound

Dockage: Yes

Picture Code: BIR at
www.crabdecksandtikibars.com/
pix

Atmosphere Meter

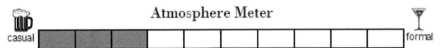

casual — formal

The arrival of crabs in the spring is grounds for celebration at Bayside Inn and all around Smith Island. It marks the opening of a new season when visitors venture out to Maryland's only inhabited island that is not attached to the mainland by bridge or causeway. Daily ferry boats from Crisfield and Point Lookout offer the only means to get there.

The island was originally mapped by Captain John Smith in 1608 and named after Henry Smith, a Jamestown man who was granted 1,000 acres of land there in 1679.

At its peak, nearly 800 residents lived on the island, but the number has dwindled, and now only 276 people call it home in the three villages of Ewell, Rhodes Point, and Tylerton. Erosion has reduced its size, so locals get around by foot or golf cart.

Nearly 8,000 acres of marshland surround the island, giving sanctuary to fledgling sea creatures and water fowl. It's considered the hub of the Bay's seafood industry, where local watermen harvest some of the region's finest crabs, oysters, and clams.

Bayside Inn is located in Ewell near the Smith Island Heritage Center and the pier where boats unload the mail, supplies, and tourists. It's a favorite watering hole for locals who like to bring down wooden hammers on hot steamed crabs cooked to order or pick the shells off perfectly pink shrimp. Tomato-based or creamy crab soup is available by the cup or bowl, and fried oysters are plump and crispy.

Given the location, it's hard to imagine ordering anything other than that fabulous local seafood, but baked ham and turkey breast sandwiches are on the menu, and the kitchen offers specials like prime rib, steak, and BBQ ribs.

At the rear of the restaurant, the carry-out shop scoops hand-dipped ice cream and sells the famous Smith Island Cake, made of 10 pencil-thin layers of moist yellow cake separated by chocolate icing. It was originally only four layers tall until local women started competing over who could stack them higher. In 2008, the Maryland legislature voted to make this rich heavenly cake the state's official dessert.

Virginia Crab Decks & Tiki Bars

ACs Café & Sports Grill

307 Plantation Drive
Coles Point, VA 22442
804-472-5528
County: Westmoreland County
Body of Water: Potomac River

Alexander's on the Bay

4536 Lauderdale Avenue
Virginia Beach, VA 23455
757-464-4999
County: Virginia Beach
Body of Water: directly on the
    Chesapeake Bay

Aqua Restaurant
& Cabana Bar

900 Marina Village Circle
Cape Charles, VA 23310
757-331-8660
www.baycreekresort.com/dining/
    aqua.asp
County: Northampton County
Body of Water: directly on the
    Chesapeake Bay

Bennett's Creek Restaurant
& Marina

3305 Ferry Road
Suffolk, VA 23435
757-484-8700
www.bennettscreekmarina.com
County: Suffolk
Body of Water: Bennett's Creek off
    the Nansemond River

Blue Crab Bar & Grill

4521 Pretty Lake Avenue
Norfolk, VA 23518
757-362-3133
County: Norfolk
Body of Water: Elizabeth River

(The) Blue Heron Restaurant

9100 Wilcox Neck Road
Charles City, VA 23030
804-829-9070
www.riversrest.com/facilities.htm
County: Charles City County
Body of Water: Chickahominy
    River off the James River

Bubba's Family Restaurant

105 Rens Road
Poquoson, VA 23662
757-868-4219
County: Poquoson
Body of Water: Floyds Bay off
    Bennett Creek off the
    Chesapeake Bay

Bubba's Seafood Restaurant
& Crabhouse

3323 Shore Drive
Virginia Beach, VA 23451
757-481-3513
www.bubbasseafoodrestaurant.com
County: Virginia Beach
Body of Water: Lynnhaven River

Captain Chuck-A-Muck's Ship Store & Grill, Secret Hideout #2

21088 Marina Road
Rescue, VA 23424
757-356-1005
www.captainchuck-a-mucks.com
County: Isle of Wight County
Body of Water: Jones Creek off the
    Pagan River

Channel Marker Restaurant

4409 Chambers Lane
Tangier, VA 23440
757-891-2220
County: Accomack County
Body of Water: Tangier Sound

Charles's Tiki Bar & Grill

40 Windjammer Lane
White Stone, VA 22578
804-436-8454
www.charliestikibar.com
County: Lancaster County
Body of Water: directly on the
    Chesapeake Bay

Chick's Oyster Bar

2143 Vista Circle
Virginia Beach, VA 23451
757-481-5757
www.chicksoysterbar.com
County: Virginia Beach
Body of Water: Lynnhaven River

CoCoMo's

1134 Timberneck Road
Deltaville, VA 23043
804-776-9311
County: Middlesex County
Body of Water: Rappahannock
    River

Coles Point Tavern

850 Salisbury Park Road
Coles Point, VA 22442
804-472-3856
www.colespointtavern.com
County: Westmoreland County
Body of Water: Potomac River

(The) Crabshack Seafood Restaurant

7601 River Road
Newport News, VA 23607
757-245-2722
www.crabshackonthejames.com
County: Newport News
Body of Water: James River

(The) Crazy Crab

902 Main Street
Reedville, VA 22593
804-453-6789
County: Northumberland County
Body of Water: Cockrell Creek off
    the Great Wicomico River

(The) Cull Ring Dockside Bar & Grill

252 Polly Cove Road
Fairport, VA 22539
804-453-5002
County: Northumberland County
Body of Water: Cockrell Creek off
    the Great Wicomico River

Cutty Sark Marina & Grill

4707 Pretty Lake Avenue
Norfolk, VA 23518
757-362-2942
County: Norfolk
Body of Water: Elizabeth River

(The) Deck Restaurant

10 Crawford Parkway
Portsmouth, VA 23704
757-398-1221
www.deckrestaurant.com
County: Portsmouth
Body of Water: Elizabeth River

Dockside Restaurant

700 Jordan Point Road
Hopewell, VA 23860
804-541-2600
www.docksideonthejames.com
County: Hopewell
Body of Water: James River

Dockside Restaurant
& Blue Heron Pub

7 Castlewood Drive
Colonial Beach, VA 22443
804-224-8726
www.docksiderestaurantand
   blueheronpub.com
County: Westmoreland County
Body of Water: Potomac River

Duck-In Restaurant & Gazebo

3324 Shore Drive
Virginia Beach, VA 23451
757-481-0201
www.vbeach.com/duck-in
County: Virginia Beach
Body of Water: Lynnhaven River

Fisherman's Corner Restaurant

4419 Long Bridge Road
Tangier, VA 23440
757-891-2900
www.fishermanscorner
   restaurant.com
County: Accomack County
Body of Water: Tangier Sound

Fisherman's Wharf

1571 Bayville Street
Norfolk, VA 23503
757-480-3113
County: Norfolk
Body of Water: Elizabeth River

(The) Flagship Restaurant

103 Constitution Avenue
Portsmouth, VA 23704
757-398-1600
www.flagshipportsmouth.
   blogspot.com
County: Portsmouth
Body of Water: Elizabeth River

Greenies Restaurant & Pub

198 West Ocean View Avenue
Norfolk, VA 23503
757-480-1210
County: Norfolk
Body of Water: Elizabeth River

High Tides on the Potomac

205 Taylor Street
Colonial Beach, VA 22443
804-224-8433
www.hightidez.com
County: Westmoreland County
Body of Water: Potomac River

Hilda Crockett's Chesapeake House

16243 Main Street
Tangier, VA 23440
757-891-2331
www.chesapeakehousetangier.com
County: Accomack County
Body of Water: Tangier Sound

Horn Harbor House Seafood Restaurant

836 Horn Harbor Road
Burgess, VA 22432
804-453-3351
County: Northumberland County
Body of Water: Great Wicomico
River

(The) Inlet Restaurant

3319 Shore Drive
Virginia Beach, VA 23451
757-481-7300
County: Virginia Beach
Body of Water: Lynnhaven River

Keith's Dockside Restaurant

38-C Water Street
Hampton, VA 23663
757-723-1781
County: Hampton
Body of Water: James River

Kinsale Harbour Restaurant

285 Kinsale Road
Kinsale, VA 22488
804-472-4476
County: Westmoreland County
Body of Water: Kinsale Branch off
the Yeocomico River

Kokoamos Island Bar & Grill

2100 Marina Shores Drive
Virginia Beach, VA 23451
757-481-3388
www.kokoamos.com
County: Virginia Beach
Body of Water: Long Creek off the
Lynnhaven River

Laffin' Gull Beach Grille

Pretty Lake Avenue
Norfolk, VA 23518
757-362-3455
www.laffingull.com
County: Norfolk
Body of Water: Elizabeth River

(The) Lighthouse Restaurant & Charlie's Quarterdeck Lounge

11 Monroe Bay Avenue
Colonial Beach, VA 22443
804-224-7580
www.baysidemarina.org/id10.html
County: Westmoreland County
Body of Water: Potomac River

(The) Lynnhaven Fish House Restaurant

2350 Starfish Road
Virginia Beach, VA 23451
757-481-0003
www.lynnhavenfishhouse.net
County: Virginia Beach
Body of Water: directly on the
Chesapeake Bay

Mallards at the Wharf

2 Market Street
Onancock, VA 23417
757-787-8558
www.mallardsllc.com
County: Accomack County
Body of Water: Onancock Creek off
the Chesapeake Bay

(The) Mooring Restaurant

347 Allen Point Lane
Kinsale, VA 22488
804-472-2044
www.portkinsale.com/Dining.aspx
County: Westmoreland County
Body of Water: Kinsale Branch off
the Yeocomico River

Ocean View Fishing Pier Restaurant

400 West Ocean View Avenue
Norfolk, VA 23503
757-583-6000
www.oceanviewfishingpier.com/
restaurant.html
County: Norfolk
Body of Water: Elizabeth River

One Fish-Two Fish

2109 West Great Neck Road
Virginia Beach, VA 23451
757-496-4350
www.onefish-twofish.com
County: Virginia Beach
Body of Water: Long Creek off the
Lynnhaven River

O'Sullivan's Wharf Seafood Restaurant

4300 Colley Avenue
Norfolk, VA 23508
757-961-0899
www.osullivanswharf.com
County: Norfolk
Body of Water: Elizabeth River

Owen's Marina Restaurant

259 Mingee Street
Poquoson, VA 23662
757-868-8407
County: Poquoson
Body of Water: White House Cove
off Bennett Creek off the
Chesapeake Bay

(The) Pelican Pub

32246 Charles M. Lankford Jr.
Memorial Highway
Cape Charles, VA 23310
757-331-4229
www.sunsetbeachresortva.com
County: Northampton County
Body of Water: directly on the
Chesapeake Bay

Pirate's Den Restaurant

6338 Riverview Drive
King George, VA 22485
540-775-4600
www.piratesdenfvb.com
County: King George County
Body of Water: Potomac River

(The) Restaurant at Smithfield Station

415 South Church Street
Smithfield, VA 23430
757-357-7700
www.smithfieldstation.com
County: Isle of Wight County
Body of Water: Pagan River

Riverboat on the Potomac

301 Beach Terrace
Colonial Beach, VA 22443
804-224-7055
www.theriverboat.net
County: Westmoreland County
Body of Water: Potomac River

River's Inn Restaurant

8109 Yacht Haven Road
Gloucester Point, VA 23062
804-642-6161
www.riversinnrestaurant.com
County: Gloucester County
Body of Water: Sarah Creek off the
York River

Rocky Bottom Grill

633 Marina Drive
Surry, VA 23883
757-294-9644
www.rockybottomgrill.com
County: Surry County
Body of Water: Gray's Creek off
the James River

Sandpiper Reef Restaurant

342 Misty Cove Road
Hallieford, VA 23068
804-725-3331
www.sandpiperreef.net
County: Mathews County
Body of Water: Piankatank River

Seabreeze Restaurant

34 Old Ferry Road
Grimstead, VA 23064
804-725-4000
County: Mathews County
Body of Water: Milford Haven off
the Chesapeake Bay

Ship's Cabin

4110 East Ocean View Avenue
Norfolk, VA 23518
757-362-0060
www.shipscabinrestaurant.com
County: Norfolk
Body of Water: Elizabeth River

Slightly Up the Creek

663 Deep Creek Road
Newport News, VA 23606
757-930-1573
www.jamesrivermarina.com/
Dining.html
County: Newport News
Body of Water: James River

Sunset Grill

1525 Bayville Street
Norfolk, VA 23503
757-588-1255
County: Norfolk
Body of Water: Elizabeth River

Surf Rider Bluewater

1 Marina Road
Hampton, VA 23669
757-723-9366
www.surfridergroup.com
County: Hampton
Body of Water: James River

Taylors Landing Surf Rider

8180 Shore Drive
Norfolk, VA 23518
757-480-5000
www.surfridergroup.com
County: Norfolk
Body of Water: Elizabeth River

(The) Thirsty Camel

394 West Ocean View Avenue
Norfolk, VA 23503
757-588-9877
County: Norfolk
Body of Water: Elizabeth River

Tim's II Restaurant & Crab House

5411 Pavilion Drive
King George, VA 22485
540-775-7500
www.tims2.com
County: King George County
Body of Water: Potomac River

Tim's Rivershore Restaurant & Crab House

1510 Cherryhill Road
Dumfries, VA 22026
703-441-1375
www.timsrivershore.com
County: Prince William County
Body of Water: Potomac River

Tommy's Seafood & Steaks

729 Main Street
Reedville, VA 22593
804-453-4666
www.tommysrestaurant.net
County: Northumberland County
Body of Water: Cockrell Creek off
the Great Wicomico River

Upper Deck Crab & Rib House

1947 Rocky Neck Road
Lancaster, VA 22503
804-462-7400
www.upperdeckcraband
ribhouse.com
County: Lancaster County
Body of Water: Rappahannock
River

Water's Edge Bar & Grill

1 Ivory Gull Crescent
Hampton, VA 23664
757-864-0336
County: Hampton
Body of Water: James River

Wilkerson's Seafood Restaurant

3900 McKinney Boulevard
Colonial Beach, VA 22443
804-224-7117
www.wilkersonsseafood
restaurant.com
County: Westmoreland County
Body of Water: Potomac River

Bodies of Water Index

Cities Index

Restaurant Names Index